WITHDRAWN

MARIANNE MOORE

Marianne Moore

QUESTIONS OF AUTHORITY

Cristanne Miller

Harvard University Press
Cambridge, Massachusetts
London, England
1995

Library of Congress Cataloging-in-Publication Data

Miller, Cristanne.
Marianne Moore : questions of authority / Cristanne Miller.
p. cm.
Includes index.
ISBN 0-674-54862-0
1. Moore, Marianne, 1887–1972—Criticism and interpretation.
2. Feminism and literature—United States—History—20th century.
3. Women and literature—United States—History—20th century.
4. Authority in literature. I. Title.
PS3525.05616Z696 1995
811'.52—dc20
95-7167
CIP

Contents

Preface

This is primarily a book about Marianne Moore, although as the first and last chapters indicate, I believe that the "questions of authority" discussed in this book are important to the discussion of poetry generally and that examining Moore's responses to these questions may illuminate the responses of late twentieth-century feminist poets in particular to similar questions. My own questions of authority are informed by a feminist poststructuralist insistence on acknowledging one's interest and perspectives; I focus, however, not on theories of critical response but on imagining the grounds of Moore's positioning and construction of a (female) poet's authority; in other words, while I recognize that authority inheres both in a writer's felt and enacted entitlement to speak and in the changing receptions of that writer's work through successive generations, I focus on the former. I do so by tracing Moore's negotiations among the several configurations of poetic agency and authority available to her at various points during her lifetime and by examining the language, structures, and arguments of her poems. To summarize my argument briefly, I see Moore as determined to establish in her writing a communally focused authority that avoided egocentric and essentialist assertions of a subjective self while also avoiding the self-erasure which is their opposite and double.

At the same time, this book gestures beyond the work of Moore toward the more ambitious project of sketching a broadly based poetic characterizing the work of a number of twentieth-century female poets. Such a poetic, like Moore's, questions authority by exploring constructions of subjectivity, lyric agency, and cultural empowerment through its forms as much as in the themes of its work. Its stance is not confessional or autobiographical. Not openly didactic in its politics, this poetic nonetheless marks a variety of political issues as primary concerns. And while not so determinedly experimental as to require a specialized audience, it self-consciously uses the structures and traditions of poetry to construct alternative relationships of power between poet and tradition, poet and speaker, poet and reader, and reader and poem. Consequently, the work of poets I see as involved in such writing typically falls outside the primary categories to which most formalist, feminist, and avant-garde critics assign the highest praise.

In this book, Marianne Moore represents both herself in her own biographical, historical, cultural, and poetic specificity and this broader poetic. In particular, I argue that Moore's work provides an example of various tactics for repositioning the gendered self within a poetic that builds upon yet distinguishes itself from the romantic sublime, the feminine sentimental, and the modernist impersonal modes—just as later poets' works additionally distinguish themselves from poststructuralist avant-garde and feminist experiential modes. Although one may find many examples of such writing, in fact most female American poets do not participate in the poetic I am outlining. Poets who have chosen a confessional mode, poets who continue to explore the romantic lyric voice, poets who write in traditional forms, poets who reject the notion of voice (or of readability) altogether, and poets who write a didactically revolutionary poetry are not the subject of this book—although they may indeed raise equally interesting questions about gendered poetic authority. Similarly, Moore may not be the first woman and poet to construct such a personal/impersonal, gendered/ungendered, disjunctive, experimental and oppositional but not openly revolutionary poetic. She is, however, I believe, the most widely celebrated poet of this century to write in such a mode, and hence plays a central role in the fashioning and reception of such a poetic for later writers.

This poetic is implicitly (and for some poets explicitly) feminist in its manipulation of received truths about identity and authority and yet, in its rejection of a self-focus and of binary categorizations, is more apt to strive for a nongendered or multiply gendered positioning than for a distinctly female subject matter or presence or the kind of simple oppositionality (us/them, female/male, black/white) that characterizes much openly political poetry. Partly because of my own stress on feminist elements in such work, and partly because of what I see as these poets' grounding in a broadly conceived feminism, I do not consider here the wide and equally rich range of poetry written by men that engages in questioning various kinds of authority. This decision is, to some extent, arbitrary; men, of course, may be and are feminists, and an interesting exploration might be undertaken of the ways in which late twentieth-century feminist male poets respond to and reconceive questions like Moore's. My focus here, however, is on the more obvious—and I believe, at this point, much stronger—convergences between female poets working in a similarly feminist but often not obviously gendered poetic. Like Moore's, this poetic asserts the limits of its own subjectivity and relative positioning, presenting multiple subject positions or voices and eschewing dogmatism, but it is also didactic in its attitudes: without assuming it can speak absolute truth and without directly addressing a need for systemic change, it constructs a poetry of assertion; it takes a stance of public political engagement.

This poetic, then, falls midway between two types of political challenge which Chandra Mohanty describes in "On Race and Voice" (*Cultural Critique* 14 [Winter 1989–90]: 179–208). It does not deal with oppositional and marginalized positioning "purely at an attitudinal, interpersonal level," nor does it frame its questions in the directly political terms of "fundamental challenge[s] to hegemonic knowledge and history" (195)—although structurally, as well as at times thematically, it in fact constitutes such a challenge. Rather than tracing convolutions of the psyche or the boundaries of selfhood, this poetic considers the relation of the individual, or of subjectivity, abstractly conceived, to public and cultural institutions (marriage, religion, language), to dominant assumptions within popular culture (about freedom, the self, the body, constructions of gender), and to the "laws" of government, science, and language (property laws, biology, quantum mechanics, grammar). It is more interested in gender as a social and political construction than in gender as an expression of self, more interested in constructing an alternative authority than in the poet's identity. It desires an open communicability while at the same time constructing a surface of sufficient complexity to make structure or style an equal bearer of poetic meaning with the poet's subjects of focus or semantic formulations themselves. Because of its tendency toward abstraction and concern with the physicality of poetry and of language, it is not a poetry of "voice"; although it indeed presents tones and perspectives unusual in poetry, it does not primarily record either private experience or self/group assertion. As a consequence of these several mixed features, this poetic is conservative to the extent that work which focuses on changing patterns of thought and desire rather than on changing behavior is inherently so.

In Chapter 1 I introduce the framework for my discussion in two sections. First, I clarify what I mean by authority and trace in slightly greater detail this poetic of intense but not autobiographical engagement and of political assertion that is more structural than narrative. Second, I sketch both the conventions of poetic authority to which Moore herself was responding and the patterns of critical reviewing that have granted this poet some kinds of authority while withholding others. In Chapter 2 I turn to Moore's multiple strategies for creating a poetry of authority based on the dual principles of impersonal information and idiosyncratic perspective or imagination. As I show, Moore's idiosyncrasy manifests itself through both didactic pluralism and complex reticence, and both of these features are in turn grounded in her definition of "clarity," with its unusual combination of the concepts of freedom and imperfection. In Chapter 3 I extend this discussion of the impersonal and personal features of Moore's poetry to argue that she constructs a verse of distinctive but not dramatized or personified "voice": she speaks directly to an audience about issues of moral and political importance without making herself personally the expert of her subject. Through an ongoing tension between constructed (or artificial) and idiomatic (or illocutionary) structures, the poet allows for subjective, playful but authoritative perception and expression without a corresponding stance of mastery for the author or self.

In the following three chapters I turn from largely structural analysis to more historical, biographical, and cultural discussions of authority in Moore's verse, organizing the chapters chronologically and by dominant themes. In Chapter 4 I examine Moore's relations with her family and the constructions of gender prevalent among Moore's college-educated, turn-of-the-century peers and argue that a critique of conventional constructions of gender not only appears frequently in the themes of Moore's early poems but affects the construction of her new aesthetic for poetry. Moore's familial and generational background are key to her extraordinary assurance in constructing this style and in her lifelong professionalism. In Chapter 5 I examine the primary didactic issue of her poetry, namely, the eradication of prejudice based on preconceptions about group or caste abilities—an issue she is most specific about with regard to nationality and race. This issue comes to the fore particularly during the 1940s, and it demonstrates both Moore's largely unacknowledged concern for national and international (moral) political issues and the problems inherent in Moore's poetic for direct political effectiveness. In Chapter 6 I turn to Moore's late poetry, arguing that this verse reveals more clearly than that of her earlier years her longstanding conviction of the importance of community to her poetic. I conclude in this chapter that the structural interactiveness, deliberate imperfection, and pluralistic openness described previously, and given political point by Moore's rejection of hierarchical constructions of both gender and race, take their most self-conscious theoretical form in her practice of quotation and their clearest thematic form in her late "love" poetry.

In the final chapter I examine the work of other, especially contemporary, poets whose work might be said to carry on poetic programs similar to Moore's, not because of direct influence or even because their verse clearly resembles hers in tone or subject, but because of analogous positioning and balancing of various political, traditional, personal, and aesthetic features within their poems. Here I discuss the work both of poets whose stance seems quite similar to Moore's (like Mina Loy, Heather McHugh, Cynthia Macdonald, and Alice Fulton) and of poets who fall at one or another of the extremes that might be said to mark the boundaries of this poetic (like Gwendolyn Brooks, Adrienne Rich, and Susan Howe).

❧

Because there is neither a truly "complete" edition of Moore's poems nor any simple method for most readers to obtain versions of her poems published before the 1981 *Complete Poems* (the only edition of Moore's work now in print), I use the *Complete Poems* version in most of my citations. On the other hand, when I give an extended reading of a poem published before 1925, I quote from either the *Poems* (1921) or the *Observations* (1924) version, since these are the poems she is most likely to have altered dramatically in the several decades between their first publication and their last. When chronology is important to my argument (as it is, for example, in the first part of Chapter 4), I quote each poem as it was first published in a book of Moore's poems or—for those never reprinted—as first published in a journal. Until a more complete edition of Moore's poems is available, such compromising between accessibility, personal preference, and historical value seems inevitable.

I would like to thank Marianne Craig Moore, Literary Executor for the Estate of Marianne Moore, for her generous permission to quote from Moore's voluminous unpublished manuscripts, and the Rosenbach Museum and Library for its permission to quote from the Moore archives. The poems "Voracities and Verities," "A Face," "By Disposition of Angels," "Efforts of Affection," and "Keeping Their World Large" are reprinted with permission of Simon & Schuster (Macmillan) from *Collected Poems of Marianne Moore*, copyright 1951 by Marianne Moore, renewed 1979 by Lawrence E. Brinn and Louise Crane; "Spenser's Ireland" is reprinted with permission of Simon & Schuster (Macmillan) from *Collected Poems of Marianne Moore*, copyright 1941, and renewed 1969, by Marianne Moore; "People's Surroundings" and "The Hero" are reprinted with permission of Simon & Schuster (Macmillan) from *Collected Poems of Marianne Moore*, copyright 1935 by Marianne Moore, renewed 1963 by Marianne Moore and T. S. Eliot. Excerpts from *The Complete Prose of Marianne*

Moore edited by Patricia C. Willis, copyright © 1986 by Patricia C. Willis, and the following poems from *The Complete Poems of Marianne Moore* by Marianne Moore are used by permission of Viking Penguin, a division of Penguin Books USA Inc.: "Blessed is the Man," copyright © 1970 by Marianne Moore; "I May, I Might, I Must," copyright © 1959 by Marianne Moore, © renewed 1987 by Lawrence E. Brinn and Louise Crane, Executors of the Estate of Marianne Moore; "O to Be a Dragon," copyright © 1957 by Marianne Moore, renewed 1985 by Lawrence E. Brinn and Louise Crane, Executors of the Estate of Marianne Moore; "Sun," copyright © 1957 by Marianne Moore; "Reminiscent of a Wave at the Curl," copyright © 1981 by Clive E. Driver, Literary Executor of the Estate of Marianne Moore; "Enough: Jamestown, 1607–1957," copyright © 1957 by Marianne Moore; "In Lieu of the Lyre," copyright © 1965 by Marianne Moore, renewed; "For February 14th," copyright © 1959 by Marianne Moore, renewed. Permission to quote from the following poems is also granted by Faber and Faber Limited: "Blessed is the Man," "Voracities and Verities Sometimes are Interacting," "I May, I Might, I Must," "O To Be a Dragon," "Sun," "Reminiscent of a Wave at the Curl," "A Face," "The Buffalo," "Enough," "By Disposition of Angels," "Efforts of Affection," "People's Surroundings," "In Lieu of the Lyre," "The Hero," "Spenser's Ireland," "Keeping Their World Large," "For February 14th."

While it is impossible to thank everyone who contributed to the many stages of my writing this book, I would like to mention those who have made repeated and substantial contributions. Moore scholars Bonnie Costello and Linda Leavell have been generous and critical readers—an extremely useful combination. I am particularly grateful to Linda for sharing her own unpublished manuscript with me, and for the careful detail of her response to a very late draft of my manuscript. Elizabeth Gregory also generously shared an unpublished essay on Moore with me. Jerold C. Frakes, Alice Fulton, Suzanne Juhasz, and Peggy Waller have proved themselves great friends and advisers in reading parts or the whole of my working manuscript, and in talking out matters of content, theory, and form.

Lynn Keller has been similarly generous in reading Chapter 7 and during our continuous discussions about poetry through our extended work together—several years ago on Moore, and more recently on "feminist measures" in general. The Alexander von Humboldt Foundation made the writing of this book possible through its generous research fellowship to the Free University of Berlin, where I was privileged to enjoy extended discussions with Moore scholar Dr. Sabine Sielke about my (and her own) manuscript, and with Professor Heinz Ickstadt about other matters concerning poetry and culture. Pomona College has granted me leave time, funded several trips to the Rosenbach Museum and Library, and provided me with terrific research assistants, among whom Carol Bork and Hilary Younkin deserve special thanks. At the Rosenbach Museum and Library, similarly, various curators and staff members provided crucial assistance, foremost Patricia C. Willis, Eileen Cahill, and Evelyn Feldman. Thanks also to Judy Harvey Sahak for opening the Scripps College Ella Strong Denison Library Macpherson Collection to me. It has been a privilege to work again with Mary Ellen Geer at Harvard University Press—an indefatigable and utterly reasonable manuscript editor. Finally, I would like to thank Maxi, Katie, and Jerry for so fully supporting an absent-minded, or absent, mother and partner during concentrated bouts of research and writing, and for filling my life with, as Moore puts it, "diversity, controversy, tolerance" and "gusto."

Abbreviations

P   *Poems* (The Egoist Press, 1921)
Obs   *Observations* (The Dial Press, 1925)
CP   *The Complete Poems of Marianne Moore* (Viking Press, 1981)
CPr   *The Complete Prose of Marianne Moore*, ed. Patricia C. Willis (Viking Press, 1987)
RML   Rosenbach Museum and Library, Moore archives
MMR   *A Marianne Moore Reader* (Viking Press, 1961)
CCE   *Marianne Moore: A Collection of Critical Essays*, ed. Charles Tomlinson (Prentice-Hall, 1969)
MMN   *Marianne Moore Newsletter*, ed. Patricia C. Willis (Rosenbach Museum and Library, 1977–1983)
IP   *Marianne Moore: Imaginary Possessions*, by Bonnie Costello (Harvard University Press, 1981)
TCL   *Twentieth Century Literature*, Marianne Moore Issue, ed. Andrew J. Kappel, vol. 30, 2–3 (1984)
SR   *The Savage's Romance: The Poetry of Marianne Moore*, by John M. Slatin (Pennsylvania State University Press, 1986)
PMM   *The Poetry of Marianne Moore*, by Margaret Holley (Cambridge University Press, 1987)
AMM   *Marianne Moore: The Art of a Modernist*, ed. Joseph Parisi (UMI Research Press, 1990)

Introduction

Poetry . . . is an assertion. The poet must use anything at
hand to assert himself.

William Carlos Williams

I seem to myself an interested hack rather than an author.

Marianne Moore

Questions of authority are questions of power. Gayatri Chakra-
vorty Spivak speculates that "'Power' in the general sense is . . . a
catachresis"—a misused, misunderstood, oversimplified term.[1] The
same might be said of authority—an aspect of power so various as
to be misleadingly denominated by a single name, especially a name
which suggests that its possessor is the exclusive initiator or "author"
of his or her power. Authority inheres in some offices (that of a
head of state, a judge, an elected official); it is perceptible in a
variety of circumstances, and exists even when it is not actively
perceived—as Marianne Moore states in "Marriage," "men have
power / and sometimes one is made to feel it." On the other hand,
the factors establishing an ordinary person's, or poet's, warrant for
public speech, for judgment, or for aesthetic or ethical leadership
do not always have a clear source, location, or substance. Moore
does not examine philosophical or epistemological roots of the
concept of authority, and neither will I; her interest, rather, lies in
constructing a position of authority that is not inherited through
the office of poet, does not stem from caste (race, nationality, class,
gender), and does not depend upon the assertion of genius or other
personal, exceptional abilities.

In this book, I use authority to mean a variety of things. First, authority inheres in that factor or those factors that poets allude to, invoke, or openly manipulate as enabling them to say what they do. Standard examples of such self-authorizing appear in the introductory verses of canonical poets well known to Moore—George Herbert, John Milton, and William Wordsworth. In *The Temple*, Herbert's authority to speak, and all praise for the worth of his verses, comes directly from God:

> Lord, my first fruits present themselves to thee;
> Yet not mine neither: for from thee they came,
> And must return . . .
> ("Dedication," 1633)

In *Paradise Lost*, Milton seeks inspiration from a "Heav'nly Muse" that seems to be a cross between the Greek deity and Christian God. Yet at the same time, he boldly states that he himself makes his epic original through his choice of a previously "unattempted" theme:

> Of Man's First Disobedience, and the Fruit
> Of that Forbidden Tree, whose mortal taste
> Brought Death into the World, and all our woe
> . . . . .
> Sing Heav'nly Muse
> . . . I thence
> Invoke thy aid to my advent'rous Song,
> That with no middle flight intends to soar
> Above th'Aonian Mount, while it pursues
> Things unattempted yet in Prose or Rhyme.
> (1667)

Here the poet is hero rather than worshipper. In contrast, Wordsworth, like most romantic poets, turns to Nature, often represented as female or through the person of a particular woman, as "The anchor of my purest thoughts, the muse, / The guide, the guardian of my heart and soul / Of all my moral being" ("Lines Composed a Few Miles Above Tintern Abbey," 1798). This is a tradition I return to later in this chapter to discuss its problematic aspects for women who themselves write poetry. Although modern poets rarely begin with formal invocations or dedications to a muse, the concepts of superhuman or otherworldly inspiration, personal heroic genius, and attunement to nature remain powerful bases of poetic authority.

According to Gerda Lerner, feminist writers of the medieval and early Renaissance periods saw themselves as similarly empowered. In *What Women Thought: The Creation of Feminist Consciousness,* she argues that early transcribers of feminist thought typically authorized their assertions, which at the time were utterly unconventional, by reference to one of three things: motherhood—hence their culturally acknowledged calling to educate the young; their talent or skill, an impulse or force presumably beyond their control, perhaps God-given; or spirituality, typically expressed through mystical visions—a nonliterary form of divine inspiration, which did not place them in competition with poets.[2]

In contrast, Moore, and other twentieth-century female poets whose work resembles hers, authorize themselves more fluidly and more skeptically—by reference to traditionally authoritative fields having little to do with poetry (biology, physics, history, law), to feminism itself (variously defined), and to a belief (often based in community experience) that although words do not reveal truth, change may occur because of them.[3] In each case, the poet openly distinguishes her constructions of authority from those of Western literary traditions—genius, nature, and supernatural inspiration—while acknowledging her debts to empowering elements in or writers of those traditions.[4] This is not a poetic of visionary wholeness or epiphany, but neither is it one of malaise or despair. It authorizes itself through inclusiveness, an assumed commonality of interest that does not claim universal insight or conclusive knowledge. To borrow terms from Moore that will reappear in this book, it is a poetic of "inquisitive intensity," of "diversity, controversy; tolerance," of "questions more than answers," but still and also of "gusto."

The concept of authority also includes that solid self-confidence, or personal but nonspecific authority, which stems from formative individual, familial, or group experiences. This is the kind of authority that Western, white, middle- and upper-class men may be said to enjoy beyond that of any other group—given their repeatedly affirming experience of themselves as holders of power, or at least of potential power—although, of course, any number of mitigating factors may either reduce the sense of authority of individual members of that class or increase the authority of people outside that restrictive category. Moore, for example, feels herself to be fully normative and highly empowered—to the surprise of many late twentieth-century readers whose conception of women's lives at the turn of the last century precludes such assurance.

By authority I also mean the credence that the reader, or, more important, a succession of publicly articulate readers, grants a poet in particular spheres—intellectual, moral, experiential, "feminine," and so on.[5] This kind of authority must be distinguished from personally claimed power; as Robert Paul Wolff points out, power can be based on force, while authority (thus defined) must be given. Or as Jerome McGann puts it: "Authority is a social nexus, not a personal possession."[6] Judith Bennett similarly distinguishes power from authority, defining the former as "the ability to act effectively on persons or things" and the latter as "recognized and legitimized power." In medieval England, she argues, women "were often powerful, but they were never authoritative."[7] A similar, although less extreme, distinction held during the early twentieth century when women held positions of power in the literary world but were not invested with authority by their peers. Bringing this distinction into the late twentieth century, Christine Battersby asserts in *Gender and Genius* that "we still associate the great artist with certain (male) personality-types, certain (male) social roles, and certain kinds of (male) energies. And, since getting one's creative output to be taken seriously involves (in part) becoming accepted as a serious artist, the consequences of this bias towards male creators are profound" (23); it continues to be harder for a woman than for a man to accumulate that nexus of artistic authority.[8]

Authority, then, is an umbrella category for a variety of feelings and forces that encourage, for example, William Carlos Williams to "assert himself" as the primary tactic, and perhaps even goal, of his poetry while they encourage Moore to avoid the label "poet" or even "author" altogether, preferring to call herself a "hack." Even

4

such an apparently transparent claim of lack of authority, however, can be complex and misleading. As I have already suggested, Moore rejects one kind of authority in frequently apologetic or self-questioning language in order to construct an alternative kind of authority that depends precisely on lack of self-assertion, the foregrounding of a questioning attitude, and an equalizing, constantly shifting access to the positions of expert and judge. While appearing to belittle herself, she instead shifts the terms of value by which one judges what is worth hearing, what empowers readers and previous speakers as well as what empowers herself. It may be, then, that Moore does not have a less powerfully felt warrant to speak than Williams; she clearly draws her privately felt authority, however, from different sources. Others, in turn, respond to these two poets' assertions differently, granting them different kinds and levels of that nexus of public authority.

Moore eschews a binary notion of empowerment, for herself in relation to traditions of the lyric poem and for her readers. To undermine these expected relationships of power, she constructs a complex intertextuality resembling that which Julia Kristeva defines in *Revolution in Poetic Language,* an intertextuality denoting the "transposition of one (or several) sign-system(s) into another" or "passage from one signifying system to another."[9] Moore, however, combines not just obviously diverse "signifying systems" in her juxtapositions of kinds of information, detail, and tone, but also literally several texts or voices through direct quotation. Her intertextuality directly links the most highly honored culturally authoritative sources (canonical literary texts, speeches by the President of the United States) with the least authoritative types of speech (random conversation overheard at public events, advertising slogans). Such intertextuality allows Moore to underline the seriousness of her message through literary allusion and fact and to avoid the directly responsive stance of an imitator or competitor while at the same time often also critiquing the source of her allusion: she speaks as compiler, for and from a community of heterogeneous voices, as herself a reader and listener of extraordinary intensity and interest rather than as "author" or personal authority. As a matter of fact and convention, Moore is a poet. She, however, prefers the stance of grateful, enthusiastic, and judicious collector. She arranges texts, or voices, to assert her own.

For all writers in this poetic, voice is of special concern, but not in that they simply seek to gain it—either for themselves personally or for other marginalized or silent people. With what might be seen as Bakhtinian dialogic pluralism (particularly to the extent that Kristeva's notion of intertextuality develops from her analysis of Bakhtin), they bring distinct voices into play in their constructions, building a poetry of fragmentation and of multivocality rather than of strong personal voice. Moreover, this heteroglossia is a means to an end; these poets accept the obligation of having something to say incurred by public speech, and use multiple voices or aspects of speech to counter the dominating tendencies that may threaten public, published assertion. Marilyn Brownstein writes of the "un-hierarchical relations in [Moore's] narrative register."[10] For these poets, a heteroglossic, pluralist, anti-imperialistic (or anti-specular) presentation or intertext of voices acts as a didactic tool of participatory education. No singular and unambiguous voice instructs, but the poems push oppositionally toward change.

As part of their construction of poetic forms that have authority and distinctive tone while remaining pluralistic, Moore and other writers manipulate what may be called variously "omission" or "silence" or "reticence" and several types of linguistic excess—wordiness, overinclusiveness, repetition, overwriting. In both these extremes, their use of language resembles what Lacanian/Kristevan theorists have demarcated as the feminine (or semiotic) in language and what an Anglo-American literary tradition has characterized as most typical of women's speech.[11] Indeed, these writers do propose tentative links between their stylistic choices and their gendered (and in some cases racial) marginality, but none appears interested in constructing a female poetic, in speaking for women or definitionally "as" a woman. In particular, they use silence and excess in their multiple manifestations as articulate tools of empowerment rather than as signs of exteriority, radical difference, or lack.

Consequently, these writers implicitly reject the philosophical basis of feminist theories developed from French and German philosophy and psychoanalysis, which tend to recognize only radically disruptive, nonverbal, extralinguistic strategies as either expressing or constructing an order beyond phallocentrism.[12] These writers' modes of silence (omission, restraint, syntactic fragmentation, unusual use of white space on a page) and of excess (lists, repetition, intrusive sound play, unusually wide ranges of diction or complicated syntax and long lines or other typographical modes of filling marginal space) may indeed be seen as oppositional to the symbolic or phallocentric realm, but not simply so. Far from rejecting outright more traditionally poetic and grammatical structures, these poets instead seem to emphasize the range of language practices available to them—from silence to excess and including various forms of articulate and traditional practice in between. They do not seek a "feminine" as opposed to a masculine language or tradition but instead reject essentializing and accept liberating strategies wherever they find them. Whether because, like Moore, they regard meaning as possible only within constraints, or because, like Gwendolyn Brooks and M. Nourbese Philip, they find precedents for combining the newly radical and the given in their (African American and Caribbean) communities' historical transformation of the English language, their rejection of binarisms includes a rejection of philosophies that cast the "feminine"—and implicitly the female—even symbolically as disempowered or outside of the language systems from which they build their poems. In my reading, they do not (to borrow from Lyotard) assign a "privileged exteriority" to the nonverbal or to nonsystemic discourse ("spontaneity, libido, drive, energy, savagery, madness") any more than to the laws of syntax and grammar, and in their poetry there is a fluid movement between these and other modes.[13] Because the writers I am discussing do feel authorized to speak within or through traditional, albeit modified, structures of language, I find theories of language and power relations that are not based on "feminine" and "masculine" characterizations of psychological development or of language most suggestive in analyzing their work.

Indeed, the most useful theoretical framework I have found comes from a field not typically seen as relevant to language and gender studies—namely speech-act theory. Especially as extended by J. G. A. Pocock's analysis of a speech-act as an act of power toward or over the receiver in "Verbalizing a Political Act: Toward a Politics of Speech," speech-act theory provides both a descriptive system for the interactive and illocutionary elements crucial to Moore's poetics, and an understanding of speech itself as an act of power within particular language communities and contexts. Pocock's analysis is useful in seeing that such a stance is oppositional without being revolutionary: as he writes, "the verbal strategy characteristic of the revolutionary is the reduction of You to a choice between We and Them, or even It"; revolution constitutes a "one-way act of power"—unlike a "two-way communication system" that opens or maintains possibilities for response between people.[14]

Generally, the writers of this poetic manipulate elements of traditional verse, or familiarity with the literary canon, through a transformation rather than rejection of previous structures, formulations, and idioms. Jan Montefiore argues in *Feminism and Poetry: Language, Experience, Identity in Women's Poetry* that women poets inevitably "write at once within and in spite of the context of a defining poetic tradition in which their gender makes them seem 'naturally' the bearers of others' meanings."[15] The poets I am interested in consciously manipulate this experimentation among multiple traditions. While this is, for them, a process involving more than two models or conceptions of language and verse, such experimentation nonetheless recalls Hélène Cixous's concept of "(the) in-between" and Luce Irigaray's negotiation away from a masculine specular economy, between the semiotic and symbolic linguistic realms.[16] Working among and between multiple traditions and modes also brings these poets into a realm of the in-between or complex negotiation in regard to political effectiveness and acknowledged authorial power.

Michel Foucault writes that "Where there is power, there is resistance, and yet, or rather consequently, this resistance is never in a position of exteriority in relation to power." Working from Foucault in his *Room for Maneuver*, Ross Chambers theorizes:

> Discourses of power are not simply open to disturbance, as communication is subject to "noise," but . . . the disturbance introduces change. It does so, moreover, without [directly] challenging the

system, since it consists of making use of dominant structures for "other" purposes and in "other" interests, those of the people . . . whom power alienates or oppresses.[17]

Calling oppositional behavior "ultimately conservative" to the extent that it works within a system (it helps the existing power structure to remain in place by making the system "livable"), Chambers nonetheless insists that "in the universe of discourse, which is that of human 'reality,' oppositional behavior has a particular potential to change states of affairs, by changing people's 'mentalities' (their ideas, attitudes, values, and feelings, which I take to be ultimately manifestations of *desire*)" (1). Oppositional narrative works to produce "shift[s] in desire," and hence change; it creates "'discontinuous local effects'" to disrupt traditional power structures and form at the level of ideas and values (xvii, xvi).[18] As this implies, it is a poetic whose oppositionality is discovered through a practice of oppositional reading—that is, a reading "that both produces that oppositionality and is responsive to it" (6). For, as Chambers argues, it is the "readability" of such texts that allows them to make use of prevailing discourse as a tactic so that they may, eventually, indeed produce the desired shift in their readers' ideas, attitudes, or feelings (2).

Just as Moore and other writers of this poetic reject simple oppositions encoding empowerment and authority, I attempt to keep my use of standard binary oppositions provisional, recognizing the inadequacy of terms like personal/impersonal, feminine/masculine, feminist/masculist, traditional/nontraditional, but preferring their known quantities to the development of new categories of analysis.[19] As Jacques Derrida has long argued, binary opposition displaces itself; a concept defined in juxtaposition to a given category is incorporated within its field of meaning, and differences between them may be deconstructed forever. As Spivak notes, however, one can use binary opposition as "provisional[ly] and polemical[ly]" as one uses any other critical tool (*In Other Worlds*, 77). My analysis attempts to keep its reliance on oppositions "provisional and polemical," denying essence or hierarchical value while nonetheless sketching boundaries.

Similarly, I attempt to sustain a balancing act in my reading of Moore's poetry. On the one hand, I trust Moore's own patterns of representing her interests, desires, and intent as fully as possible, assuming that she (like other poets) is intelligent and self-conscious as a poet and critic of poetry. Moore, of course, neither can nor attempts (or wishes) to articulate all aspects of her poetic design— not to mention that it changes with time, as she does. Nonetheless, even her partial, unconscious, contradictory explanations may illuminate aspects of her poetic. I attempt, as well, to recreate the contemporary discourse and background Moore may be responding to rather than attributing anachronistic principles to her structures and designs. At the same time, I take neither her words nor historical materials as simple fact, any more than I regard a single theoretical position as adequate or all-illuminating.

Finally, while I hope to point readers in the direction of making their own links between the quietly radical innovation and oppositionality of Moore's poetry and the work of various contemporary female poets, the point of this book is neither to establish a new "tradition" nor to trace Moore's influence. My detailed analysis of Moore's own questions of authority and how others have questioned the authority she constructs is meant to suggest useful ways to read the work of other poets that falls between the overlapping boundaries conventionally established by formalist, feminist, and avant-garde critics. If indeed this study of Moore's verse is useful, readers will want to provide their own candidates for similar analysis, moving far beyond the brief suggestive analyses of various poets that I include in the final chapter. Most of this book, then, will explore patterns of assertion, speculation, and questioning in Marianne Moore's work, and in the rest of this chapter I will provide a historical and critical context for that exploration.

For Marianne Moore, as for all modernist poets, the romantic poet and poem provided the scale against which poets and lyric poetry were measured. During the romantic era, the relation between the poet's singular gift and public responsibility was conceived in psychological and personal terms. By writing about "his" own revelations or self, the poet instructed others about truths in the world. Walt Whitman's magnificently unabashed "I celebrate myself and sing myself / And what I assume you shall assume" is only the most obvious expression of this stance. For the romantic poet, the poem provides a ground for the author's transcendent claims to Beauty, Truth, and Nature through the profundity of his perception. Intensified self-consciousness and the Wordsworthian overflow of feeling become the route by which the poet may temporarily escape the entrapment of a trivial, personal, and historical rather than a transcendent self. The poem, then, does not express but preeminently constructs the self as Poet. As Jonathan Culler argues in *The Pursuit of Signs*, even the prototypical romantic act of invoking an "other" through apostrophe constitutes either an imposition of self onto the world or an interiorization of the world into the self, that is, in either case a radical act of egocentrism rather than of communion. Although apparently focused elsewhere, the poem's images work primarily "to dramatize or constitute an image of self . . . One who successfully invokes nature is one to whom nature might, in its turn, speak."[20]

The notion of "successfully" invoking nature depends upon the romantic conception of individual genius, which in turn constitutes the link between selfhood and art. As Svetlana Boym writes in *Death in Quotation Marks: Cultural Myths of the Modern Poet*, "Geniuses are endowed with the ability to read 'natural laws'; moreover, they themselves create according to natural laws with the help of grace and inspiration. Hence, in Romanticism art and the artist's personality turn into 'correlated variables' . . . they can be viewed as metaphors of one another, with tenor and vehicle thoroughly blurred."[21] This association of romantic, idealized selfhood with poetry was so powerful up through the middle of the twentieth century that one could not easily think of writing except as an egotistic endeavor. Moore, for example, writes home from college on April 4, 1908:

> Writing is all I care for, or for what I care most, and writing is such a puling profession, if it is not a great one, that I occasionally give up—You ought I think to be *didactic* like Ibsen or poetic like "Keats,"

or pathetic like Barrie or witty like Meredith to justify your embarking as selfconfidently as the concentrated young egotist who is a writer, must—writing is moreover a selfish profession and a wearing (on the investigator himself). (RML VI.14.05)

The shifting of pronouns from first person to second to third person masculine ("I care," "you ought," "writer must . . . himself") may indicate a gendered base for Moore's discomfort with becoming a "writer" as defined by these traditions. Moore's contemporary Genevieve Taggard writes similarly of herself as "a serious-minded egoist (i.e., artist)."[22]

Much has been written about how the masculine engendering of the romantic poet's authority presents difficulties for the woman writer, and indeed the extent to which romanticism itself is historically a masculine phenomenon.[23] As Margaret Homans argues in *Women Writers and Poetic Identity,* for the romantic poet the self and its imagination are central, and this self is defined through the poetry as masculine; logically, "where the masculine self dominates and internalizes otherness, that other is frequently identified as feminine" (12). The poet's self and imaginative projection are male, and the precursor of the poet is a father from whom this son learns and against whom he must rebel. In contrast, feminine or womanly forces appear alternately as Nature, as a figure of desire, or as a human figure whose role is a mixture of the other two—none of these options empowering to a woman who herself will write.[24] Given this, as Homans calls it, "phallogocentric community" of selfhood at the heart of the romantic poet's identity, it was difficult for a woman outside this community of fathers and sons to create a female central self in the genre of the lyric poem or to imagine other structures to replace this "centrism" of the individual perceiving self (34, 36).[25] For a woman who was a poet, the parameters of this notion of central selfhood set a trap: as Homans puts it, the very "desire to be at the center generates hierarchical thinking" and "this hierarchy is at the heart of male supremacy" (36).

An alternate and obviously feminine tradition of poetry, that of nineteenth-century American sentimentalism, was equally unacceptable to at least some ambitious female poets. Such poetry was extremely popular throughout Moore's youth and arguably the dominant form of women's poetry well into the twentieth century.[26] Cheryl Walker describes this poet as preoccupied with "disillusionment, ambivalence, and renunciation"; she writes in the first person about experiences that are assumed typical of women and that establish her as preeminently female (motherhood, death of a child, courtship and marriage, unsatisfied longings; *Nightingale's Burden*, 141). By stereotype—although as Joanne Dobson points out, rarely in fact—the "poetess" is frail and sensitive to the point of sickness or manic-depressive inability to cope with the daily events of adult life. She writes of her feelings and her experiences, substituting depth of emotion for range of topic or breadth of experience, eschewing intellectual, political, or public issues in her work. According to Walker, these poets "present[ed] themselves poetically as creatures who lived mainly out of the world—in domesticity, in love relationships, in nature" (*Nightingale's Burden*, 150). As such attitudes suggest, they assumed their experience of a core subjective self as key to their expression; like their contemporary and predecessor poets, they perceived poetry as a vehicle for simultaneously expressing, exploring, and constructing identity in selfhood—despite their emphasis on a type of experience (the mother's; the mourner's) rather than the more individuated or transcendental experience of romantic "genius." Although the high visibility, professionalism, commercial success, and striking honesty of some of these poets might make them far more attractive as models for a "modern" poet than the stereotype would suggest, the stereotype was firmly entrenched by the turn of the century, and even the most unconventional of these poets supported aspects of that type.[27]

The self-fashioning of the "poetess" as creature of nature and of the emotions contributed to the Freudian/Lacanian sense of her lack when compared to the "poet" of intellectual and aesthetic authority. Christine Battersby's *Gender and Genius*, which traces the anti-female roots of the concept of genius from ancient Roman to modern times, explores the dynamics of these gendered associations. Svetlana Boym, too, analyzes the concept of genius as "quintessentially virile"; as she writes, genius shares a root with genre, gender, genetics, and genitalia. The poetess is by definition not a genius; she is a sort of literary *nouveau riche* who lacks the genetic blue blood of the artistic aristocracy. Genius is a sign of genetic artistic superiority, crucial to the genesis of "true" poetry and available to one gender only. (*Death in Quotation Marks*, 195)

The poetess responded to such characterization by claiming an alternate authority for her speech that was based precisely on those characteristics (femininity, nature, domesticity) used to shut her out of the category of genius, thereby marking a space for herself but also widening the gap between women and "poets."

Not surprisingly for such consciously polarized constructions, the authority of the poetess resembled that of the romantic poet in its self-absorption—despite its portrayal of the subject as morally selfless. Although it constructed an essential rather than a transcendent self, this self also used the objects it described or addressed to represent the essence of—in this case—a gender as much as a calling. Unlike the (implicitly masculine) "poet," however, the specifically feminine "poetess" constituted by this construction offered little room in which the ambitious and curious mind might stretch; its nature was represented as private and personal (although common to women) rather than as transcendent and universal (that is, common to men). In other words, while poetesses attempted to create a female world and expression distinct from that of men, they in fact fashioned their separation in terms that linked them with masculist assumptions and norms, both by defining themselves in terms of lack and through the shared notion of a unique and fully bounded creative self.

The tradition of the "poetess" described above is one of the nineteenth century, but there are clear links between this genre and the sentimental poetry of the first decades of the twentieth century, especially that of Sara Teasdale, Edna St. Vincent Millay, Elinor Wylie, and Louise Bogan. Although (and perhaps because) it was commercially successful, such sentimental poetry was a primary target of modernist revisionary aesthetics, far more than the romantic verse of, for example, Wordsworth, Keats, or Shelley, which modernists also rejected as flawed or outmoded but never as trivial. In her important revisionary study *Sentimental Modernism,* Suzanne Clark argues that such targeting had a clear cultural as well as aesthetic base. Popular assumptions about gender and about the dominant tradition of women's writing linked a watered-down, "feminine" romanticism of emotionality with women who wrote poetry: "The gendered character of this condemnation seemed natural: women writers were entangled in sensibility, were romantic and sentimental by nature, and so even the best might not [be seen to] altogether escape this romantic indulgence in emotion and sublimity."[28] As Clark's prose indicates, sentimental verse was seen to incorporate the excess and self-indulgence of romanticism, but not its virile genius.

Perhaps because of the disgust with which masculist modernist poets and critics viewed sentimentalism, several early twentieth-century women who were poets, editors, and critics turned decisively away from modes of feminine writing—Moore among them. For poets like Moore, however, sentimentalism was problematic not just because it was looked down upon by her male peers but because it did not provide the nonessentializing, nonautobiographical structures and strategies she sought. Like its nineteenth-century predecessor, twentieth-century sentimental poetry focused on essentializing constructions of both self and gender (whether as true portraits or as what writers like Sandra Gilbert, Alicia Ostriker, and Walker refer to as masks or personae). One might argue that Moore makes some use of sentimental traditions in her late poetry. For the most part and during her formative years, however, sentimental representations of gender, of subjectivity, and of poetic authority as identified with attitudes of essentialism offered Moore little she found helpful.

Just as the concept of sentimental literature is now undergoing profound revision, that of modernism is being reevaluated both as a hegemonic tradition against which "postmodern" and "marginal" poets rebelled and as a counterhegemonic response to various kinds of social change and to previous poetic traditions uninterested in the dilemmas of the modern world. In a series of decisive essays on gender and modernism, Rachel Blau DuPlessis describes "high modernists" (Eliot, Pound, Yeats, Lewis, Lawrence, Williams) as "the most problematic nonhegemonic group" within literary tradition because while "modernism has a radical poetics and exemplary cultural ambition of diagnosis and reconstruction," it is also "imbued with a nostalgia for center and order, for elitist or exclusive solutions, for transforming historical time into myth." Specifically in regard to gender, DuPlessis argues that "in writings of male modernists, femaleness is as fixed and eternal a category as ever before in Euro-literature . . . Their radical forms are made relatively accessible—readable—by the familiarity of gender limits, the iconographies they inherit and repropose."[29] This conservatism also reveals itself in the related "high" modernist notion of authority, or an authoritative self.

As quoted in the epigraph to this chapter, William Carlos Williams identifies poetry as not just "assertion" but the poet's assertion of "himself." Although he and most other modernist poets consciously rejected romantic notions of transcendent selfhood, they rewrote the privilege of poetic authority in equally self-empowering modernist form: "the poet must use anything at hand to assert himself." The authority of the self was recast as "impersonal," descriptive, and historical; the poet constructed a verbal snapshot or collage rather than a self-portrait revealing that transcendent mixture of intuition and intellect. His attitude was factual rather than sublime, but he maintained a posture of masculine self-assertion.

The concept of authorial impersonality provided a solution for masculist modernists because it disguised elements of subjectivity (culturally coded as "feminine") in their poetry, while providing an alternate, historically viable mode of authority. For female poets, however, this offered no solution to the romantic subjugation of female "nature" to male genius. The impersonal mode had characterized phallic authority for centuries (as in laws, textbooks, and newspapers); in its grounding assumptions, women were presumed to be as incapable of fully rational intellectual understanding as of romanticism's fully subjective (transcendent) identity.[30] Similarly, modernist "impersonality" maintained an emphasis on individual "genius" in the poet's ability both to perceive connections between disparate literary and cultural moments and to present them originally in poetry.

Through her responses to romantic, sentimental, and masculist modernist modes of authority, Moore developed for herself an anti-poetic mode of expression that rejected the self-centered, culturally imperialistic assumptions of both the romantic and modernist eras as well as the essentialist mode of popular women's poetry in the United States, while still claiming an authority for itself. Neither ignorant of the implications of her own biographical and social/cultural (re)sources nor apologetic about them, Moore assumed her right to speak for herself without feeling she had to speak of herself or from one part of herself only: she claims to be a "hack" rather than an "author" only to the extent that she redefines the value of these terms. Moore does not seek natural genius or inspired loveliness but ostentatious constructedness in a poem, including structural inconsistencies or imperfections and remarkable openness to the nonpoetic.

Without yet considering what Moore's stylistic choices and strategies may imply to her or to a changing audience, one may note a general pattern of contradictory inclusiveness as a primary element of her response to previous and contemporary poetic movements.[31] This is perhaps most strikingly revealed in her diction, which ranges from an erudite and precise Romance-Latinate vocabulary, to the less erudite but still formal tones of what Marie Borroff has described as an advertising or feature article style, to downright chatty, colloquial utterances.[32] One is initially most struck by the erudition and formality of Moore's language, but her less frequent informal tones are equally significant to her poetic. In conjunction with this range of diction, Moore's syntax covers the full range of expression, from highly complex sentences to sentence fragments to short statements of simple, direct speech—again, with the balance falling on the side of the complex. Moore writes in sentences more often than in fragments, and within the sentence Moore's syntax tends to be hypotactic; she proceeds by argument, by subordinating one thought or idea to the next, and by accumulating finely delineated distinctions through phrasal parallelism and repeated embedded clauses that modify or sharpen her major clauses. On the other hand, her sentences or sentence fragments themselves are often paratactically juxtaposed in a manner suggestive of collage and characterizing much modernist poetry. Her poetry, then, demands from its reader both careful attention to the complex syntactic development of an argument and imaginative leaps from one statement to the next. One can see in these features, as in others, Moore's manipulation of the languages of restraint and excess.

Moore's poetry is typically phrasal, using (as Borroff enumerates) relatively few dynamic finite verbs, a high number of participial and complex noun phrases, and lists resembling Whitman's catalogues in their inclusiveness but omitting the pointed rhetorical reiterations that keep Whitman's syntactical progression clear. These elements contradictorily make her verse both highly compressed (much information is compacted into very tightly constructed syntactic units) and yet lavish in its inclusion of precise detail. The combination leads to a particularly dense surface of language and, again, to a contradictory sense of what her poetry or voice is "like." Moore's syllabic stanzaic structures, heavy use of line-end and internal rhyme, extremely varied line lengths, unusually frequent quotation, and explanatory notes to poems increase this effect of density.

Yet Moore's poetic is remarkably engaging and interactive, suggesting an aesthetic of correspondence, conversation, and exchange rather than one of mastery. One sees this particularly in the poetry's use of quotation and in its speech-like features even, as Grace Schulman argues, when the poems do not include a first-person speaker.[33] Many poems address an unnamed "you," and others imply address by their argumentative tone. Moore's prominent use of negatives to begin a poem and her use of self-correcting syntax contribute largely to this effect, as do her exclamations, questions, imperatives, and colloquialisms. Humor also contributes to the spoken quality of Moore's poems, marking even an uncharacterized speaker as present; especially for the modernist period, Moore's verse is notably playful and witty.

Finally, Moore's verse is didactic, yet includes multiple judgments and perspectives. The poems almost without exception make some point, but not through aphorism. Moore believes in teaching through argument and example, revealing the play of her own mind around the complexities of a subject and then leaving it to the reader to put the multiple, often contradictory pieces of that play into a concluding frame. In some poems, the multiplicity of this play is extreme—to the point where the reader cannot decisively choose a single refraction of the poet's prismatic perspective. In other poems, the primary argument is clear, and complexity lies in its abstraction and detail. The result is a style that calls attention to its difference, its departures from its own rules or patterns as well as from those of traditional verse. This is a highly constructed and controlled, elegant poetry that paradoxically makes indecision, awkwardness, what one might even call imperfection key to its aesthetic. It maintains a strong flavor of informal "gusto" that effectively counteracts the hierarchical elevation its formality and stylization might otherwise imply.[34]

Moore's style marks the middle as well as the end of a story about influence and authority: what Taffy Martin has called the "myth" of Moore as "writing master" or formal perfectionist has had a powerful impact on succeeding writers and perhaps particularly on women who, until quite recently, saw in Moore almost the only example of a publicly successful female American poet—winner of every major poetry prize offered in the United States.[35] Consequently, to understand later poets' rejection or choice of a poetic similar to hers, one must consider how Moore's reputation and oeuvre became part of the multifaceted tradition within and against which they wrote. To do this, one must understand how Moore's poetry has been received, or how her authority has been, and continues to be, constructed by her readers.

Moore's most highly regarded poetry is that written in the 1910s, 1920s, and 1930s and prized for its iconic clarity, impersonality, experimental form, and ironic, spirited tones.[36] While often at odds with one another because of conflicting interests and competition, Moore's most famous peers unanimously praised her poetry during these years and later.[37] At the same time, their praise of this work is often combined with an indirect condescension toward Moore based on what they saw as her eccentric personal life as well as, implicitly and explicitly, on gender. Such evaluation began with

Moore's contemporaries and was vigorously supported by the New Criticism.[38] It imagined an almost otherworldly, antiseptic Moore—one who, as William Carlos Williams writes in 1925, "wip[es] soiled words" clean, "taking them bodily from greasy contexts"; she separates words out, treating them "with acid to remove the smudges" of the everyday world.[39] Similarly, Randall Jarrell, writing in 1969, reads Moore's poems as "entirely divorced from sexuality and power, the bonds of the flesh"; she, like her words, is wiped clean—without body and without power.[40]

The alterity that Williams and Jarrell depict takes various forms in Moore criticism, typically combining elements of female, neutered, and nonhuman "otherness" in ways that reduce or deny her authority as poet.[41] Williams, for example, who writes oftener about Moore than anyone else, in a 1923 poem tells poets "evad[ing] the law" to show up at her door crying "Marianne, save us! / Put us in a book of yours" ("Marianne Moore"); in a 1936 letter he quotes himself saying, "Marianne was BEAUTIFUL! I found myself drifting off into the trance which only beauty creates more than once. There is a quality there which is unspeakably elevating—" (MMN VII [1983], 18, 33). Similarly, in his 1951 *Autobiography*, Williams writes that "Marianne was our saint . . . in whom we all instinctively felt our purpose come together to form a stream. Everyone loved her."[42] Although Williams always means to praise, in each of these passages Moore disappears as an actor in her own right: she saves others; she elevates others by her beauty; and, in a very suggestive unfinished metaphor that conflates the alterity of the feminine with that of the nonhuman, she provides the bed in which others may "form a stream" clarifying their purposes. Eliot calls Moore "one of the strangest children I have ever had anything to do with" in their 1935 exchange over her *Selected Poems* (RML V.17.26). Gilbert Snow refers condescendingly to Moore's "aesthetic shrinking from the present industrial ugliness" (*New York Herald Tribune Books*, May 17, 1925); Winthrop Sargeant in a 1957 *New Yorker* essay calls Moore a "daring performer on a flying trapeze . . . soaring and pirouetting above the world of reality." These men represent Moore as an object of wonder, a modernist version of the age-old pedestal of difference, in terms uncomfortably reminiscent of the poetess.[43]

Although one might see such idolatry merely as a tribute to the force of Moore's achievement and character, idealizations of women carry connotations almost as misogynistic as open attacks because of the centuries of stereotyping in which women were respectable only insofar as they were inhumanly good, beautiful, and nonthreatening. As Sandra Gilbert and Susan Gubar describe, throughout centuries of literary production "the ideal woman that male authors dream of generating is always an angel"; "whether she becomes an *objet d'art* or a saint . . . it is the surrender of her self—of her personal comfort, her personal desires, or both—that is the beautiful angel-woman's key act."[44] Given the patterns of our literary tradition, it is perhaps not so surprising that despite Moore's legendary acerbic wit and intimidatingly encyclopedic knowledge—not to mention her skill as a poet—her peers idealized her into the safety of various nonthreatening images. As Robert Penn Warren rhymes: "For many years you charmed us, / And never harmed us." A poet need not compete with a saint, a circus performer, or a child.[45]

Related to the tactic of personal idealization is that of calling attention to gender in inappropriate contexts or with unnecessary ostentation, and this, too, happens repeatedly in public and private reviews of Moore's work, often in the context of high praise.[46] To mention just a few instances: in 1923, Eliot ends his review of *Poems* with the gratuitous "'magnificent' compliment" that "Miss Moore's poetry is as 'feminine' as Christina Rossetti's, one never forgets that it is written by a woman; but with both one never thinks of this particularly as anything but a positive virtue" ("Marianne Moore," CCE, 51). Randall Jarrell condescends more openly, using class as well as gender stereotypes: "Some of [Moore's] poems have the manners or manner of ladies who learned a little before birth not to mention money, who neither point nor touch, and who scrupulously abstain from the mixed, live vulgarity of life" ("Her Shield," CCE, 122). Wallace Stevens writes that "Miss Moore's form is not the quirk of a self-conscious writer. She is not a writer. She is a woman who has profound needs" (quoted in Molesworth's *A Literary Life*, 273). Although he does not mention gender specifically, Hugh Kenner limits Moore's intellectual capacity in a way implying gender. After praising her highly as an experimenter with nonorganic forms and, with Williams, as one of the two "inventors of an American poetry," he concludes that "having been held together by a temperament, [Moore's poetry] grows dilute as the temperament grows more accommodating"; it "deteriorates, as it were, through insufficient grasp of its own principles." Moore, Kenner writes, is "other from us" in her "limited, remarkable achievement," begging the question of who "we" are (*A Homemade World*, 114, 117). As has so often been claimed of women writers, Moore does not understand her own accomplishment.[47]

By the 1940s and 1950s, such stereotypes were firmly enough in place that even an intimate friend like Elizabeth Bishop may have perceived the older poet in part through their distortions, and certainly contributed to them. In particular, both her memoir "Efforts of Affection" and the poem "Invitation to Miss Marianne Moore" highlight the older poet's otherworldliness in a way that helps to engrave an image of the poet as quaintly harmless.[48] For example, in her memoir Bishop relates that Moore has "shiny bright" eyes, "like those of a small animal"; she "was innately flirtatious," has a "*chinoiserie* of manners," and kept an "'old-fashioned' apartment—" (51–53). With a sense of wonder resembling the disguised condescension of Hugh Kenner, Bishop sees Moore as having "a unique, *involuntary* sense of rhythm, therefore of meter, quite unlike anyone else's"; she refers to Moore's "quick decisions" and then corrects this to read "decisive *intuitions* . . . as to good and bad, right and wrong"—as though Moore did not think or decide (54, 60; my emphasis). Although Bishop does castigate feminist readers for not paying enough attention to "Marriage" (a poem that "says everything they are saying and everything Virginia Woolf has said") and briefly describes Moore's early suffrage activity, the essay encourages readers to think affectionately of a feminine "beloved 'character'" rather than to give attentive respect to a poet or thinker of note (55, 60).[49]

Bishop's "Invitation to Miss Marianne Moore" has a similarly belittling effect: repeating that her mentor should "please come flying," Bishop portrays Moore as a fairy-tale good witch—complete with pointed black shoes, cape, and "angels" "riding / on the broad black brim of your hat."[50] The poem suggests that certain conditions must be propitious for this poet's journey: "The flight is safe . . . the grim museums will behave / like courteous male bower-birds," "Manhattan / is all awash with morals this fine morning." Moore will "Mount[ ] . . . above the accidents, above the malignant movies, / the taxicabs and injustices at large," listening to "a soft uninvented music, fit [only, she implies] for the musk deer." The light mockery of this poem is affectionate, and Bishop even makes herself the butt of it to the extent that she offers as entertainment things they will do together:

> We can sit down and weep; we can go shopping,
> or play at a game of constantly being wrong
> with a priceless set of vocabularies,
> or we can bravely deplore, but please
>   please come flying.

Nonetheless, the overall effect of the poem is to make Moore nonhuman (like the musk deer), fantastic (she flies), and fragile ("the weather"—actual and moral—must be "all arranged")—not a person but a phenomenon: "like a daytime comet / with a long unnebulous train of words."

Several years later, although with a condemnatory rather than an affectionate edge, Adrienne Rich depicts a similar Moore in "When We Dead Awaken: Writing as Re-Vision": she was "maidenly, elegant, intellectual, discreet."[51] More recent critics maintain the same view. For example, Cheryl Walker writes that "it doesn't really matter that [Moore] *failed* to insist upon her femaleness . . . many male poets have led quiet lives, applauded gentility, preferred intellectual reflection over gestures of social outrage, and amused themselves with playful experiments"—that is, have been irrelevant to intellectual and political activity as traditionally defined (*Masks*, 7; emphasis mine). Perhaps following the letter but not the spirit of Costello's essay praising Moore's transformation of "feminine" values and language, Betsy Erkkila claims instead that Moore fosters the otherworldliness of "traditional notions of feminine virtue and reticence"; she "maintained a childlike moral innocence"; her "'imaginary gardens' and fundamental Protestant faith set her apart, aesthetically and morally, from the sordidities of the times" (*Wicked Sisters*, 103, 148, 126).[52]

On the other hand, Moore has contemporary defenders. For example, Rachel Blau DuPlessis sketches an argument similar to mine in its contours, writing that "Moore produced a distinctive intellectual, analytic writing fueled by [her] articulate suspicion of foundational assumptions of gender in poetic texts and traditions."[53] Joanne Diehl finds that Moore "covertly reinscribes the male imagination's conceptualization of the feminine" by divorcing "conventionally condoned aspects of the female . . . from those that threaten men," and yet that her poetry is revolutionary in its "radical questioning of institutional structures" and hierarchy (*American Sublime*, 47, 50). Jeredith Merrin writes of Moore's imaginative "maternal transformation and assimilation of congenial male sources" to create a poetry of thoroughgoing "resistance to *all forms* of egocentricity and domination," reflecting a "woman-centered" but not woman-focused world (*Enabling Humility*, 136, 139, 137). Jeanne Heuving argues that Moore engages in a "doubly paradoxical" poetic "quest . . . to write a universal poetry which includes her perspective as a woman and to construct a universal consciousness out of a 'direct treatment of the thing'" (*Omissions Are Not Accidents*, 21). Sabine Sielke invokes French feminist theory to argue that Moore constructs a sense of female subjectivity that is not based on corporeality ("Intertextual Networking"). My work is enriched by the concurrences and debate among these and other feminist readings.

The relative paucity of affirming feminist work on Moore until recently, and even now of book-length studies, may result as much from current trends in feminist criticism and what it typically recognizes as feminist poetry as from the characteristics of Moore's own verse.[54] Critical perspectives like those of Gilbert, Walker, and Erkkila tend to celebrate a poetry that has explicitly female-focused and political or historical/biographical subject matter, like that of Adrienne Rich, as most interestingly and radically feminist.[55] As a consequence, poets (especially heterosexual or not actively sexual poets) writing outside this mode tend not to be the focus of feminist critical study.

In contrast, my book is concerned with a non(auto)biographical and formally experimental poetic. Such a poetic resembles that of poets linked with LANGUAGE theory (for example, Beverly Dahlen, Rachel Blau DuPlessis, Kathleen Fraser, Lyn Hejinian, Susan Howe, Leslie Scalapino, and Rosmarie Waldrop) in stressing language as such and the play of language outside the given economies of exchange/interpretation. On the other hand, the poetic I explore tends to take a more inclusive and pragmatic approach than LANGUAGE poetry to its relationship with a community of readers, attempting to balance the value of experimental surface textures with both loosely didactic intent and accessibility.

While I am convinced, and argue in the following chapters, that Moore's verse is intensely political and that her basic principles are feminist in her own understanding, they are not so in a systemic or global context. This poet focuses her critique on the foibles or more serious flaws of the individual without typically extending that criticism to the institutional structures that encourage the behavior and beliefs she deplores. Yet although Moore is in part blocked from direct political involvement by her fundamentally capitalist and Christian belief that individuals are more powerful finally than institutions, she also for this reason sees enormous possibilities for action and for power in the individual will, and she regards the "new" century in which she lived for seventy-two years as a continual challenge to act.

TWO

"Inquisitive Intensity"
in Marianne Moore

The impersonality of the artist is the vainest of delusions.

George Moore, quoted in CPr, 77

In these non-committal, personal-impersonal expressions of
   appearance,
the eye knows what to skip;
the physiognomy of conduct must not reveal the skeleton;
"a setting must not have the air of being one,"
yet with X-ray-like inquisitive intensity upon it, the surfaces
   go back;
the interfering fringes of expression are but a stain on what
   stands out,
there is neither up nor down to it;
we see the exterior and the fundamental structure—

"People's Surroundings," CP, 57

*M*oore rejects the Romantic role of poet-authority early in her college days of experimental versification primarily because it celebrates an unexamined egotism she associates with an outmoded lyric and with hierarchical principles.[1] Similarly, as a woman distinctly *in* the world and ambitious to be respected as a writer and critic within the brotherhood of poets, Moore rejects the voice of female experience that would publicly define her as belonging to the oversimplified category of Woman and "poetess"—despite the fact that some of her female peers (notably H.D.) combined feminist principles with a continuation of some aspects of this tradition. Between these two traditions, Moore forges a verse that, unlike the sentimental poet's, speaks with an authority divorced from openly personal experience and yet, unlike the masculist poet's, at the same time acknowledges the contingencies of her perspective and positioning. Moore creates a poetry that is both personal and impersonal, that engages its subjects and readers from a stance of contradiction. Similarly, her poetry balances between what late twentieth-century critics would identify as poststructuralist and modernist conceptions of language, of poetry, and of the self. John Slatin argues that, far more than most of her contemporaries, Moore "uses poetry as a medium for speculation about poetry" (SR, 244); I argue in addition that, for Moore, speculating about poetry inevitably involves speculating about gender and other forms of cultural identity that both assume the power of, and confer power upon, one kind of poet or speaker or poem over another. The role of subjective positioning, with its concomitant assumptions of authority, is central to such speculation.

Moore's authority is that of the morally minded, politically astute outsider who is accepted on the inside. Although she would call this stance ungendered, its outlines and at times its content stem from her culturally anomalous position as an early twentieth-century professional, and by principle feminist, poet, working within the main literary and cultural stream. Rachel Blau DuPlessis speculates that "Moore may have postulated herself as a kind of cultural inter-gender . . . figuratively. A creature neither he (with its political crudeness) nor she (with its accumulated opprobrium) but some third thing—maybe closer to 'she' but without the burden of stereotype and denigration."[2] Elizabeth Gregory sees Moore as like her peers in attempting to redefine those values that place European and historical qualities above those of the modern and American world, or to "exorcise" a sense of "cultural secondariness," at the same time that, as a woman, Moore "invest[s] in the revaluation of secondariness" and "dismantling" of hierarchies more extensively than American and modernist men.[3] Charles Altieri speculates that Moore saw "that her male colleagues were perhaps a bit too drawn to versions of constructivism that stressed those powers of the 'composing-antagonist,' and thus conferred on 'the poet' the right to impose his order on the bland fields horizontal before him . . .

27

woman's place afforded an imaginative position where alternative forms of imaginative power become available."[4] I similarly see Moore as like yet unlike both her male and female peers. Such positioning rests upon Moore's complex and never explicitly stated belief that women and minorities in particular should play a public role without falling prey to the morally crippling belief that they may speak for others like them. In speaking from a "woman's place," Moore speaks as herself, a woman, rather than for women. The primary experiment of Moore's poetry consists of her attempt to create a lyric poem in which the female writer may assertively articulate diverse feelings and beliefs, appealing to and invoking a strong sense of (largely female) community, without adopting the guise of cultural or transcendental, hence "universal," authority. She wishes neither to write in masculine drag nor to replace that masculine self of authority with a culturally feminine one.

The contrast of the apparently impersonal and transparently personal is key to the structure of Moore's verse because it is inseparable from other bipolar constructions of empowerment and authority—especially the masculine/feminine, self/other, and perfect/imperfect. Moore seeks a shifting middle ground among these boundaries, emphasizing the "personal-impersonal expression of appearance," not fact. One of Moore's most accessible poems illustrates this distinctive and experimental balance. "To a Steam Roller," first published in 1915, begins with a cutting critique in the dead certain tone of irony.

> The illustration
> is nothing to you without the application.
>   You lack half wit. You crush all the particles down
>   into close conformity, and then walk back and forth on them.
>
> Sparkling chips of rock
> are crushed down to the level of the parent block.
>   Were not "impersonal judgment in aesthetic
>   matters, a metaphysical impossibility," you
>
> might fairly achieve
> it. As for butterflies, I can hardly conceive

of one's attending upon you, but to question
the congruence of the complement is vain, if it exists.

(P, 6)

Like the steam roller itself, the speaker is excessive in describing how a machine-like intelligence crushes all in its path, or accepts only information "crushed" into "close conformity" with the traditions of "the parent block," even though the humorous puns on "chip off the old block" and "half-witted," the very long last line of each stanza—appearing especially long in the first stanza because of its sequence of monosyllables—and the outrageousness of the controlling metaphor soften the critique. Were it not impossible, such an effectively flattening intelligence might almost "achieve" the "impersonal judgment in aesthetic / matters" claimed for centuries by poet-critics who insist that one may indeed know what is and is not a good poem by measuring (crushing?) it against "the level of the parent block."

Up to this point, the speaker has spoken with an authority and absolutism equivalent to the steam roller's. The poem concludes, however, with the modest admission that the speaker may be wrong: "butterflies"—creatures of fancy and delight, far more suited to "illustration" than to "application"—may indeed "attend[ ] upon you," "complement[ing]" the steam roller's dogged reliance on conformity and repetition and thus at least potentially transforming it into some other kind of more imaginative thing. The speaker seems to have been reminded by mention of the "metaphysical impossibility" of "impersonal judgment" that her or his judgment may also be fallible. Incongruities do "exist" and, even in a brief and witty satire, should be acknowledged.

While this poem has nothing to do with gender or subject-identity ostensibly, it may well be read as a piece of didactic instruction on how to read. Even the most intransigent-seeming quality or aspect may carry its unlikely, incongruous complement. This does not prevent the steam roller from being a steam roller, but it inevitably changes one's vision of that object. When reading a poem

29

or judging someone radically different from oneself, this poem warns, acknowledge the possibility of a "complement."[5]

Moore's satire of the steam roller may constitute a critique of all judgment that sets itself up as absolute, and at the same time of any simple distinction between rational and fanciful or objective and subjective ways of knowing. As she states in "Idiosyncrasy and Technique," "One writes because one has a burning desire to objectify what it is indispensable to one's happiness to express": writing manifests "burning desire" yet it objectifies its expression (CPr, 507). This combination of objectifying form (seen in both the pronoun "one" and the word "objectifies") with embedded need or desire reveals the complexity of Moore's authorial stance. Like her "Student," who is "too reclusive for / some things to seem to touch / him; not because he / has no feeling but because he has so much," her poems are only apparently objective, while in fact the site of "burning" feeling (CP, 102). As Moore quotes from George Moore in a review of his work, "the impersonality of the artist is the vainest of delusions" (CPr, 77). Or as she more wryly puts it, "One asks a great deal of an author . . . that he should not induce you to be interested in what is restrictedly private but that there should be the self-portrait; that he should pierce you to the marrow without revolting you" (CPr, 328).

As with all "self-portraits," those created by Moore's verse rest in part on contextualizing factors outside the frame of the poem, and particularly on Moore's contradictory self-positioning as both author and not-author.[6] Moore insists that she is not a "Poet"—as though the word for her must be capitalized and set off in quotation marks or otherwise distinguished from the ordinary. She claims, instead, merely to have "a way with wording," or to have put together "statements that took my fancy which I tried to arrange plausibly," or to present facts about things and people "in lieu of the lyre."[7] A 1958 poem calls itself "a grateful tale—/ without that radiance which poets / are supposed to have—/ unofficial, unprofessional" ("In the Public Garden," CP, 191). In the same year, Moore writes: "When under the spell of admiration or gratitude, I have hazarded a line, it never occurred to me that anyone might think I imagined myself a poet" ("Subject, Predicate, Object," CPr, 504). In

1960, Moore comments that "what I write . . . could only be called poetry because there is no other category in which to put it," herself substituting the phrases "observations, experiments in rhythm, or exercises in composition"; her work is "if not a cabinet of fossils, a kind of collection of flies in amber" (MMR, 258, xv). As early as 1934, when asked "what distinguished her as a poet from the ordinary man," Moore responded, "Nothing." Similarly, in 1968, in response to receiving the National Medal for Literature, Moore commented, "I'm a worker with words, that's all."[8]

Yet because her poetry is philosophical, moral, and at times didactic in a national and international sphere, Moore seems indeed to take on the "Poet's" mantle. Willard Spiegelman describes didactic poets as those who hold "their mirrors up to nature not simply to reflect it but to occasion reflection and right action in their readers. Poet as teacher, reader as student." Although Moore does not openly set herself up as a teacher, her poems contain moral reflection and pronouncement; like the poets Spiegelman describes, she combines "irony, wit, self-deprecation . . . skepticism" and a healthy dose of "American common sense" with a didactic stance.[9] Moreover, she is indefatigable in publishing what she has written, placing her words in the public sphere.[10] "Literature is a phase of life," she confidently proclaims in "Picking and Choosing."

Moore does not hang back from "life" or pronouncements about it. As the next lines of "Picking and Choosing" reveal, however, one may be too confident: "If"

> one is afraid of it, the situation is irremediable; if
> one approaches it familiarly,
>   what one says of it is worthless. Words are constructive
> when they are true; the opaque allusion—the simulated flight
>
> upward—accomplishes nothing.
>
> (P, 18)

Moore rejects the falsifying "familiar[ity]" that takes a privileged stance or interpretation as its due, calling instead (later in the poem) for "the most rudimentary sort of behaviour," "a 'right good / salvo of barks,'" not the "opaque allusion." As such positive certainty indicates, Moore's refusal to call herself "poet" or her work "poetry" does not result from lack of confidence or an overweening awe at the splendors of her predecessors and peers but from principled choice about the kind of aesthetic she will construct and her conception of the role of "literature" in the public world.

Understanding this aspect of Moore's pronouncements and poetic is crucial to the argument I make. Moore is not primarily apologetic, self-belittling, or modest in refusing the title "poet." This behavior may resemble but it does not, I am convinced, stem from the poet's lady-like or "feminine" character. My argument here, then, is in direct contrast to a reading like Betsy Erkkila's, which interprets both Moore's statements about her poetry and the style itself as working within the conventions of feminine modesty, virtue, niceness, and restraint.[11] On the contrary, and especially in her early years, Moore's stance seems to me more belligerent than modest.[12] When she was first forging, developing, and defending her stylistic and aesthetic choices, it was a matter of crucial importance for Moore to be clear about the communities with which she sought to identify her work and those which she rejected—and she is unwaveringly clear about rejecting the role of "poet" and the aesthetic of poetry as commonly defined.[13] As Joanne Diehl writes, Moore "engages modesty as a trope";[14] and this trope grounds her construction of an alternative authority.

The vocabulary of poststructuralism describes well the effect of Moore's assertiveness in combination with her lack of transparent self-portraiture or personalized judgment. In fact, Moore appears to offer her work for such analysis by providing no immediately recognizable subject-identity for her multiply constituted text to center around. In poststructuralist terms, Moore's politics and practice are deconstructive and anti-essentialist. Unlike her peer modernist poets (whom she in other ways closely resembles), Moore sees an object's or poem's meaning as unstable, changing with the conditions and culture of its reader, just as she sees a text's production as influenced by the conditions and communications of its author's life.[15] Here the poststructuralist concept of the "death of the Author" is useful. Although, unlike Barthes and Foucault, Moore believes that a writer bears a direct moral responsibility for his or her work, like them, she does not see herself as the sole creator of her poems, or her poetry as stemming from an act or moment of transforming genius.[16] As one sees in her extensive use of mosaic- or collage-like quotation and in her public statements about her art, she conceives of herself as compiler or editor rather than as "poet."[17] She inscribes herself in her verse without making herself its subject or assuming she can control (or has originated) its full meaning.

In "To a Steam Roller," as in all of Moore's poetry, the speaker is not necessarily the poet, or any other characterized individual. We know only that she or he is educated, witty, fallible, and intensively engaged. There are no romantic apostrophes, no meldings of the self into a greater being or force, no grandly representative stances of a speaking soul or poet-self, and no open references to personal experience. Even when Moore uses an "I" of distinctively singular feeling or experience ("I, too, dislike it," or "You can make me laugh," or "I don't like diamonds"), the tone is so casual, the "I" so fleetingly foregrounded, and the lack of contextual positing so complete that it does not encourage the reader to imagine a centrally subjective self—transcendental or sentimental.[18] The portrait is of an aesthetic, philosophical, political position rather than of a personality or "I"—even though that "position" has marked attributes of idiosyncrasy and charm.

Early Moore criticism tended to read this lack of an identifiable speaker in Moore's poetry as "self-effacement" or Christian "selflessness," and recent feminist criticism has repeated a version of this claim.[19] Joanne Diehl makes this case most strongly, arguing that Moore's is a poetic of disguise: her style "theatricalizes itself in the name of self-effacement"; it creates "a generic mask that provokes readerly response, directing that responsive feeling away from the author and back toward the textual field" (*American Sublime*, 53). Because the vocabulary of masking has become so prominent in feminist criticism, and in Moore criticism, this point has a particular significance.[20] To hold that any poetic that admits the centrality of subjective perspective yet does not focus on that subject is self-disguising assumes that a poet's experience or feeling necessarily constitutes the subject of a text. I argue, in contrast, that while these areas of information do indeed illuminate a text, it is not because they constitute it. Moore avoids referring to herself in her poetry not because she represses or because her feeling, identity, and experience are irrelevant to what she would say, but because she rejects both the romantic and the sentimental poetics that ground themselves there. Moore does not don a mask; she asserts her perspective, identity, and values through the mode she finds most conscionable and effective.

The primary alternatives to the psychoanalytic framing of Moore as a poet of self-effacement come from poststructuralist theory and from comparison with the visual arts. For example, Carolyn Burke identifies Moore's nonpersonalized (although rarely impersonal) presence with Kristeva's positing of shifting and fluid boundaries of selfhood as the basis of nonpatriarchal textual production.[21] DuPlessis similarly presents Moore as undercutting conceptions of the self as a unified, adequate organizer of experience and information while still inscribing herself and gender politics in her poems ("No Moore of the Same," 23). Implicitly poststructuralist and feminist is Gary Lee Stonum's recent analysis of Emily Dickinson as a writer who befuddles critics by explicitly declining elements of poetic inscription and public behavior that would categorize her as an "author":[22] Moore, too, rejects a role of mastery over her text and toward her reader. Like Dickinson, she recognizes the traditional (and to some extent inevitable) power relationship between author and reader and attempts through multiple strategies to undermine it. In *Painterly Abstraction in Modernist American Poetry*, Charles Altieri speculates that "modernist abstraction seemed to [Moore] capable of sustaining principles of idiosyncratic assertiveness that were not as likely as expressivist models to be shaped by prevailing cultural codes or to depend for their reinforcement on the social structures one hopes to change" (263). Abstraction offered Moore a mode in which to attempt a nongendered poetic while maintaining an idiosyncrasy that inscribes individuality. Linda Leavell provides extensive documentation for her similar claim that Moore felt stronger ties to and was more influenced in her aesthetic by avant-garde visual and plastic artists than by the modernist literary community: for example, Moore's lack of a singular subject resembles the lack of singular perspective in Cubist painting (*Prismatic Color*, 73–74). Like these critics, I see Moore's non-"authorial," abstract, shifting representation of identity or self as necessarily conjoined with, not effacing, a distinctive, idiosyncratic, and personal presence.

In ways pertinent to Moore's poetic, Gayatri Spivak suggests both that it is "strategic" to posit an occasional essentialism or autobiographical speaking subject and that "the way to counter the authority of either objective, disinterested positioning or the attitude of there being no author (and these two opposed positions legitimize each other) is by thinking of oneself as an example of certain kinds of historical, psycho-sexual narratives."[23] One counters the force of traditional perceptions of identity and authority by representing the self both as "I" and through multiple types of narratives. Moore does precisely this. Using an unemphatic "I," she juxtaposes a variety of types of diction, reference, and narrative—historical, scientific, religious, popular, and cultural—in resisting the boundaries of a set authoritative position or truth. Rather than proclaiming the Whitmanian (and Poundian) "I contain multitudes," Moore presents multitudes without conceiving of an authoritative self as the container. As she writes in the poem I use for my chapter title, "People's Surroundings . . . answer one's questions," but some phenomena constitute "questions more than answers." Hence to conclude with a question is not necessarily to equivocate or hide but may be the most honest form of self-positioning—especially to the extent that questions frame the kinds of answers possible. It is the reader's task to sort through the various things and positions Moore presents— "non-committal, personal-impersonal expressions of appearance"— in search of the equally important answers and questions, the "surroundings" themselves and what structures them.

Again, Moore's stance toward a poet's or poem's authority is contradictory. No individual alone authors, or authorizes, a text. At the same time, she believes that the writer has a moral and civic duty to say something of worth and that this statement (indirect as it may be) will always in some sense dominate the poem. Her implied or explicit "I" is both strategic in acknowledging that all perspectives are positioned or stem from some personal place, and structurally and morally necessary as representing her crafting role

in the poem. It is abstractly personal. Returning to "People's Sur-
roundings," although "the physiognomy of conduct" does not nec-
essarily "reveal the skeleton," when an "X-ray-like inquisitive inten-
sity" is turned upon it, "the surfaces go back; / . . . we see the
exterior and the fundamental structure."[24] Moore then concludes
this poem with thirteen lines of celebratory exclamation listing a
variety of professions, titles of privilege, and places (ranging from
"cooks" to "queens" to "asylums and places where engines are
made"). She does not, that is, openly reveal anything "fundamental"
about this puzzling and ambitious poem. If it is, however, the
"structure" rather than the apparent moral of the poem that is
fundamental, we may see some point in the insistently "personal-
impersonal" tone; we may find the abstract self-portrait.

The middle of this poem's five sentences catalogues a variety of
"personal surroundings" and is forty lines long; its list of "surround-
ings" ends as follows:

> straight lines over such great distances as one finds in Utah or in
>   Texas,
> where people do not have to be told
> that a good brake is as important as a good motor;
> where by means of extra sense-cells in the skin
> they can, like trout, smell what is coming—
> those cool sirs with the explicit sensory apparatus of common
>   sense,
> who know the exact distance between two points as the crow flies;
> there is something attractive about a mind that moves in a straight
>   line—
> the municipal bat-roost of mosquito warfare;
> the American string quartet;
> these are questions more than answers,
>
> and Bluebeard's Tower above the coral-reefs,
> the magic mouse-trap closing on all points of the compass,
> capping like petrified surf the furious azure of the bay,
> where there is no dust, and life is like a lemon-leaf,
> a green piece of tough translucent parchment,
> where the crimson, the copper, and the Chinese vermilion of the
>   poincianas

set fire to the masonry and turquoise blues refute the clock;
this dungeon with odd notions of hospitality,
with its "chessmen carved out of moonstones,"
its mocking-birds, fringed lilies, and hibiscus,
its black butterflies with blue half circles on their wings,
tan goats with onyx ears, its lizards glittering and without
    thickness,
like splashes of fire and silver on the pierced turquoise of the
    lattices
and the acacia-like lady shivering at the touch of a hand,
lost in a small collision of the orchids—
dyed quicksilver let fall,
to disappear like an obedient chameleon in fifty shades of mauve
    and amethyst.

                                       (CP, 55–56)

By writing of "surroundings" (Spivak's "narratives") of history, myth, nature, art, class, profession, and gender rather than about individual experience or personality, Moore suggests that such things in fact go a long way toward making up that conglomerate called the "personal" self. It matters crucially, for example, whether a female self lives in "Utah or in Texas" with their "cool sirs" or in "Bluebeard's Tower" with its "odd notions of hospitality," even though both places fall into Moore's category of constituting questions rather than answers and both may prove isolating to a *woman* "of common sense"—particularly to a poet. At the same time, both would attract a poet, the first because of its clarity (associated through Moore's description with wit) and the second for its lush beauty. There is clearly some danger in being either subsumed or seduced by these at best "odd[ly]" hospitable offerings of a patriarchal world.[25]

    Yet despite such danger and despite the poet's lack of a dramatic, centering "I," "People's Surroundings" is so distinctively singular in its idiosyncratic lists of details and occasional flights of verbal loveliness that one cannot help feeling the poet's own presence more strongly than any thing she describes. This poem is in some ways about creating a presence or personal voice out of things utterly beside (or outside) but nonetheless partly constituting the self. As Moore writes in "The Accented Syllable" (1916), "tone of voice" is "that intonation in which the accents which are responsible for it are so unequivocal as to persist, no matter under what circumstances the syllables are read . . . if an author's written tone of voice is distinctive, a reader's speaking tone of voice will not obliterate it" (CPr, 32). In "People's Surroundings," the poet utterly dispenses with questions of identity while creating a presence of unembodied but utterly distinctive authority: as the poem says, "the interfering fringes of expression are but a stain on what stands out."

Moore's insistence that an observer will see "the fundamental structure" or "what stands out" if she or he looks sharply, that "an author's written tone of voice" or "intonation" will "persist," makes the question of whether this is a strategy of construction or of disguise more than a semantic quibble. Indeed, Moore structures much of her verse (particularly her early verse) antagonistically. Again, as Diehl writes, "the poems attest to a view of the world that is essentially adversarial, a view that requires a code of conduct suited for survival" (*American Sublime*, 59). Moore typically presents her convictions in negative form or only by stating what she holds *not* to be true; she proceeds in several poems by contentious argument; she repeatedly describes situations in which conflict of some kind must be met. Yet Moore does not see the "self" as a refuge against a hostile outer world and therefore does not imagine her most essential "armor" as that which protects her from others; the difficult surface of her poetry is not meant to keep a reader out or to protect a vulnerable private poet but to promote "inquisitive intensity" and hence enable perception. In this poetic of contradiction, of exploded dichotomous boundaries, negation serves to affirm; difficulty enables clarity; and multiple surfaces of apparent impersonality or armor establish a self-portrait that will "persist, no matter under what circumstances the syllables are read."[26] Given that apparently sincere and transparent portraits will be read according to gender, racial, and class stereotypes—hence, according to a reader's preconceptions rather than to unequivocally distinctive characteristics of the writer—Moore's strategies for blocking such preprogrammed response may indeed provide the clearest form of self-portrait possible in her eyes. Moreover, structures of negation, contradiction, and multiple surfaces help establish the interactive element of Moore's poetic: by presenting her views in terms of what they differ from or what they are not, Moore models and encourages a similarly engaged response from the reader. The argument thus engendered may be simultaneously antagonistic and cooperative. As Moore writes, "we employ antithesis as an aid to precision" (CPr, 397).

It is here that a fuller understanding of the principle of "clarity" in Moore's verse helps to distinguish my position from that of critics who see Moore's poetry as essentially masking. Moore's most frequently expressed desire for her poems was that they be clear. In a 1919 letter to Ezra Pound, Moore writes: "Anything that is a stumbling block to my reader, is a matter of regret to me" (January 9, 1919; RML V.50.06). An early version of "Poetry" ends with the line: "enigmas are not poetry" (RML I.03.36). In the poem "An Ardent Platonist" (published in 1918 and not reprinted), Moore argues that "to understand / One is not to find one formidable . . . to be philosophical is to be no longer mysterious; it is to be no / Longer privileged, to say what one thinks in order to be understood." In "Idiosyncrasy and Technique," she reasserts this conviction with characteristic indirection and negation: "Since writing is not only an art but a trade embodying principles attested by experience, we would do well not to forget that it is an expedient for making one's self understood" (CPr, 508).

As the convolution of many of Moore's statements promoting clarity suggests, her perspective on this concept is not the obvious one. Costello, in fact, claims that while "Moore's method is to appear to be simply getting it said, like everybody else," she instead "revises the forms and structures peculiar to verse . . . and those inherent in ordinary language . . . to hinder the automatic flow of statement into established orders that may seem to be 'natural' but are in fact language-bound" (IP, 160–161).[27] In college, Moore writes her family that "by artistic I mean with a view to the relations of things—with a respect for the main issues of life and a sort of contempt for hard and fast definitions" (November 29, 1908; RML VI.14.11). "Feeling and Precision" (1944) makes clarity its theme, but in modified form: "We must be as clear as our natural reticence allows us to be" (CPr, 396). Years later, Moore tells Donald Hall, "I think the most difficult thing for me is to be satisfactorily lucid, yet have enough implication in it to suit myself" (MMR, 261). Moore's clarity is always complex, always involves "implication."

Given the poet's conviction that responsible authority never insists or proclaims itself as unilateral, it is hardly surprising that her notion of clarity points the reader toward personal discovery, often through contradiction, rather than presuming to provide illumination itself. The difficulty of Moore's clarity, however, also no doubt stems from the inevitable difficulty of constructing something new—a new poetic mode, a new set of relations among a writer, a text, and an audience, and a new mode of authority that depends on the interaction of all three for its full construction. Colin McCabe describes the relation of "clarity" to such a project in his foreword to Gayatri Spivak's *In Other Worlds*:

> No matter how great the commitment to clarity, no matter how intense the desire to communicate, when we are trying ourselves to delineate and differentiate the practices and objects which are crucial to understanding our own functioning and for which we as yet lack an adequate vocabulary, there will be difficulty . . . there will be a certain difficulty in reading *any* work which is genuinely trying to grapple with some of our most urgent problems which do not yet— and this constitutes their most problematic intellectual aspect—have the clarity of the already understood.[28]

Moore articulates a similarly contextual notion of what is clear in a 1931 review of Pound's first thirty Cantos: Pound, she concludes, achieves the clarity of "saying something 'in such a way that one cannot re-say it more effectively'"—a property more important to her than "eas[e], for hurried readers" (CPr, 273).[29] Moore makes her points in the most "effective" way possible, given that she has no use for "the clarity of the already understood."

Clarity and a revisionary aesthetics constitute the subject of two poems Moore wrote during the 1930s. In "The Hero," she distinguishes the traditional grail-seeking, dragon-fighting, war-making or prophetic "hero" from one who faces ordinary, daily difficulty with "a sense of human dignity / and reverence for mystery." The model hero of her poem is a "decorous frock-coated Negro" tour guide, responding gently but mechanically to the insistent and superficial questions of a tourist. While this tourist is "fearless," a wanderer or "hobo," out to see the world's "sight[s]," the metaphorically sight-less hero has an altogether different kind of vision: "He's not out / seeing a sight but the rock / crystal thing to see—the startling El Greco / brimming with inner light" (CP, 8–9).[30] The hero is the ideal tour guide because he is not distracted by the tourist or by Martha and George Washington's graves. He indicates mysterious "inner light." Similarly, in "When I Buy Pictures" Moore's speaker "may regard myself as the imaginary possessor" only of "what would give me pleasure in my average moments"—pictures "in which no more is discernible / than the intensity of the mood," or in which "the approved triumph" is not "easily" honored (CP, 48). This poem ends (in its final version) with lines echoing the conclusion of "The Hero": the art Moore seeks "must be 'lit with piercing glances into the life of things'; / it must acknowledge the spiritual forces which have made it" (CP, 48). A triumph too easily "honored" will not lead one to its spiritual sources. Or as Moore quotes Ruskin in 1927: "To see clearly is poetry, prophecy, and religion all in one" (CPr, 184).

Defining clarity as "inner light," "the rock crystal thing to see," a triumph not easily honored, and as poetry itself, Moore indicates that surface difficulty, indirection, tactics of presentation based on antithesis may be at times the clearest way to move readers to their own visions. The readers who interest Moore are not tourists, and a writer cannot point to "inner light" as to George Washington's grave; the reader must be as motivated and questing as the writer. Difficulty of surface enables interpretation by preventing a too-simple or merely assumed understanding of the topic at hand—as also of the writer.

Such a notion of clarity complements Moore's belief that no individual can adequately know about a subject of importance, regardless of his or her experience or scholarship. In her view, the honest observer will always be in part baffled by an observed thing or event. This ontology may be based partly in Protestant Christianity. As Michael Edwards suggests, in the Christian "fallen" world, all meaning is fictive: "meaning is an absence, that has to be laboured for"; more than most, even non-Christian, writers, however, Moore insists on the "fictionality" of her own "account." She "suspend[s]" the world "re-creatively" between apparently factual description and consciously idiosyncratic representation.[31] Her poetry exhorts the individual to see, not to accept information or doctrine as received.

Through a combination of paradox, precision, and wit, and like her use of multiple "surroundings" or narratives, Moore's extensive use of scientific information in fact undermines the centrism both of "fact" as such and of a centrally important perceiving self, thereby again revealing the complementarity of her concepts of authority and clarity. Relying heavily on *National Geographic* and other popular magazines, encyclopedias, newspapers, and her own extensive notes taken from reading, lectures, and museum visits on a wide range of historical, scientific, and cultural topics, Moore fills her poems with facts. "The Plumet Basilisk," for example, compares the Costa Rican "dragon" with that of Malay:

> Ours has a skin feather crest;
> theirs has wings out from the waist which is snuff-brown or sallow.
> Ours falls from trees on water; theirs is the smallest
> dragon that knows how to dive head-first from a tree-top to some-
> thing dry.
>
> Floating on spread ribs,
> the boat-like body settles on the
> clamshell-tinted spray sprung from the nut-meg tree—minute legs
> trailing half akimbo—the true divinity
> of Malay. Among unfragrant orchids, on the unnutritious nut-
>
> tree, *myristica*
> *fragrans*, the harmless god spreads ribs that
> do not raise a hood. This is the serpent-dove peculiar
> to the East;
>
> (CP, 20–21)

In such verse, the authority of the poet does not stem from a moment of revelation, much less from the poet's translation of such observation into an intuition of universal truth. Nor is the poem about the poet's presence in a landscape (or situation) that allows for revelation. Her notes, in fact, force recognition that no such landscape exists except as created through the author's (or reader's) library, museums, and zoo.[32] Instead authority here lies in the accuracy of the information Moore passes along, and in the suggestiveness of the commentary she embeds in the apparently objective detail—for example, the lines quoted above calling "their" basilisk "the true divinity of Malay" and a "serpent-dove." Such interpretive comments do not call attention to themselves and receive no extension into a formal argument or thesis, much less explanation of what seems to be their contradictory claim: a "true divinity" is not clearly the same thing as a "harmless god" or what in Christian mythology seems an incongruous linking of evil and good—the "serpent-dove." Similarly, Moore's omission of a predicate specifying the relation of the lizard to "true divinity" allows the phrase to register associatively before the reader sees the more positive identifications with less clearly "true" divinity that follow. Identifying the several references to myth and divinity within the poem and constructing from them an argument about Moore's purpose in presenting such detailed but, as it were, unexcavated information becomes the reader's task, and having constructed such an argument the reader must then share responsibility with Moore for its claims. Authority lies somewhere between the sources of Moore's information, her suggestive use of that material, and the reader's construction of an intellectual or moral argument from the poem's suggestions.

And yet Moore acknowledges the originatory control she has exercised in "The Plumet Basilisk" at the same time that she rejects its self-aggrandizing or essentializing forms. Only a few first- and second-person pronouns occur in this poem, each casual yet revealing the importance of Moore's crafting hand. In her sole use of the first-person singular, the poet stresses her role as speaker:

Now, where sapotans drop
   their nuts out on the stream, there is, *as*
I have said, one of the quickest lizards in the world—
                   (CP, 21–22; emphasis mine)

Sounding more like a lecturer than a seer, the poet reminds her reader that the information presented thus far is not disembodied fact, as that of textbooks may seem to be: it has a specific and personal source, which may be credited or blamed for its perceptual angle. Moore's "I" is even foregrounded by its position at the beginning of a line, and yet because this brief aside is grammatically gratuitous, it is easy to read right over it. Moore seems to be reminding her audience both that "I am saying this" and that this is not simply "my" vision, or nature appropriated by "my" need or desire.

Similarly, the poem's two uses of "you" serve both to place each reader personally in the landscape and to distance readers from any singular vision, as the ambiguous personal and impersonal, singular and plural meaning of "you" in English allows. In the first instance, Moore claims that unlike the serious dragon-like "tuatera," the "frilled lizard . . . and the three-horned chameleon, are non-serious ones that take to flight // if you do not": readers here may reveal themselves as serious or not in response to these lesser mutations of the ancient dragon. In the second use of "you," Moore gives her readers a more important position. The Costa Rican basilisk

is our Tower-of-London
jewel that the Spaniards failed to see, among the feather capes

and hawk's-head moths and black-chinned
    humming-birds; the innocent, rare, gold-
defending dragon that as you look begins to be a
    nervous naked sword on little feet, with three-fold
separate flame above the hilt, inhabiting

fire eating into air.

(CP, 23–24)

The dragon's transformation is one that all may see, yet the vision is overlooked by those with only appropriation or dominion on their minds. "Spaniards failed to see" the "jewel" of nature visible to any "you" who will look at it; as with the steam roller's flattening insistence, imperialism or the egotism of attempted conquest blocks vision, destroys all jewel-like "sparkling chips of rock."

Without the preceding "I," one might mistake this passage as implying that any modest observer (not a conqueror) may gain a pure or unmediated experience of nature, see it on its own terms, know it. Yet Moore's earlier reminder that we see only what she *tells* us, together with the highly metaphorical quality of this passage ("you" see not just a lizard but a "jewel," a "naked sword" on "feet" that is mythically "gold-defending") must disabuse the reader of any such ideal. Like the poem itself, the basilisk that "you" see and that Moore claims as "ours" is a work of art, a moral guide, every bit as much as it is a creature scientifically observed and precisely rendered onto a page. In part, this is sleight of hand: Moore simultaneously asserts her objectivity and reveals it to be bogus. On the other hand, as she states in "Armor's Undermining Modesty," "What is more precise than precision? Illusion" (CP, 151).

The implications of Moore's use of "you" here go against the grain of most readings of Moore's animal poems, which argue that these poems function through accurate representation to show respect for a different order of being from which the reader may learn to be unselfconscious, unpossessive, ungreedy, and so on.[33] In such readings, Moore depicts an animal with "scientific" accuracy, becoming—as Lynn Keller quips—a speaking "eye" rather than the subjective "I" (*Remaking it New*, 98). This is certainly an accurate description of Moore's method, but only in part. In addition, this lizard, like others of Moore's animals, evokes highly metaphorical and fanciful description from its author. Even the poems lacking a textual "I" reveal their author's subject position in the wild idiosyncrasy of their descriptions. The "Pangolin," for example, is a "near artichoke," resembling both a wrought-iron vine and "the hat-brim of Gargallo's hollow iron head of a / matador" (CP, 117, 118); "The Frigate Pelican" resembles both Handel and "charred paper" (CP, 26). In other poems, "Peter" the cat is a "dangerous southern snake," resembling "seaweed," an "eel," and a "mouse," but with "alligator-eyes" and springs of "froglike accuracy" (CP, 43–44); "Snakes, Mongooses, Snake-Charmers, and the Like" presents its subject as "long fingers all of one length," resembling "the shadows of the alps /

45

imprisoning in their folds like flies in amber, the rhythms of the skating-rink" (CP, 58). Because the perspective making these disparate images cohere with one another and with the more closely "factual" material of a poem is embedded metonymically in the text rather than apparent from self-reflective statements in it, one may be seduced into overlooking the presence of that singular perspective and misread the poem as factual.[34] One may fail to see the butterflies hovering over the steam roller. The very density of the detail, however, cautions "you," the reader, to "look" more carefully both at the detail itself and at who it is that "tell[s]" us what we see. Animals do not exist in a world separable from that of the humans who perceive them: we may indeed learn from them, but only through a combination of observation and imagination.

Authority, for Moore, admits its personal bias, thereby destroying any clear distinction between the personal and impersonal, or subjective and objective knowledge. So-called facts, like mythology, or like idiosyncratic perception, have their limits, and the nonimperialistic, nonhierarchical poet who nonetheless wishes to take a public and moral stand must position herself among those limits as among the facts themselves. Moore writes in one of her notebooks that "the most desirable thing in the world is to confuse a know-all," and one can see her use of information, with its objectivity but simultaneous indivisibility from both the perception of the author and the figurative nature of language, as doing precisely that (RML notebook 1250/24). Poems of information will necessarily confuse anyone who wants to accept them as equivalents to the encyclopedia or magazine articles from which many of their parts come, because those readers will not look beyond the surface of their information—which is interesting but in itself pointless. The "know-all" by definition trusts information as sufficient in itself.

Moore's college course work in biology and her lifelong interest in science undoubtedly underlie her only apparently paradoxical love and distrust of facts. Moore came to her maturity in the age that developed quantum mechanics and the concept of scientific relativity, and she was passionately interested in such theories. As Lisa Steinman confirms in *Made in America*, at least basic ideas of quantum theory were broadly known by the twenties, and Moore reveals in her reading notebooks (1916–1943) that she had read broadly in this area, noting reviews of Einstein's biography, several issues of the *Scientific Monthly,* and books by Bertrand Russell—who was important in popularizing recent discoveries in science—as well as numerous other books on science (*Made in America,* 67, 187n51). Although she studied biology and wrote about plants and animals, Moore's verse is more closely related to developing theories in physics than in biology. According to quantum theory, an object manifests itself differently according to the context of the experiment in which it is seen: for example, light behaves as particles under one set of experimental circumstances but as waves under another. Accordingly, it is impossible to know the object of observation except through the mediation of an experimental situation; there is no dualistic separation of object from observer or tools of observation, of nature from knowledge. To be known accurately, then, the object must be seen in multiple and paradoxical or what Niels Bohr has labeled "complementary" ways.[35] Moore's use of negation, of antithesis, of contradiction in almost every aspect of her poetic structure resembles Bohr's concept of complementarity: phenomena are known most clearly by being seen from multiple and paradoxical points of observation. Moore's familiarity with Cubism's presentation of multiple perspectives simultaneously would only have strengthened her attraction to such principles.

Redefining clarity, for Moore, dovetails with redefining authority: to speak clearly is to have authority, both positive values for Moore but only to the extent that clarity does not entail transparency and authority does not rest on inflexible notions of identity and truth. The matter of tone is crucial in negotiating this tension in Moore's work, for most readers do not "hear" in her poems a "voice" or self-representation typically associated with "female" (or nongendered and feminist) empowerment, or with oppositional, nonauthoritarian thinking of any kind; hence they suppose it does not exist. The elaborate syntax, technical and Latinate vocabulary, highly stylized syllabic structures, and lack of a dominant personality or personalized perspective tend to push readers instead toward a philosophical reading of the poems, or toward a New Critical aesthetic of poem as isolated object of perfection or icon of author-ity. Yet it is the very high seriousness of the writing, in the context of its rejection of clearly delineated authority and poethood ex-plored above, that calls its artificiality and art's potential preten-tiousness into question. Michael Edwards goes so far as to speculate that Moore's syllabics suggest "that our forms, our aesthetic trans-figurations, are vulnerable and even rather comic, and that it would be correct if, while we delighted in them, we also saw the joke" ("Marianne Moore," 123).

In a paradox typical of Moore's structures, all the highly control-led elements of her verse enumerated earlier also suggest a sense of impending chaos, of meaning that is always on the verge of (or has slipped into) unmanageability, of hard-wrought and faulty human endeavor rather than polish, perfection, and effortlessly lyric beauty.[36] There is a compelling undertone of humor in all this manipulation of poetic technique, a tongue-in-cheek quality—as though Moore wants to demonstrate that she can in fact have it both ways in poetry. To borrow a construction of DuPlessis's re-garding her own verse, Moore uses the arts of poetry with consum-mate skill to "Depoeticize: reject normal claims of beauty. Smooth-ness. Finish. Fitness. Decoration. Moving sentiment. Uplift."[37] One must be particularly sensitive to nuance in Moore's tones to see the complementarity of these processes.

Such problems are most pronounced in a poem like "Blessed Is the Man" (1956). Quoting, as she states in "Idiosyncrasy and Tech-nique," from the "First Psalm," and hence both invoking and revising biblical wisdom, the poem appears to be a kind of manifesto, a word from on high. Similarly, given its quotations from Stalin, Presidents Lincoln and Eisenhower, and Eisenhower's campaign manager, the poem appears to be about civic duty or authority in its most public and systemic form.[38] Yet even with these obvious links to the hegemonies of religion, proscriptive language, and high public office, the poem attempts primarily to carve out a space of moral authority for the individual poet or "man," and this authority is defined primarily by the types of exclusiveness and privilege it rejects.[39]

Moore's poem both manifests and praises a matter-of-fact, une-gotistical mode of communication that is more likely to distance than draw a reader, partly because of its introductory emphatic negatives: "Blessed Is the Man"

who does not sit in the seat of the scoffer—
    the man who does not denigrate, depreciate, denunciate;
        who is not "characteristically intemperate,"
who does not "excuse, retreat, equivocate; and will be heard."

(Ah, Giorgione! there are those who mongrelize
    and those who heighten anything they touch; although it may
                                        well be
        that if Giorgione's self-portrait were not said to be he,
it might not take my fancy. Blessed the geniuses who know

that egomania is not a duty.)
    "Diversity, controversy; tolerance"—in that "citadel
        of learning" we have a fort that ought to armor us well.
Blessed is the man who "takes the risk of a decision"—asks

himself the question: "Would it solve the problem?
    Is it right as I see it? Is it in the best interests of all?"
        Alas. Ulysses' companions are now political—
living self-indulgently until the moral sense is drowned,

having lost all power of comparison,
    thinking license emancipates one, "slaves whom they themselves
        have bound."
        Brazen authors, downright soiled and downright spoiled, as if
                                        sound
and exceptional, are the old quasi-modish counterfeit,

Mitin-proofing conscience against character.
    Affronted by "private lies and public shame," blessed is the author
        who favors what the supercilious do *not* favor—
who will not comply. Blessed, the unaccommodating man.

Blessed is the man whose faith is different
    from possessiveness—of a kind not framed by "things which do
        appear"—

who will not visualize defeat, too intent to cower;
whose illumined eye has seen the shaft that gilds the sultan's tower.
(CP, 173–174)

Using seven instances of "not" and four negative prefixes in its first nine lines, the poem almost buries its single opening positive declaration that the blessed man "will be heard" in its emphatic restrictions against certain kinds of speech; the blessed are heard because they speak without scoffing, denigrating, equivocating, or being intemperate or egomaniacal. As I have suggested earlier, although somewhat paradoxically in this context, negation expresses affirmation: effective self-presentation lies in rejecting a negative attitude, intemperance, and repeated self-portraiture. Moore then states what qualities the blessed should have in the form of what "ought to armor us": "'Diversity, controversy; tolerance'" are a "citadel of learning" that should serve as self-protection. Put into the frame of the preceding injunctions, tolerance, diversity, and controversy appear to be armor against egomania, intemperance, and one's own inclination to denunciate or retreat rather than armor against another's harsh words. The fort of learning is one that tolerantly lets all comers in, building its defenses against the impulse of the self to tyrannize.[40]

Following this hopeful statement about defense, Moore continues in the line of community interaction. The blessed man "takes the risk of a decision" on the basis of interests beyond his own: for Moore, the practical query "Would it solve the problem?" includes the concern "Is it in the best interests of all?" As though acknowledging how rare such a process of reasoning is, Moore follows these questions with a formal lament: "Alas." The political, in contrast to the blessed, live "self-indulgently," have "lost all power of comparison," and mistake "license" for true emancipation, hence becoming "slaves whom they themselves have bound." Such "brazen authors" are "counterfeit," "soiled and downright spoiled," attempting to protect their "conscience against character" through "*mitin*" or mothproofing. Such false armor lies in direct contrast to the true armor of tolerance and diversity, although neither ensures protection.

Having made "Ulysses' companions" "authors" rather than states-

50

men, Moore continues to define the ideal "author" as one who thinks differently from "the supercilious" and who "will not comply." Here, appropriately, she quotes for the second time in the poem from Louis Dudek in imagining the author's trials: like any other public figure, the author suffers "private lies and public shame." At this point, Moore's "Notes" ask the reader to perform a curious doubling act in reading the poem. Rather than stating that Dudek is the source of this quotation, she refers the reader back to "note 13," ensuring that the reader will link the two passages. The blessed man who "takes the risk of a decision" is the same as the author "who will not comply," and both lines stem from Dudek's original statement as Moore quotes it in her "Notes": "'poetry . . . must . . . take the risk of a decision'; 'to say what we know, loud and clear—and if necessary ugly—that would be better than to say nothing with great skill'"; the blessed speaker is the public-minded (not egotistical) poet (CP, 289). Although she returns to the subject "man" for the rest of the poem, Moore seems to focus on the poet, and certainly calls attention to her poetry by ending with the sole full rhyme of the poem: the blessed man or poet "will not visualize defeat, too intent to cower; / [his] illumined eye has seen the shaft that gilds the sultan's tower."

Just as it is not immediately clear why it might be a good thing to see the "sultan's tower" (because it represents a good value in itself? because seeing it represents "power"—an echoing rhyme word?), it is not clear why a poem arguing against power based on elitist rhetoric and professionalism should be dominated by high-flown and formal rhetoric. Such language makes the poet seem ambiguously placed in relation to (if not co-opted by) the statesman-like sultan's tower. Yet Moore states that the poet must foster "diversity, controversy; tolerance," and that risking a decision demands setting oneself in relation to a community and to a process of figuring. As Dudek says, the poet attains "speech of a minor kind one understands and profits by," rather than truth by revelation or purely aesthetic value ("The New Laocoon," 118). In that process one admits the personal aspects of judgment and taste (is it right *as I see it?*) without withdrawing from the responsibility of a public stance. Moreover, the end of the poem distinguishes poet from statesman. Because one can see the "shaft" of light that "gilds the sultan's tower" only when one stands at a distance from it, the poet cannot also be the sultan. One notes also that the sultan's tower is not in fact gold; light "gilds" the tower. Appropriately, then, the poet's vision is fixed not on the apparently valuable tower but on the transforming light. Living within that suggestively phallic tower and gilding spotlight would block the poet's vision. For Moore, desirable authority inheres not in the publicness of the spotlight but in observing those within it.

Moore herself is simultaneously authoritative and invisible in this poem, and one hears both aspects of presence in its tone. The poem expresses formulaic, not personal, principles and emotion ("ah . . . Alas"), and it repeats a proscriptive or generic "man" and "author," keeping the private self, the woman, out of its spotlight.[41] This may be because the principles of the poem make it impossible for Moore to speak in it as a woman, or personal self; she uses the stereotypes of, for her, nongendered "man" to reject all traces of self-interest. As she writes in the margin of a draft of this poem, "Become self consc[ious] & momentum fails" (RML I.01.20). Yet in this same margin, Moore writes that "one's art is an exp[ression?] of one's needs." To the extent that "the blessed man" is a poet, the poem is also about herself, the female poet, and her "needs," yet any specifying of her personality or self would potentially lead back to the cult of the poet and the hierarchy of selfhood—for her a moral and poetic dead end. In this poem's formal tonality and reticence, one may perhaps read Moore's dissatisfaction with the traditional roles of both male and female poets, one too self-aggrandizing, the other too private. In the abundance of her negations and in her linking of diversity as a "fort that ought to armor us well," Ulysses' unlucky companions, and moral behavior as moth-proofing, all with Eisenhower's farm policy, one sees the play of a singular mind at work. Through its juxtapositions, its formality, and its occasional brief colloquialisms and "fancy," this mind asserts its (perhaps wistful) vision of the nongendered poet as one who speaks from personal conviction to prompt diversity rather than to quell it.[42]

Although nothing in the poem itself is feminist, Moore's mapping of ideal poethood coincides in part with late twentieth-century feminist notions of identity. The poet here is an outsider who both chooses that position and does not allow the consequences of that choice to lead to embitterment or self-righteousness. While choosing alterity rather than being relegated to it certainly implies privilege, such choice may magnify the importance of the position. In "Marriage," Moore distinguishes people's duties by specifying their different relations to power: though "some"—in the context of "Marriage," presumably female—"have merely rights" which they must struggle to maintain, others with greater access to power "have obligations," presumably to exercise their rights in the interest of the less empowered. One might read "Blessed Is the Man" as revising that distinction through a broader notion of the power of speech: all people who would "be heard" (and thereby lay claim to the authority inevitably attending public speech) have "obligations" to curb their potentially excessive influence or power—and such obligation to curb themselves rises above any "mer[e] right" to speak.

This poem protests against dominance, against hierarchy that rests on an assumption of privilege, at the same time that it recognizes imbalances of power inherent even in the act of speaking. These static *im*balances create the need for a constant struggle to undermine them by promoting instead the *un*stable balances of controversy and diversity. Although it is not clear that Moore sees the contrast, her position is the exact opposite of masculist power as represented in the party politics she alludes to in the "Notes" to this poem, where men are voted, appointed, and born into hierarchical positions that they struggle to maintain against all comers.[43] Yet the authority of the blessed man, or author, is like that of the public representative in democracy: it is unstable, always liable to become illegitimate through authoritarian self-aggrandizing.

While a poem like "Blessed Is the Man" may discourage feminist or author-focused readings because of its impersonal pontificating, poems of direct address and simple syntax using a first-person pronoun may equally discourage such readings. The early poem "Is Your Town Nineveh?", for example, is read almost exclusively as a statement about Moore's private life or about her religious beliefs, although it deals openly with the relation of individual freedom to moral and public responsibility.[44] The poem begins with its title: "Is Your Town Nineveh?"

> Why so desolate?
>   And why multiply
>   in phantasmagoria about fishes,
>   what disgusts you? Could
>   not all personal upheaval in
>   the name of freedom, be tabood?
>
> Is it Nineveh
>   and are you Jonah
>   in the sweltering east wind of your wishes?
>   I, myself have stood
>   there by the aquarium, looking
>   at the Statue of Liberty.

(P, 24)

In this poem, the opening scorn of judgmental distance in the first three questions is softened in the fourth by the more philosophical (although still chastising) question about the relation of "personal upheaval" to "freedom," and of both to moral law. Jonah is "desolate" presumably, first, because God commands him to go to the wicked city of Nineveh, second, because God does not destroy Nineveh after Jonah has told its inhabitants God would do so, and finally, because God does destroy the gourd that grew to shade Jonah's head. Engaged in an ongoing battle of wills with God, Jonah loses at every stage. These losses in the biblical story are meant to instruct that Jonah's proper role should be obedience to God's will. He is not to think or feel in the name of his own freedom, but to act as an instrument of the higher authority he represents.

The first stanza of Moore's poem may parrot the authority of a domineering god who threatens the Jonah-like "you" with the loss of all "personal upheaval in / the name of freedom." In the second stanza, however, the poem's tone changes from attack to identification, from condemnation to sympathy. The speaker who appeared to echo a patriarchal and punishing god now admits to being another Jonah. Consequently, the meaning of freedom undergoes a shift. At first, freedom seemed to be the escapist "phantasmagoria" of a Jonah who will renege on his responsibility and flee—even if it is only to the whale, or the fantasy of one. From an orthodox believer's perspective, this is egotistical irresponsibility, deserving to be "tabood." As soon as one takes Jonah's position, however, such "personal upheaval" is more attractive. The will to challenge authority leads to disruption, which leads in turn to the possibility of experience, and of freedom.

In its last lines, the poem introduces the aquarium and the Statue of Liberty—symbols of enclosure and freedom, and indeed Moore has written of New York as signifying both. In two 1915 letters to her brother, she refers to her recent trip to the city as her "sojourn in the whale" (December 19 and 26, 1915; RML VI.21.13)—although she regards this sojourn as a delightful adventure rather than punishment. Later in a poem named for the city, Moore characterizes the wealth of "New York" as lying in its "'accessibility to experience.'" New York is the city of the "savage's romance," not of law or authority. With or without such extratextual information, one may hear ambivalence or unfulfilled desire in "Is Your Town Nineveh?". Moore indicates that the poem is about conflict over the notions of duty and freedom without revealing what the specific basis for that conflict might be, or her own relation to it.[45] Moreover, although Jonah here seems clearly to be a prototype of the poet, since both prophet and poet may be seen as spokespersons for a higher authority, Moore leaves ambiguous whether it is the rebellious or the dutiful Jonah who best represents the poet for her, or if in fact both aspects are necessary. Unlike "Blessed Is the Man," "Is Your Town Nineveh?" contains no clear statements of priorities or beliefs. There is no essentializing or romanticizing of the questioner, no ritual of confession, and no transcendental moment at the end of the poem. Retreating from the role of chastiser or observer of another's punishment, the speaker becomes a participant in the dilemma the poem stages. Similarly, although Moore presents a final balanced image of where the speaker "ha[s] stood," the past perfect tense does not indicate where the speaker stands now, or what the relation of this speaker is to Moore herself. This unfixed position is key, I believe, to Moore's positioning generally in her poems.

By framing a series of questions about freedom and responsibiity, and then placing the speaker in the center of them, without concluding, this poem simultaneously minimizes and foregrounds the author's place in the poem. The poem's "I" is not depicted specifically enough to serve as the poem's focus—without, that is, retreat into biographical detail not revealed in the poem—and the poem's structure allows for multiple interpretations of the poet's stance. This poem multiply encircles the moral question of how any subject and especially any poet balances the freedom of individual desire with duty. Moreover, it implies that an espousal of any single response would be deadening. The aquarium stands in sight of the Statue of Liberty; Moore's speaker has stood between them. In other places, Moore defines freedom in terms of restriction: "freedom in art, as in life, is the result of a discipline imposed by ourselves"; "you're not free / until you've been made captive by / supreme belief" (CPr, 426; "Spenser's Ireland"). One cannot choose one without choosing the other—a philosophical position neatly dramatized by a quester keeping both the aquarium and the Statue of Liberty in view.[46]

Moore establishes an unprivileged positioning of authority based on ordinary research and private conviction through the structures and topics of her poetry generally and through her writing process as well as through thematic and stylistic elements of individual poems. She writes, for example, about a television production of Mozart's *The Magic Flute*, or a carriage she sees in a museum, or Yul Brynner. There is no element of privilege in watching TV—or, in other poems, going (or listening) to a baseball game or admiring a race horse one has read about in the newspapers. The poet-speaker may or may not have witnessed the occasion under discussion, but such primacy is irrelevant because individual experience is not the poem's focus. Moore engages in little elaborated transformation of classical literature, biblical tradition, or other cultural mythology demanding specialized knowledge from her readers. For example, "Virginia Britannia" rewrites the history of the colonization of the

United States, but with only fleeting reference to recognizable moments or figures of dominant history. "The Hero" debunks notions of Western heroism and provides a new model for heroic action without more than listing a few classical heroes. Poems like "The Labours of Hercules" or "For February 14" (with its address to St. Valentine) assume that the reader knows the stories alluded to (that Hercules had to perform impossible tasks; that February 14 is "Valentine's" day and, later in that poem, that Noah's ark preserved animal and human life from the flood). Yet these are tales of much greater familiarity to most readers in the United States than, for example, Eliot's myth of the "Fisher King" or Pound's Breton and Chinese legends. Moreover, the myths themselves serve as no more than background analogy for the contemporary and immediate point of Moore's poems: that eradicating prejudicial stereotypes is a task of heroic proportions, or that thanksgiving for ongoing life may be a more considerate gift than commodified tokens of worth or rarity. Moore does not invoke traditional literary authority.

I suggested earlier that several aspects of Moore's verse encourage a poststructuralist reading. Her lifelong process of revising her work similarly promotes the perspective that no text is definitive or more than temporarily fixed. Moore radically changed the form of poems already published and anthologized (for example, converting "Picking and Choosing," "England," and "Peter" from syllabic into free verse in 1967 for her so-called *Complete Poems,* with no mention that the poems existed in an earlier form); she frequently altered the shape of syllabic stanzas by adding to, cutting, or rearranging them; she dramatically revised poems, cutting lines or whole stanzas or, in the most notorious example, reducing her poem "Poetry" from a length of two pages to a skeletal three lines.[47] In Moore's oeuvre, nothing marks one version of a text as being more authoritative than others—including chronology, since one might argue either that the first or the last (or the "best"—always problematically defined) text constitutes the "real" poem. As she puts it in a draft copy of "Blessed Is the Man," "we change bec we are alive, not because / it looks well to alter the style of our pronouncement" (RML I.01.20).[48]

Moore's lack of a formal title for many of her poems has an effect similar to that of frequently revising texts. Making a poem's opening words double as its title obviates the traditional necessity for the author to produce a summary or introduction to the poem's themes. The poem does not announce itself but simply begins. "The Fish," to take a famous example, begins: "The Fish // wade / through black jade"—and then never mentions fish again. This poem is not about fish at all but, one might argue, about human destructiveness and the fragile balance of what survives it. Yet the reader must draw such conclusions for her or himself. Taken as a statement about the poem, the title misleads, again destabilizing if not the text itself certainly the reader's sense of it.

Such destabilizing gestures return us to Moore's relation to her audience, and hence to the poem "Is Your Town Nineveh?" This poem's concern with freedom, the unstable positioning of the speaker at the end, and the structural insistence on a reader's response (through its five direct questions in only twelve lines) suggest a link between contemporary theory and Moore's aesthetic politics that is best summarized by J. G. A. Pocock. In his essay "Verbalizing a Political Act," Pocock describes speech as not just an act but an act of power toward its addressee.[49] In *The Poem as Utterance*, R. A. York describes similarly the relationship between writer and reader. Because a text fictionalizes its reader, or writes a role for its reader into its structures, the relationship between them is necessarily based on a differential of power: "The image of the writer is that of someone who has the authority to write, to impose himself, to persuade or seduce his reader, and he has to show that he has that authority, or, better, he has to gain it in his writing."[50] To return to Pocock, the extent to which a speech-act (or text) leaves itself open to or invites independent response determines the kind or degree of power it exercises.[51] Pocock then theorizes that "the preservation of a structure of two-way communication . . . [is] a necessary feature of any form of human freedom" and, further, that it is the ultimate imperfection of language as speech-act that underlies the possibility of such structural openness (33, 31). As he describes, this "imperfection" inheres in the nature of language as inevitably borrowed, not originating with a speaker, and hence never completely controlled by her intentions, although speech-acts (and speakers) may minimize or attempt to control such imperfection through controlling the contexts of interpretation (as, for example, in repressive dictatorships or under a system of slavery).

In his analysis of oppositional narratives, Ross Chambers interprets imperfection as the sign of oppositionality, describing a dynamic very similar to Pocock's. As he puts it, "The oppositional narrative (this is a law) is one that is always aware of the possibility of its own failure because . . . it must address a more powerful other whose attention or inattention . . . means life or death for the narrative." Texts (or writers) that are empowered don't need to worry about failing; in contrast, by marking itself as imperfect, acknowledging the possibility of failure, a text may also be identifying itself as oppositional. Moreover, and because of the performative character of communication, a text that manifests an oppositional act "invites reading as an oppositional act" and hence raises the possibility of ultimately changing "political, social, [and] historical realities."[52]

Such linking of interactive conversational engagement and oppositionality or freedom seems to me precisely apt as a description of the structural intent of Moore's poems. In addition to the inevitable uncontrollability of language, however, Moore's forms seem to me to manifest a more directly willed "imperfection" precisely to ensure the continuation of that "structure of two-way communication" (albeit a fictional one) and hence the possibility of independence for both poet and reader. There is an assumption, as Pocock puts it, of "a polity of shared power" here (31): the reader must enter into the structure, answer Moore's questions, consider the choice between duty and freedom, in order to make sense of her poem at all because its clarity is not perfect, not that of a command. As Moore puts it, the mind is "enchanting" in part because of its "conscientious inconsistency," because it is "not a Herod's oath that cannot change"; or, in another poem, she reminds that "The Gordian knot need not be cut."[53] In the very late "Love in America," Moore even defines "tenderness" as coming from "one with ability / to bear being misunderstood—/ take the blame" (CP, 240)—in other words, not just fallibility but the willingness and capacity to reveal it to others are crucial for this poet.

Conceiving of this interaction in terms of acts of power—even if

Moore's intent is to eradicate to the extent possible the power differential between poet and reader, or the conventional authority of the "author"—provides yet another way to conceive of the balance of the personal and the impersonal in her work. While Moore speaks "to" a reader, she also constantly reminds her reader that the conversation is fictional, merely a structure; it is only with a text— and hence the reader may have innumerable opportunities for response to it, thereby fictionalizing the author as well as responding to her fictions. The reader responds with an act of power toward the poet—an act both enabled and necessitated by the deliberate imperfections of the brilliant but contradictory surface of Moore's form. Read oppositionally, questioningly—which is, I believe, in Moore's terms, properly—Moore's poetry engages the reader in a controversy, a two-way communication that negotiates power, freedom, and authority between them. Without such readerly "inquisitive intensity," one sees only questions, only the sultan's tower, only a poetry of indecisive assertiveness that appears to want not to be clear.

THREE

An "Unintelligible Vernacular": Questions of Voice

Poetry is an unintelligible unmistakable vernacular like the language of the animals—a system of communication whereby a fox with a turkey too heavy for it to carry, reappears shortly with another fox to share the booty.

"*Ideas of Order*," *CPr, 329*

And America . . .
the wild man's land; grass-less, links-less, language-less
country—in which letters are written
not in Spanish, not in Greek, not in Latin, not in
shorthand
but in plain American which cats and dogs can read!

"*England*," *P, 19*

$\mathcal{A}$lthough some elements of Moore's verse are radically destabilizing, or postmodern, in their representation of the creative process, the poet-self, and the text, other elements mark it clearly as situated within its own time, or modern—in particular Moore's conviction that both accurate observation and communication on topics of moral importance are possible, even if ultimately inadequate.[1] For modernists, communication was typically conceived as a matter of voice rather than of audience or systems of communication, and Moore's oppositional poetic also situates itself in relation to notions of voice. In "The Accented Syllable" Moore defines "tone of voice" as "that intonation in which the accents which are responsible for it are so unequivocal as to persist, no matter under what circumstances the syllables are read" (CPr, 32). She then continues, in a modernist strain, by saying that "voice is dependent on naturalistic effects" and that "an intonation must have meaning behind it to support it, or it is not worth much" (CPr, 34). On the other hand, by characterizing the language of poetry—its "unmistakable vernacular"—as also "unintelligible," a "system of communication" requiring a fellow "fox" to "share the booty," Moore veers again toward the postmodern, or at least maintains the tension between modernist and postmodern elements of her verse. In this chapter I focus on Moore's juxtaposition of illocutionary, directly interactional and vernacular elements of verse with others that lean toward unintelligibility, representing the poem as artificial, constructed, a product of convention. Combining these elements constitutes another of her several tactics for restructuring the lyric poem so that it directly engages an audience in a mode reminiscent of conversation without invoking an authority of personal presence, natural voice, or iconic elevation.

The rejection of a voice-based lyric has become the rallying point for much late twentieth-century experimental poetry, a rejection based on dismantling the ideology of authenticity and the identification of conventional language structures with the expressions of a self that underlie voice-based poetry.[2] Marjorie Perloff reviews the history of the importance of the concept of "natural" voice to the modern (and postmodern) period in *Radical Artifice,* pointing to the ways that one generation's innovative constructions become the "natural" voice of the next generation, and suggesting that all notions of "nature" in verse are constructed. Like Gayatri Spivak (and with reference to Fredric Jameson and James Clifford), Perloff argues that all notions of authenticity, or authentic voice, constitute institutionalized "domains of truth," fictions of a colonizing or capitalist first-world criticism—whether based on a conservative concept of the traditional as natural or a liberal concept of that which has resisted incorporation into a commodity system, the "primitive" or "other" as natural.[3] Verbal formulas and poetic structures (colloquial idiom, "free" verse, the fiction of immediacy) gain authority as representing the natural or sincere even though they are no more than conventions agreed upon by literary and critical communities.

Moore's position in relation to the desirability of either a natural or a personal voice is complex. On the one hand, as Hugh Kenner states so decisively in *A Homemade World,* for Moore "the poem is a system, not an utterance, though one can trace an utterance through it. A thing made, then, not a thing said."[4] On the other hand, she shares in what Perloff describes as the overwhelming commitment of "Modernist poetics . . . to the 'natural look,' whether at the level of speech (Yeats's 'natural words in the natural order'), the level of image (Pound's 'the natural object is always the adequate symbol'), or the level of verse form ('free' verse being judged for the better part of the century as somehow more 'natural' than meter and stanzaic structure)" (*Radical Artifice,* 27). Not only does she frequently use animal and botanical subjects, Moore too at times eulogizes the "natural"—for example, repeating in her own words Pound's dictum "never, NEVER to write any word that you would not actually say in circumstances of urgency" and telling Grace Schulman in 1967 that she desires her verse to proceed "in straight order, just as if I had not thought it before and were talking to you. Unstrained and natural."[5] Yet Moore does not identify a particular diction and syntax as natural. Her concept of natural language instead has to do with speech—which is to say, with upbringing, temperament, and education; no two people, then, will have the same "natural" way of expressing a thing, and there is no underlying authoritative nature against which all speech is measured.

Hence, although Moore frequently refers to the desirableness of the natural in her poetry, she typically also inserts a qualifier—like the word "unintelligible" to describe her description of poetry as "vernacular." For example, after asserting to Schulman that her verse should be "natural," Moore concludes that "some of my things *do* sound thought up and worked over" (*Poetry of Engagement,* 46). Or in the 1921 version of "Poetry," while insisting that it is the "genuine" which makes poetry interesting at all, Moore concludes that even though natural and cultural "phenomena are important," "One must make a distinction":

> when dragged into prominence by half poets, the result is
> > not poetry,
> nor till the autocrats among us can be
> > "literalists of
> > the imagination"—above
> > > insolence and triviality and can present
>
> for inspection, imaginary gardens with real toads in them, shall we
> > > have
> > it. In the meantime, if you demand on one hand, in defiance of
> > > > their opinion—
> the raw material of poetry in
> > all its rawness and
> > that which is, on the other hand,
> > > genuine then you are interested in poetry.[6]

> > > > > > (P, 22)

"Raw material" or "real toads" alone do not constitute a poem. One must also have the "imaginary," not a real, garden; a poem is indeed something made; a poetic voice is not a natural one; the fiction of presence is a fiction. Similarly, in "The Accented Syllable," while insisting on "natural effects" for poetic voice, Moore acknowledges that "naturalistic effects are so rare in rhyme as almost not to exist" (CPr, 34)—this from a poet who would become famous for her rhymes on "unaccented syllable[s]," or attempts to create a naturalistic (a word that marks its difference from "natural") effect within an ostentatiously constructed form. Moore's frequently quoted description of the evolution of her syllabic stanzas reveals precisely the same tension: "I never 'plan' a stanza. Words cluster like chromosomes, determining the procedure. I may influence an arrangement or thin it, then try to have successive stanzas identical with the first" (MMR, 263); thus one stanza of a poem is "organic" or "natural" and the rest follow what is for them an arbitrary and abstract pattern.[7] Like Moore's concept of "freedom," the natural "in art, as in life" seems not simply to occur but to result from "discipline imposed by ourselves" (CPr, 426).

Moore's concept of naturalistic effects in verse as both spontaneous and constructed helps to explain the tension between spoken or directly engaging and constructed or distancing tones and structures in her verse, or her repeated use of illocutionary or spoken structures within a poetic form and dominant diction that contradict any impression of idiomatically ordinary or immediate presence. Moore writes "speech" much as Henry James does in his late novels: the voice accents are striking only if one does not attempt to imagine any of the characters actually talking that way, in any particular dramatic scene.[8] The stress here is not on authenticity or naturalness in an imitative sense but on a process of thought. Moore's verse indeed follows the rhythms of syntax, but these are not necessarily the rhythms of speech. As Robert Pinsky delightfully notes in "Marianne Moore: Idiom and Idiosyncrasy," Moore's speech at times resembles an "almost parodic version of social discourse" in which "the artificiality . . . is the point."[9] As Pinsky briefly notes and Jeredith Merrin argues at length, such meditative "speech" is among Moore's strongest ties to the seventeenth-century prose and verse that she claimed as among her few important influences.[10] Moore's poems most strikingly communicate with their audience in the structure of implied dialogue or response rather than in the idiom or rhythm of speech.

This tension or balance in Moore's work between the interactive and the abstract may stem from notions of language and of rhetoric similar to those of early pragmatists. Moore was, for example, strongly drawn to the work of William—as well as Henry—James, whose great respect for scientific empiricism and precision in language was matched by his conviction that language could viably enable the exploration of moral and spiritual realms.[11] Answering a questionnaire late in her life, Moore lists James's *Psychology* as one of the books that "did most to shape [her] vocational attitude and [her] philosophy of life" (CPr, 671). Moreover, she may have been familiar with some of the essays and books published by Gertrude Buck (Vassar College professor, 1897–1922) on the philosophy and psychology of rhetoric, which anticipated aspects of pragmatics and also drew on the work of James.[12] To summarize briefly, in contrast to the dominant model of rhetoric as battle, an interaction in which conversational "opponents" maintain fixed positions until one position is proven false and hence must be abandoned, Buck constructs models of rhetoric as an activity of social dependence and emotional interaction.[13] Buck based her theory on an organic model of rhetoric that might not in itself have attracted Moore, but her conclusions about the process of communication are strikingly similar to the poet's. Drawing on James, she viewed the mind as adaptive, changing, dynamic. Buck wrote, for example, in 1899 that persuasive discourse is "the act of establishing in the mind of another person a conclusion which has become fixed in your own, by means of putting up in the other person's mind the train of thought or reasoning which has previously led you to this conclusion"; as LeeAnn Lawrence puts it, in this structure, "speaker and audience are thus co-equal partners in a process of discovering the argument" ("Organisms Vs. Machines," 34, 33) rather than combatants in a battle the rhetorician seeks to win.

In her early poetry, Moore makes the effectiveness of various models of communication her theme. In "In This Age of Hard Trying," for example, Moore claims that a storyteller's "by- / play was more terrible in its effectiveness / than the fiercest frontal attack" (1916; reprinted in P, 14). In another poem, the "Ardent Platonist" is decisively not "formidable"; he "say[s] what [he] thinks in order to be understood"; "A philosopher, he was but // An apple which has not begun to mellow"—or tart rather than contentious (1918). In her most combative early poems, Moore's verbal artillery is directed against a specific "you" which cannot be mistaken for the reader, and the reader is implicitly invited to join in the critique or condemnation, which seems to be more of the addressee's hostile methods than of the person or a fixed position. In the most pointed example of such critique, "To Be Liked By You Would Be A Calamity," the speaker's response to a threat of violence is "to put my weapon up, and / Bow you out" (1916; reprinted in Obs, 37). The context is one of combat, but the speaker proffers a pointed and effective nonviolent response—a gesture of "steel." Distinction, will, intention, "steel" are crucial, but they are not used to attack the reader or addressee.[14]

Buck's model of rhetoric also interestingly anticipates Pocock's speculation that "the preservation of a structure of two-way communication . . . [is] a necessary feature of any form of human freedom" ("Verbalizing a Political Act," 33). Moreover, her formulations indicate that such speculation was already in the air at the turn of the century—perhaps because of some recognition that (as M. H. Abrams writes in *The Mirror and the Lamp*) there is "something singularly fatal to the audience in the romantic point of view . . . the poet's audience is reduced to a single member, consisting of the poet himself."[15]

Turning from theories of rhetoric to those of language structure, one again sees that Moore emphasizes what contemporary language theory describes as the discursive implication of all language use. The linguistic field of pragmatics claims that all language inevitably occurs as discourse, written language merely representing one side of a dialogue rather than the whole dynamic process; as R. A. York puts it, written language always carries with it in the form of implications and presuppositions the context of its own participation in dialogue. H. P. Grice, in particular, has argued that speech depends on a process of "conversational logic" or "implicature" which allows the possibility of response. Conversation is ordinarily "governed by the co-operative principle," that is, we expect those with whom we converse to "speak sincerely, relevantly, clearly, while providing sufficient information."[16] I argued at the end of the previous chapter that Moore's verse is interactive at an abstract level; she omits those elements of deixis and explanation that facilitate ordinary conversational response, or the "already understood" kind of clarity. One is reminded by Grice's theory of Moore's own statement to Donald Hall: "I think the most difficult thing for me is to be satisfactorily lucid, yet have enough implication in it to suit myself" (MMR, 261); unlike Grice's "implicature," the "implication" she means is to suit her, not to make her meaning transparent for a reader. At the same time, Moore constructs fully lucid structures of interactive effect repeatedly in her verse.

Structures of speech that depend for their meaning upon interaction with an audience—rather than, for example, upon truth-value, narrative development, or providing information—are called illocutionary, and the speech-like or interactional element of Moore's poetry stems primarily from such structures. As Richard Ohmann explains, illocutionary speech-acts "implant meaning in the stream of social interaction"; they cannot carry out what they say without the willing involvement of a listener or reader: "whereas the rules of grammar concern the relationships among sound, syntax, and meaning, the rules for illocutionary acts concern relationships among people."[17] There are many illocutionary elements of language, but the most obvious and powerful is the direct address. This form occurs frequently in Moore's poetry. For example, the poet exclaims: "Bury your nose in [the musk ox's coat]" or "but think!" in "The Arctic Ox (Or Goat)." "Tom Fool" begins "Look at Jonah." In "The Wood-Weasel" Moore admonishes "don't laugh" in the middle of identifying the weasel as a skunk; "Propriety" contains the phrases "Come, come" and "Pardon me"; and "Mercifully" urges "Play it all; do."

Like directives and exclamations, questions similarly imply dialogue with an audience. As indicated previously, "Is Your Town Nineveh?" consists largely of questions, and Moore's "Blessed" man is one who continually asks "'Would it solve the problem? / Is it right as I see it? Is it in the best interests of all?'" I distinguish here between rhetorical questions (such as the oft-quoted "What is more precise than precision?"—that is, questions that the poet immediately answers herself) and questions that require some audience response, for these are the questions that pull or welcome a reader into a poem. Such direct questions to the reader abound in Moore's poems: "Are they weapons or scalpels?" "What can one do for them— / these savages?" "Shall / we never have peace without sorrow?" "What is the good of hypocrisy?" "Have you time for a story?" ("Those Various Scalpels," "Marriage," "In Distrust of Merits," "Peter," "Charity Overcoming Envy"). Although the poet in some sense answers all her own questions, by resting her procedure on their open form she establishes an interactive rather than a closed or iconic frame.

Moore's poetry contains an equally frequent "you" of direct address, but like rhetorical and "real" questions, her "you" may take two forms, only one of which refers to an immediate audience. Especially in her early years, Moore wrote several poems addressing specific historical or mythic figures, for example, David and other biblical heroes, Blake, Disraeli, Molière, Yeats, Robert Browning, George Bernard Shaw, George Moore, and an unpublished poem to

Ezra Pound.[18] Such use of "you" is not illocutionary because "you" is clearly not the reader; these poems make the reader an eavesdropper on a private conversation. It may be partly for this reason that Moore dropped the named address in revising these poems and later dropped the majority from her publications.[19] Some of Moore's poems addressed to abstract or inanimate figures have this same quality of specificity that makes the reader an eavesdropper rather than a participant—for example, "To a Steam Roller"; or "To Statecraft Embalmed," with its opening dismissive "There is nothing to be said for you"; or "To Military Progress" with its equally dismissive "You use your mind / like a millstone to grind / chaff" (CP, 35, 82).

Although such poems of exclusive address formally resemble the romantic apostrophe, they include no distance of exaltation or sublimity and no revelation of a perceiving self, taking a mundane or ironic rather than transcendental perspective.[20] In those poems addressed to individual men (Moore addresses none to individual women), the poet takes a variety of stances in relation to masculine privilege but never substitutes her authority for theirs. These are perhaps Moore's only poems in which she attempts to place herself in direct relation to a tradition or to other poets, but that placement is typically more appreciative than competitive.[21]

Others of Moore's poems address a less specific "you" that may well include the reader in its sweep. In "Critics and Connoisseurs" the poet comments dryly, "I have seen this swan and / I have seen you" (CP, 38); in "A Grave" Moore warns an unspecified "Man" which may stand for men or, more likely, for all humanity that "you cannot stand in the middle of this" (CP, 49); and "Nevertheless" begins by including the reader in a statement of the obvious: "you've seen a strawberry / that's had a struggle" (CP, 125).

The use of "I" also implies a subject's personal relation to its audience even though its use is not necessarily illocutionary: "I" may speak to itself or to an audience distant in place and time. Yet, just as Moore's "you" does not suggest the high lyric apostrophe, her "I" rarely soliloquizes. Instead, the "I" often reveals a state of mind or a personal preference: to take a famous example, "Poetry" begins, "I, too, dislike it"; "To a Prize Bird" begins "You suit me well, for you can make me laugh." In other poems, the "I" confides, "I am troubled, I'm dissatisfied, I'm Irish"; or "I am hard to disgust, / but a pretentious poet can do it" ("Spenser's Ireland," "Mercifully"; P, 22; CP, 31, 114, 243). The present tense of the verbs in these instances contributes to the immediacy of the speaker's presence in important ways, but even with the past tense Moore at times creates a vividly familiar, conversational presence. For example, in "Then the Ermine" she writes, "I saw a bat by daylight; / hard to credit // but I knew that I was right" (CP, 160). Other uses of "I" commit the speaker to the audience's presence through the illocutionary acts of promising or swearing. For example, the last half of "Bowls" consists of parallel repeated phrases (foregrounded by their placement at the beginning of lines): "I shall purchase . . . / shall answer . . . / and acknowledge . . . / and I shall write" (CP, 59). This use of a personal and informal "I" distinguishes Moore's lines from the promotional prose that Marie Borroff claims as its closest model. Such prose constantly addresses a "you" and occasionally includes the community of "we" but almost never includes the voice of a thinking, remembering, feeling, resolving, self-correcting individual "I." Moore's poetry, in contrast, both repeatedly promotes such a presence and makes it either so grammatically gratuitous or otherwise apparently irrelevant to a poem's topic that it is often overlooked.[22]

Yet particularly a grammatically superfluous "I" calls attention to the presence of a thinking, organizing, perceiving subject. We read, for example, "He said—and I think I repeat his exact words" in "The Past is the Present," or the previously discussed "as / I have said," in "The Plumet Basilisk" (CP, 88, 21–22). Other similar phrases call even stronger attention to the speaker's presence, as though he or she were presently in the act of "presenting" the poem: "Saint Valentine" begins: "permitted to assist you, let me see . . ." (Moore's ellipses); "Voracities and Verities Sometimes are Interacting" concludes, "One may be pardoned, yes I know / one may, for love undying" (CP, 148).

Directives to the self and corrections addressed either to a reader, a self, or both also establish the fiction that the poetic process is still going on and thus suggest communicability; even as we read, the poet changes her mind about which words to choose. In "Peter," for example, Moore calls attention to the speaker's apparent slip doubly—through questioning and in an explicit correction. Following a claim that the cat "may be dangled like an eel," she writes: "May be? I should have said might have been" (CP, 43). In "Efforts of Affection" the poet ponders: "Thus wholeness— // wholesomeness? say efforts of affection," and in "Enough: *Jamestown 1607–1957*," the poet parenthetically scolds herself for what she has just written: after mentioning a path "enticing beyond comparison" she exclaims, "Not to begin with. No select / artlessly perfect French effect // mattered at first. (Don't speak in rhyme / of maddened men in starving-time)" (CP, 147, 185). In "Propriety," the poet wavers between "Brahms and Bach, / no; Bach and Brahms. To thank Bach // for his song / first, is wrong" (CP, 150). Such highlighted changes in wording, especially when combined with the simple present tense, imply a (fictional) unedited process of talking about the subject at hand.

Margaret Holley notes that Moore nearly dropped her personal use of "you" and "I" during the decades of the 1920s and 1930s, yet the poems of this period merely assume a different, not a distanced, relation to their audience. "We," a common pronoun of this period, indicates a similar proximity with readers, although it less clearly marks a context of exchange. For example, "The Hero" (1932) begins "Where there is personal liking we go . . . / We do not like some things, and the hero / doesn't . . ." (*Selected Poems*, 19). "An Egyptian Pulled Glass Bottle in the Shape of a Fish" (1924) begins with the immediacy of deixis as well as assertion: "Here we have thirst / And patience from the first, / And art, as in a wave held up for us to see" (Obs, 20). "The Monkey Puzzler" (1924; later retitled "The Monkey Puzzle") uses only the impersonal "one" until its last line, which finally admits the reader into the speculating poet's company: "but we prove, we do not explain our birth" (Obs, 30). The mode of these poems is more of casual lecture than of conversation or harangue, but nonetheless spoken.

Moore's abundant use of negative constructions also implies a spoken context: the speaker disagrees with or corrects a previous claim. This is a property of all negatives. As Chaim Perelman and Lucie Olbrechts-Tyteca state, "negation is a reaction to an actual or virtual affirmation by someone else"; "negative thought only comes into play if one's concern is with persons, that is, if one is arguing" (quoted in *Language and Style*, 124). Negatives often suggest emphatic as well as immediate presence, and Moore tends to foreground her negative constructions in ways that emphasize them. For example, Moore begins the poem "In This Age of Hard Trying, Nonchalance is Good and" with unusual exasperation—marked by her colloquial modifier "really" and by extension of the usual colloquial "isn't" into its more emphatic form: "'really, it is not the / business of the gods to bake clay pots'" (P, 14). In "Marriage" the reader is told: "One must not call [Hymen] ruffian / nor friction a calamity"—the line break calling attention to the parallel second negative, and hence emphasizing both (Obs, 77). Moore underlines her negative instruction with consonance in "Charity Overcoming Envy": "The Gordian knot need not be cut" (CP, 217). Her only frequently used syntactic inversion stresses negative constructions: for example, "No 'deliberate wide-eyed wistfulness' is here" in "An Octopus" (Obs, 86) and "Not afraid of anything is he" in "The Pangolin" (CP, 120).[23] Double negatives may be even more emphatic in their objection to a stereotype or misperception. For example, in "Poetry," "we / do not admire what / we cannot understand" (P, 22); "Peter" concludes with the triple implied negative, "to do less would be nothing but / dishonesty" (P, 52); and "The Mind Is an Enchanting Thing" ends by conclusively rejecting a familiar piece of Western history: the mind is "not a Herod's oath that cannot change" (CP, 135).

Even more frequent than double negatives is Moore's combination of an explicit negative with the implied negative of a conjunction like "but," "although," or "yet." For example, "An Egyptian Pulled Glass Bottle in the Shape of a Fish" specifies "not brittle but / intense" (CP, 83) and "Light is Speech" concludes "we / cannot but reply" (CP, 98). "New York," in a spectacular example of this construction, repeats five parallel negative phrases ("It is a far cry from . . . / It is not the dime-novel exterior, . . . / it is not that . . . / it is not the atmosphere . . . / it is not the plunder") before finally concluding "but 'accessibility to experience'" (CP, 54). Such conjunctions in isolation also function as implied negatives. For example, "He 'Digesteth Harde Yron'" begins "Although the aepyornis / or roc . . ." and "Those Various Scalpels" ends with the question "But why dissect destiny with instruments / more highly specialized than components of destiny itself?" (CP, 99, 52).

Perhaps most remarkable about the use of negatives in Moore's poems is the degree to which they are foregrounded. Every phrase quoted above begins a line, most begin stanzas, and several begin a poem. Several poems end, as well, with an emphatically negative construction. Negatives introduce and conclude Moore's poems, making them sound not just interactive but contentious. Such emphatic negations assume, or perhaps force, equally emphatic agreement or disagreement on a reader's part.[24]

As with her negatives, Moore generally emphasizes the illocutionary or speech-like aspects of her poetic voice at the beginning or (less frequently) end of her poems. From examples cited above, one culls as first lines: "There is nothing to be said for you"; "really, it is not the / business of the gods to bake clay pots"; "I, too, dislike it"; "There! You shed a ray / of whimsicality"; "you've seen a strawberry / that's had a struggle"; "I don't like diamonds"; "permitted to assist you, let me see . . ."; "Look at Jonah"; "I am hard to disgust, / but a pretentious poet can do it"; and "Have you time for a story . . .?". Illocutionary end lines quoted above include: "but we prove, we do not explain our birth"; "it's / not a Herod's oath that cannot change"; and "I am troubled, I'm dissatisfied, I'm Irish." Beginnings and endings are the two greatest points of emphasis in any poem. Making them speech-like—and particularly making a poem's first lines colloquial and personal or of direct address—gives a spoken cast to the whole of the poem, even when the diction is primarily technical or formal within and when not a single sentence of the poem might actually have been spoken. The poem's form announces a speaker's presence at the outset, as it were, and then moves on to what is to be said.

Such insistent illocutionary force is in several ways reminiscent of a similar mode in Walt Whitman's poetry.[25] Many of the illocutionary devices characterizing Moore's work also characterize Whitman's, especially her use of repeated negative constructions, questions, exclamations, promises, and other forms of direct address, and unusually long poetic lines that follow prose or spoken rhythms more obviously than poetic ones. Similarly, both poets delight in the accumulation of detail in lists and display a broad range of diction—including word coinages or usage that is far from speech-like (think of Whitman's Americanization of French words). The differences between their modes of verse, however, reveal clearly Moore's distance from any ordinary or unexamined sense of poetic voice, as well as from a characterized speaker that centers an ongoing, dramatic relationship between reader and poet, such as the one that Whitman attempts to establish. Where Whitman's poetic is based on the line and his line on an end-stopped syntactic and rhetorical unit—all supporting his fiction of natural presence, and the organic growth of his poems—most of Moore's verse is syllabic, organized around the poetic stanza, multiple complex rhyming structures, and an apparently arbitrary counting of syllables in a line.[26] Consequently, while Whitman seems almost to instruct his audience how to hear and "read" his voice, Moore plays syntax against lineation in ways that make reading (and especially reading aloud) an adventure.[27] One must continually decide whether to mark written aspects of the verse (rhyme, line-endings) vocally and hence disrupt the syntactic flow, or to forgo vocalizing any aspect of lineation, and hence read the verse like prose. Moreover, some of Moore's syntax is so complex and so bereft of the clearly lineated rhetorical parallelism of Whitman's complex sentences that one can unravel all its parts only after prolonged textual study, if at all, and the voice alone cannot carry the syntactic embedding and parallelism.

In Moore's poetry, syntax or phrasing, and hence any sense of "voice" or form as an extension of the physical body (Whitman's revolutionary version of organicism), functions in tension with lineation and stanza form rather than in harmony with them. James Scully notes that writers "attempt to solve those problems they have set for themselves, but set in concert with their historical circumstances, social values, class outlook, jobs, and the innumerable opaque or transparent 'aesthetic' and 'extra-aesthetic' encouragements and discouragements visited on them"; a poem is the "site of an exchange" between the "poetic" and "extra-poetic."[28] The tension between illocutionary and other language structures in Moore's verse strongly marks that she has "assume[d] responsibility for" the structure and "social transaction" of her text ("Line Break," 100). In an era of modernist nearly wholesale adoption of the free verse line as a "natural" basis for poetry, Moore's complex rhyming and syllabic stanzas proclaim her double oppositionality in asserting formal limitation as integral to her poetic.[29]

While illocutionary structures, not rhythms of speech, most distinctly mark Moore's poetry as spoken, poetic conventions of meter and rhyme most distinctly mark it as constructed, in spite of Moore's radical experimentation in constructing "naturalistic effects" in and through such forms. One might look, for example, at Moore's much-anthologized "The Fish." The last three stanzas read:

All
external
   marks of abuse are present on
     this
      defiant edifice—
   all the physical features of

ac-
cident—lack
   of cornice, dynamite grooves, burns
     and
      hatchet strokes, these things stand
   out on it; the chasm side is

dead.
Repeated
   evidence has proved that it can
     live
      on what cannot revive
   its youth. The sea grows old in it.
               (P, 15)

Here no stanza and no line is syntactically self-contained; every sentence, every major phrase, and even some words are enjambed. The syllabic count of 1, 3, 8, 1, 6, 8 bears no organic relation to the poem's words, although one might imagine an impressionistic wave-like movement between short and longer lines. The stanza pattern also uses its limitations playfully—as in Moore's dividing the word "ac- / cident" mid-syllable. The poet's craft reveals itself in precisely this play, in her ability to place words appropriately within the severe limits of such a logically unpredictable form—for example, giving "defiant edifice" a line of its own; suspending the sentence-concluding adjective "dead" across a stanza break; or, earlier, dividing the alliteratively lovely phrase "sun, / split like spun / glass" among three lines to slow the reader's movement through it. And this crafted enjambment of the syntax against the abstract grid of syllables indicates how fundamentally arbitrary that grid is.[30] Playing counted syllables against syntax depends on a process of reading, not hearing, the poem. Moore did write exclusively free verse for a few years during the twenties, but then returned to syllabic stanzas for her next forty years of writing.[31]

Like Moore's stanzas, her rhyme highlights the craft of her poetry and the static conventionality of verse in which rhyme sounds occur with a regularity that might be mistaken for natural. In a brilliant use and parody of this convention, rhyme occurs with visual regularity in much of Moore's verse but, because of the uneven line lengths of a syllabic stanza, varying lapses of time and stress occur between rhyme sounds and hence the ear does not know when to anticipate the end of a line, or a rhyme: it might be after one syllable or after twenty-eight. Moreover, because her lines are as apt to end with a function word (or, before the 1940s, even mid-word) as with the conclusion of a phrase or the kind of substantive monosyllable creating the "masculine" rhyme most valued in traditional prosody, Moore's end-rhymes are often syntactically unstressed. As I note in the concluding "cower / tower" rhyme of "Blessed Is the Man," Moore may also pun on conventional terminology for rhyme as either masculine (strong, full, perfect) or feminine (unstressed, polysyllabic, weak) through her typical reliance on "feminine" rhymes in combination with obviously artificial constructions of "masculine" rhyme or with particular placements of such rhymes. For example, returning to "The Fish," the technically masculine rhyme of "ac-" and "lack" calls attention to the wrenching of the word necessary to fulfill this convention. The mixed rhymes of "all / external" and "dead. / Repeated" are more typical of Moore's rhyme combinations of all styles and classes of words. Moore is also one of the great experimenters with rhyme in English, rhyming monosyllables with mid-word syllables, and creating a variety of consonantal, homophonic, sight, and two-syllable rhymes. Because her rhymes often occur within lines or line-internally between lines, Moore's (grammatically and aurally unaccented) end-rhymes receive even less relative stress. One hears the syncopation of sound and word repetition, but one is more apt to note the *patterns* of Moore's rhyming visually than aurally.[32] With both rhyme and syllabic stanza patterning, Moore uses a traditional form paradoxically to minimize the sense of regularity or tradition in her verse—and, again, thereby doubly emphasizing the constructed quality of her verse.

Quotation and allusion, especially when interwoven as densely as they are in many Moore poems, also stress the written aspects of Moore's forms.[33] This density of interwoven voices would be impossible in speech, where pitch, tone of voice, and so on cannot accurately mark distinctions between what is and is not borrowed. Similarly dependent on a written mode are the explanatory notes she attaches to large numbers of her poems, and the detailed index she compiled for *Observations,* containing proper names, subjects mentioned, but also what seem to be her favorite phrases or lines. The reproduction of such elements in poem after poem, highlighting idiosyncratic principles of selection, complex intertextuality, and the labor of compilation, creates a background of effects that work against a spoken quality. These elements provide the base against which the counterpoint of her poems' spoken structures and phrases are more sharply and clearly heard.

As noted previously, one finds the same tension between highly constructed and colloquial features within the registers of diction in Moore's poems as within their structural and formal elements. As Borroff persuasively argues in *Language and the Poet,* a polysyllabic, Romance-Latinate, phrasal mode dominates proportionally over an also present "common" or colloquial one, even in those structures that imply exchange or "speech."[34] Similarly, stative verbs ("to be," "have," "can") occur more frequently then active ones, and a phrasal structure of parallel noun series and appositive phrases dominates Moore's syntax. Even in her late, more colloquial poetry of often shorter and simpler syntactic units, a phrasal, noun-based structure predominates.[35]

Moore's practice of embedding aphorisms—blunt, short, memorable phrases encapsulating a single thought—between or within long and complex sentences reveals in microcosm the kind of tension I see in the poems as a whole between idiomatic and constructed elements. These brief phrases are often seen as being of particular significance in Moore's verse—of course because they are memorable, but no doubt also because they are so refreshingly clear. A recent extreme example of such reading occurs in Richard Howard's list of the "great ethical crystallizations which occur like geodes" in Moore's verse.[36] Borroff similarly reads the "slogans or mottoes" that Moore creates in several of her poems as providing encapsulated truths, moments of assurance that what has been will be (*Language and the Poet*, 133–135). Given Moore's definition of "clarity" as a process working against received truths, and given the insistently illocutionary structure of her verse, however, it seems unreasonable to read such phrases as isolated moments of forever stable truth. Instead, they provide a temporary clarifying function in a poem—offering a respite, as it were, from syntactical complexity or detail. To be fully understood, they must be returned to the complexity of the context in which they are embedded, so that their aphoristic clarity becomes a prismatic rather than a lazer-like ray for illuminating various aspects of their context.

"In the Days of Prismatic Color" (1919), a poem about style, incorporates a few illocutionary features with several of the most formal elements of Moore's verse. It is, therefore, particularly useful for analyzing how the various elements of Moore's language work together to create the kinds of effects, and poetic, that I have outlined. The poem begins with a fourteen-line sentence (initiated in the poem's title) that is insistently illocutionary with its repeated "not . . . but" constructions but primarily complex in syntax and Romance-Latinate in its diction: "In the Days of Prismatic Color"

> not in the days of Adam and Eve but when Adam
>   was alone; when there was no smoke and color was
> fine, not with the fineness of

    early civilization art but by virtue
of its originality, with nothing to modify it but the

mist that went up, obliqueness was a varia-
    tion of the perpendicular, plain to see and
to account for: it is no
    longer that; nor did the blue red yellow band
of incandescence that was color, keep its stripe: it also is one of

those things into which much that is peculiar can be
    read; complexity is not a crime but carry
it to the point of murki-
    ness and nothing is plain. A complexity
moreover, that has been committed to darkness, instead of grant-
                                                    ing it-

self to be the pestilence that it is, moves all a-
    bout as if to bewilder [us] with the dismal
fallacy that insistence
    is the measure of achievement and that all
truth must be dark. Principally throat, sophistication is as it al-

ways has been—at the antipodes from the init-
    ial great truths. "Part of it was crawling, part of it
was about to crawl, the rest
    was torpid in its lair." In the short legged, fit-
ful advance, the gurgling and all the minutiae—we have the classic

multitude of feet. To what purpose! Truth is no Apollo
    Belvedere, no formal thing. The wave may go over it if it likes.
Know that it will be there when it says:
    "I shall be there when the wave has gone by."
                    (P, 23; Moore marks omission of "us" as error)

The poem's first phrase of Anglo-Saxon diction and simple syntax—
"it is no / longer that"—implies that the modern world is one of
smoke, modification and, at best, refinement in contrast to the
glorious earlier "Days." Rather than ending her sentence here, how-
ever, Moore continues it until she has reached the point or goal of
such distinguishing. Once we realize that we have lost the Edenic
simplicity of "prismatic color," we must also understand that such

79

loss is not necessarily bad: unlike Adam and Eve's disobedience, "complexity is not a crime" if kept within bounds. Intervening between the opening contradictions and the conclusion on complexity comes a statement that the rainbow (that "blue red yellow band / of incandescence") has become a thing "into which much that is peculiar can be / read." This claim, in its passive-voice form, suggests that complexity results only partly from changes in the world; human perspective has changed as well. In "the days of prismatic color," Adam might have seen merely a "rainbow," the simple name that Moore's complex phrasing avoids, rather than this scientific phenomenon. The third and paradoxically plain-style phrase "nothing is plain," then, may mislead: one understands the relation of plainness to perception only by considering who is doing the viewing, and in what actual and ideological "light."

Although the remaining three stanzas of "In the Days of Prismatic Color" depict the "murkiness" Moore deplores, they contain shorter and simpler sentences than the first three, and less radical contrasts in mode. The poem moves from the perfect clarity of Adamic "prismatic color" to dismal complexity. Yet, characteristically, rather than counter such complexity directly, providing an affirmative guide to plainness or unraveling the "dismal fallacy" of vision that is too complex, Moore states the fallacy itself, leaving the reader to convert the fallacy into a statement of truth—in this case by inserting rather than deleting negatives: "insistence is [not!] the measure of achievement and . . . all truth must [not!] be dark." The next full sentence, through apposition, identifies "sophistication" as synonymous with the complexity of murkiness and seems to reestablish the notion of a paradise of perfect clarity: "sophistication is as it al- // ways has been—at the antipodes from the init- / ial great truths."[37]

Up to this point, the poem seems predictable: the simplicity of Eden is lost, and sophistication is a dragon-centipede attempting to persuade all that its dismal vision is the only true one. Startlingly, however, the speaker then identifies this centipede with "the classic multitude of feet." Rather than saving us from darkness and returning us to the simplicity of ancient sunlight, traditional poetry's "classic // multitude of feet" emerges from sophistication's lair. In contrast, the poet asserts that "Truth is no . . . formal thing"; it is what will survive disaster or change, what will "be there when the wave has gone by."[38] The poem—far from asserting the desirability of what had seemed to be an Adamic paradise of clarity and classic form—suggests that "Truth" is different from both the lost clarity of Eden and the sophisticated simplicity of canonical, iconic form.

The authoritative ring of this poem's concluding short statements lies at odds with the poet's refusal to describe a complexity that is not murky or to name the rainbow, and that oddity is reflected in tonal changes. Although the poem begins in a measured, reflective tone, the apparently illogical meandering of the passive-voice claim that rainbows may be variously read introduces a note of irony. The reader, it implies, knows others "of those things" that may be interpreted peculiarly. This ironic edge then turns defensive: the claim that "complexity is not a crime" as long as it does not degenerate into "murkiness" suggests that someone (Adam?) has asserted that it is. Once the subject has changed to murkiness, the tone is ironic throughout, although a dry humor prevents sharpness. Extreme complexity will not admit to being "the pestilence that it is"; fallacy is "dismal"; sophistication is "principally throat" at the same time that it seems to consist largely of feet. Moore's final response to classic (and perhaps classical) form—already portrayed as a pestilent centipede—marks an exasperation beyond irony: "To what purpose!" At this point, the syllabic structure of the poem dissolves. With four lines instead of five and only a rough approximation of the shape of the earlier stanzas, the final stanza seems itself to have gone under the wave and to mimic in its form the poet's question: to what purpose are these formal niceties of verse?

Having reached the end of the poem, one may return with it to the beginning and ask what the purpose is of Adam without Eve, or of days of prismatic color. Greek sculpture—as the apex of Greek art—is generally considered a model of simplicity, of clean and pure lines. In "An Octopus" (1924), Moore writes that "The Greeks liked smoothness, distrusting what was back / of what could not be clearly seen, / resolving with benevolent conclusiveness, / 'complexities which still will be complexities / as long as the world lasts'; / ascribing what we clumsily call happiness, / to . . .['] a power—' / such power as Adam had and we are still devoid of" (Obs, 88). Using the later poem as a crib for what Moore may have been thinking in 1919, one might regard the Greeks as desiring, through proud sophistication, to recreate the "smoothness," "conclusiveness," and "power" that Adam had when alone, and that ignores the murkier "complexities" of post-Adamic or ordinary human experience. Deliberating on what characterizes a world in which Adam is no longer alone, and in which his names no longer constitute the only viable articulation of phenomena and experience, leads to a clearer understanding of the play of contradictory elements in Moore's style as well as of this poem.

Twice in this poem, Moore portrays a set of power relations that may suggest patriarchy in primal form. First, she presents a mythic world in which woman (or otherness of any kind) does not exist to obscure man's vision, where appearance and reality fully converge. This is the world of light, of name-giving, of Adam, of the Genesis God, of fulfilled phallocentricism, and it is undeniably beautiful in its prismatic clarity—indeed an ideal (although not, I believe, Moore's—despite its strong appeal for her). At the end of the poem, patriarchal authority takes the more subtle form of Apollonian critic, sophisticate, and poet; this world appears to be equally phallocentric, although with less ease: its "gurgling and all the minutiae" proclaim that "insistence / is the measure of achievement" and, although this artist insists that "all truth is dark," the premier mark of his profession is to (re)create Apollo Belvedere—the sun god and original lyric poet, parallel to the Christian Adam in his ability to name and suggestion of pure light.[39] Between the purity of crystalline light and the sophistication of Apollonian art lies shadow, the place where "complexity is not a crime" and some things may yet be "plain."[40]

Moore never describes such a middle ground, let alone identifies it with feminism, the appearance of Eve, or her own prose-like revision of traditional "feet," yet the poem powerfully suggests these associations. Here Moore identifies truth with a process of negation, contradiction, and modification, all verbal characteristics in distinct contrast to Adamic language or Lacan's symbolic, with its representation in the law. Moore's truth lies in a world of complexity rather than of name-giving. By calling attention in the first line to

Eve's absence from Adamic isolation and clarity, Moore suggests that the complexity of her art may be identified with the presence of women—not as essentialized beings but insofar as their presence represents the inclusion of otherness, "complexity," or the murky world in which both men and women live, speak, and create.[41]

"In the Days of Prismatic Color" makes use of most of Moore's range of formal characteristics, including syllabic structure, rhyme, a high proportion of Romance-Latinate diction, and quotation. There is nothing colloquial or informal, far less anything "natural," in the overall tone or surface of this poem. The lines appear to be of arbitrary length, and the stanzas of arbitrary shape: none is end-stopped but the last, and that stanza breaks all the other norms of length, line length, and rhyme. As is typical of Moore's verse, the end-rhyme is so unobtrusive in the syntactic phrase and so slant that it is easy to miss even when examining the written surface: *was* rhymes with *because*, for example, in stanza one, apparently setting a rhyme scheme of abcbd. In stanza three, however, the first line sets the rhyme sound which is echoed in unstressed syllables in lines 2 and 4, and line-internally as well. By stanza five, end-rhymes are aabaa: *init-/*ial, *it*, *fit-/*ful, and the near-rhyme "classic." There are no end-line rhymes in the concluding stanza, although internally "no" appears twice, is echoed in "know," and rhymes with "go" and "Apollo"—perhaps to emphasize the conclusiveness of the poet's rejection of this icon and of verse traditions (not just the breaking of the stanzaic pattern but the preference of internal over line-end rhyme). On the other hand, both thematically and in its few illocutionary effects—strongest, as usual, at the beginning and end of the poem—"In the Days of Prismatic Color" portrays a process of thought (or argument) and implies an exasperated speaker at odds with an addressee, or a world, that values Adamic light above the nuance of shadow or complexity linked with Eve. The poem does not have a natural speaking voice, but it carries on a passionate argument with someone.

"Voracities and Verities Sometimes are Interacting" (1947) stresses elements of diction and syntax at the other end of Moore's scale: it structures itself as direct address to an audience, maintains a fairly even balance of Anglo-Saxon and Romance-Latinate phrases, and appears at first to be transparent in meaning because its individual phrases are short and clear. As in "In the Days of Prismatic Color," however, both ends of her range are present and both are necessary to a full understanding of the poem's subject and tone.

Like the earlier poem, "Voracities and Verities" begins with an illocutionary negative claim:

> I don't like diamonds;
> the emerald's "grass-lamp glow" is better;
>   and unobtrusiveness is dazzling,
>   upon occasion.
>   Some kinds of gratitude are trying.
>
> Poets, don't make a fuss;
> the elephant's "crooked trumpet" "doth write";
>   and to a tiger-book I am reading—
>   I think you know the one—
>   I am under obligation.
>
>   One may be pardoned, yes I know
>   one may, for love undying.
>
> Tiger-book: Major James Corbett's *Man-Eaters of Kumaon*.
>   (Moore's footnote; CP, 148)

The first stanza of this twelve-line, symmetrically structured poem proceeds by fairly obvious associative leaps. Stating her personal dislike makes the speaker think of what she prefers and on what principle: a "'grass-lamp glow' is better" than the outright brilliance of diamonds, and "upon occasion" even unobtrusiveness dazzles; in contrast, showy or obtrusive "kinds of gratitude are trying." The poem's speaker at this point sounds peevish: she doesn't like typically valued things, and is picky about how one expresses thanks. The voice is personal, and its motives private.

Because the poem provides no reason for the vehemence of these pronouncements, one turns to the powerful iconography of diamonds for explanation—that is to say, the poem virtually requires readers to leave the text to locate a context for interpretation. Diamonds have a more prominent place in modern advertising and mythologies of the feminine than any object except, perhaps, the rose (and Moore wrote her debunking poem on the rose's beauty years earlier). In the late 1930s, Harry Oppenheimer (director of several South African mining companies, including De Beers Consolidated Mines) met with the president of one of the leading advertising agencies in the United States to start a campaign to persuade Americans to buy more, and more expensive, diamonds, targeting middle-class young men and women to persuade them that diamonds were an integral part of any romantic courtship.[42] Within a few years diamond sales in the United States had increased by 55 percent, and the advertising continued to escalate during the 1940s, in spite of the war. Moore was fifty-nine when she began writing this poem. According to the popular wisdom created by this marketing campaign, for a woman to announce publicly her (or a poetic speaker's) dislike of diamonds is to distance herself doubly from the norm—as rejecting beauty and as rejecting the object that symbolizes her most appropriate and highest social status: wife. For a middle-aged unmarried woman with a background in grass-roots feminism to make the claim underlines this double distancing. Moreover, to make such a claim at all seems defiant—as though the speaker must have more than the stating of the trivial fact itself in mind. The speaker may dislike flashiness, or the advertising of affection through jewelry, or any symbol invoking eternal marital bliss, or the institution of marriage (diamonds are exclusively heterosexual and romantic in their advertised symbolic resonance).[43]

The second stanza of this poem begins with a similarly impatient and acerbic pronouncement but on an ostensibly unrelated topic. Moreover, it expresses gratitude, although presumably in a way that is not "trying." "Poets" are told not to "make a fuss" about their calling; like diamonds, they are not so special.[44] Even an elephant "doth write"; poetic inspiration is not the gift of a glorious muse. The speaker, for example, is obliged to a book on man-eating tigers—and by asserting this source for herself she indirectly requests that other poets reveal what nonpoetical materials they are indebted to, that is, that all acknowledge their mundane or idiosyncratic as well as their canonical sources. The second stanza of this poem seems to work in direct parallel to the first: the speaker dislikes

diamonds and fussing poets, likes emeralds and the unpretentious-
ness of animals (elephants and man-eating tigers), and dislikes some
forms of gratitude while feeling free to express others. The opposi-
tion of the stanzas may indicate that poets should be like the
emerald rather than the diamond: they should move beyond the
presumed glory of their own calling and give instead a "grass-lamp"
radiance. Such a light does not imitate or reflect nature, but suggests
in jeweled form its most common and unremarked expanse—per-
haps not coincidentally, an expanse that provided the title for
Whitman's insistently democratic *Leaves of Grass*. Or, as Diehl writes,
Moore may be striving to "disengage composition from a cultural
model . . . in which the dominant system of capitalist economics
becomes the model for poetic acquisition" (*American Sublime*, 50–51).
The acquisition of any fetishized commodity, whether diamonds or
popular success, depends on the institutionalization of "fuss."

The final couplet of "Voracities and Verities" adds another twist
to these speculations. Quite the opposite of the opening scorn for
diamonds, this statement emphatically presents high romance, using
a phrase that is biblical in its ring and both archaic and stereotypi-
cally poetic in its syntactic inversion ("love undying"). The same
speaker who dislikes diamonds and "some kinds of gratitude," and
who scolds poets who think of their calling in too elevated a way,
reiterates showily, if also apologetically, "One may be pardoned, yes
I know / one may, for love undying."

As in "Prismatic Color" and many other of Moore's poems, one
looks to the contrasting or odd statement rather than to the domi-
nant tone for a key to the poem's tonal riddle—and here the
contrasting tone is abstract, polysyllabic, Latinate, unidiomatic: "Vo-
racities and Verities Sometimes are Interacting." The title of the
poem gives a broad frame in which to consider its notions of
gratitude, obligation, and love. As it contends, one cannot always
separate voraciousness from verity, although the world of advertising
(in which diamonds *mean* marriage, or love) would have one conflate
the two. In the light of attempts to distinguish greed from truth,
the poem becomes as concerned with reading as with obtaining, or
writing. On the one hand, poets should control their voracious
desire to claim all glory of literacy for themselves—as though only

dazzling inspiration allows one to write. On the other hand, readers should trust their individual "grass-lamp glow" for illumination about what is written. Such illumination is also precious. It may be that by opening this address to poets with a discussion of gems, Moore implies that any illumination involves desire for possession—just as all acts of writing or reading may be voracious (Moore surely appropriates the tiger book). When "interacting" with "verities," or honesty about the context of one's rapacious appetite to own what one reads or writes, voraciousness may not harm (or one may be pardoned for it), but it nonetheless exists. In particular, "Voracities and Verities" interact in one's response to the public iconographies of love and of poethood—each category plural because there is more than one kind of greed and of truth about anything complex. Moreover, these categories "are interacting" in an ongoing sense; they will not settle into fixed ratios but instead change with each new act of loving or poetic appropriation.

The poignancy or emotional weight of the poem comes from this instability, from the "interacting" one feels even as the speaker's almost fussy statements repeat themselves in our repeated readings: "I don't like diamonds . . . don't make a fuss . . . You know the [book I'm obliged to]" the speaker states testily—as though any display of feeling would be a mere annoyance. Yet by presenting love in this context of "voracity" and "fuss" and by presenting it in the form of a defensive apology, this speaker implies that "love undying" is the greediest, most possessive, potentially most fuss-making as well as most rewarding experience of all.

The last lines of the poem, then, in conjunction with the title, make this a poem about greedy, everlasting love. That the poem is more personal in tone than many of Moore's (using "I" to state a personal preference, directly addressing its audience, using several colloquial phrases) seems apt. The exasperated tone of the speaker, though, is odd. Why be contrary, irritated, apologetic, defensive, in a love poem? This is classic Moore: intimate subject and personal address yet unsentimental, even off-putting tone. She communicates immediately and about a matter of deep importance but in propositional form, juxtaposing both feelings and propositions on such different topics that the poem seems abstract rather than personal.

"Voracities and Verities" rejects romance with all its trappings (including romantic poethood) while still affirming the ongoing presence of love.

Curiously, the affirmation at the end of the poem seems to require less contextualizing than the earlier negative statements do. Nonetheless, it has at least two possible private impulses that shed light on its argument, at least to the extent that we identify the speaker with the poet. First, "Voracities and Verities" was published in 1947, during Moore's mother's terminal illness. Although the poem was completed months before her mother's death, the poet quite likely had this impending loss in mind. Second, in 1946 Moore sent a copy of "Voracities and Verities" to Louise Crane to thank her for her recent gifts to the Moores. Two months before sending the poem, Moore had written her good friend a letter of typical warmth, wit, and gratitude—here for help she had given in rearranging the Moores' apartment and making some necessary purchases.

> I don't know why I was so purblind, Louise, about the couch. Looking at things just now, it seems to me what you suggested so insistently is the *only* good thing to do—put the couch where it was, & have the bed where the couch is . . . The wise things we do on your initiative, Louise, are not for stumbling words like these to touch upon. It is so dear of you to cogitate on our needs till you almost get us into competition with J Sloane & the House Beautiful . . . The double entendre was quite exhilarating, Louise—that about the "new bed"! Mother is lost and dazed—in a faery wood—about her Lady Seymour blankets. (I know not what to expect when she sees the bed.) And I am so happy I am unaccountable. (September 13, 1946; RML VI.13.03; ellipses mine)

Following several similar letters and frequent mention of the new bed (which Crane may have paid for; the finances of the arrangement are not clear), Moore sent Crane her poem, accompanied by the remark: "Since I'm thanking *you*, Louise, you don't have to thank *me* for the peculiar poem (I can't think of a worse favor than enclosing a friend a poem.)" (November 2, 1946; RML VI.13.05). Seen in the light of this private exchange with Crane, "Voracities and Verities" functions as a double love poem, expressing direct gratitude and love to her generous friend and indirect love for her mother whom that friend has helped her cheer. The fact that Moore received her "tiger-book" as a gift from Crane (Molesworth's *Literary Life*, 354) strengthens a metonymic reading of the poem that sees the author as "under obligation" to those she loves as well as to intertextuality.

One may read farther, however, by conflating the private and cultural or public texts. In the cultural context of love and "diamonds," the poet seems to compare the "unobtrusive" love of female friendship, or of familial bonding, with the ostentatious love of marriage partners or heterosexual relationship.[45] What matters is "love undying," and Moore's (or her speaker's) dislike of "diamonds" (like her distrust of marriage in the poem by that name) suggests that one is less likely to find "love that will / gaze an eagle blind" ("Marriage") in bejeweled coupledom than elsewhere.[46] Poets who "fuss" over their own poethood or fame seem like the love that announces itself in diamonds—and both are associated with "institutions" or "enterprises" that have a private basis but take public and commercial form. What Moore rejects here is roles: of the woman wanting publicly visible engagement or marriage, and of the poet playing genius or "great man."

In this poem, Moore's speaker states preferences that are as rich as what she disdains. In preferring emeralds to diamonds, she still values precious stones; in acknowledging her debt to a tiger book she claims intertextual reference and influence—albeit to a distinctly noncanonical text. This poem is not a call to asceticism or silence. Instead, here is a love poem that does not gush from a writer who calls attention to her speaker as a grateful reader. Rather than enumerating the qualities of people or poetry she loves, the speaker waxes enthusiastic over man-eating tigers. And this is not different from love, or from poetry. Far from transcendent, Moore's poem suggests that voracious enthusiasms are not always true but that nonetheless one may always be pardoned for the excess of "love undying."

In the context of this poem's deflationary and self-mocking (as well as impatient and irritable) gestures, let me turn to a device of

Moore's poetry that may be both tonal and structural, idiomatic and formal—namely, humor. While not illocutionary, Moore's wit functions interactively: a barbed remark or innuendo depends on the assumed presence of a listener who will share the fun. The reader is expected to acknowledge the possibility that acquaintances resemble steam rollers, or verse epic a centipede, or that poets compete with elephants. The satire or broad humor of Moore's poems also marks them as distinct in tone from the elevated romantic lyric and the sentimental lament; to borrow a phrase from Marie Borroff, they are instead peculiarly "solemnity retardant." Borroff makes this remark in discussing Moore's use of scientific and technical vocabulary, but I find it apt for several aspects of her style: "If words like *amphibious, apteryx,* and *melanin* are non-colloquial, they are also non-solemn. And they not only lack solemnity themselves, they inhibit the production of solemn effects in the contexts in which they appear" (*Language and the Poet,* 88).[47] Even nonscientific words like "pestilence," "torpid," and "minutiae" have this effect in "Prismatic Color," or the anti-lyrical precision of "phenomena," "triviality," and "inspection" in the poem "Poetry."

As a sign of playfulness, Moore's humor may also establish a particularly interactive author-reader relationship. J. G. A. Pocock suggests that a concept of play may counter "the repressive tendencies of language" to prevent two-way communication—in other words, play functions to maintain the possibility of independent response ("Verbalizing a Political Act," 39).[48] One might indeed read Moore's humor in exactly this way. Rather than outright rejecting literary traditions or patriarchal culture, Moore playfully asserts her own serious perspectives and judgment, using idiosyncrasy as a sign of the power of her, or any, response. In such a reading, Moore, in earnest jest, makes a book on man-eating tigers rather than Milton or Shakespeare the sign of her intertextuality in her address to "poets," or represents traditional verse form as the "feet" of a centipede that "the wave" will surely wash away. Moreover, the idiosyncrasy—if not obvious playfulness—of her stanzaic forms and rhyme reassures readers that Moore does not attempt to establish new forms of authority to bow to: like classical "feet," her syllabics may well be washed away, since they function not as "Truth" or nature but as reminders of the artificiality of all poetic form. They deflate traditions that take themselves too seriously, make too oppressive a "fuss," intimidate response. And in doing so they puncture any hierarchical elevation of poet over reader, or poetic over critical response.

While little of Moore's verse is outright funny, almost all of it contains sparks of wit and much contains broader, congenial veins of humor or playfulness.[49] Moreover, Moore's choice of both "gusto" and "idiosyncrasy" as key terms defining artistic excellence signifies the importance of this element to her poetic.[50] "Gusto" fits exactly the singular associative leaps, puns, and word play that characterize Moore's verse—as well as what Joanne Feit Diehl calls her "wildly exuberant conception of style."[51] This is not the playfulness of a romantic idealization of childhood or of Freudian socialization and repression of asocial tendencies; nor is it a play-acting of disguise. Instead, idiosyncrasy, gusto, an appreciation of the humorous even in contexts far from funny establishes a site of creative possibility, opens a space beyond fixed truths, conventions, perfection. As Steinman notes, Moore defines creativity broadly as "a kind of mental playfulness" and even values science for its element of play (*Made In America*, 116). Play serves Moore as a field where knowledge, art, personal inclination, and the duty of the public speaker combine. Or, to return to Moore's vocabulary, it combines ferocity and grace with gusto in maintaining the communicative openness she sees as crucial to responsible art.

Moore attempts to bring her reader into the considering, weighing, contending process of thought that drives a poem. This involves not just the interactive effect of repeated illocutionary structures but a redefinition of poetry, or art, as accessible, open, imperfectly beautiful or polished, and playful. In such a poetry, the poet's authority results not from expressions of genius, passages of lyric loveliness, personal experience and attributes, or demonstrated knowledge of a tradition or the tools of a craft, but instead from the poet's degree of success in engaging the reader profoundly and actively in the concerns and the construction of her poems. Such a poetry draws a reader not to identify, sympathize, or simply enjoy, but to figure out just where the poet stands—when *is* complexity a crime? why do poets fuss, and why shouldn't they?—and through that process to understand more about her or his own positioning. In the following chapters I turn from the structures of the poems themselves to ways in which Moore's responses to contemporary social issues—particularly politicized concepts of gender and race—both figure in and shape this poetic that attempts to construct and to share a nonhierarchical authority.

FOUR

"Your Thorns Are the Best Part of You": Gender Politics in the Nongendered Poem

> I know they did say I was the best woman poet in this country; but you see . . . that means nothing, just nothing at all; because here in America not more than two, or perhaps three, women have ever even *tried* to write poetry.
>
> *Marianne Moore*

> To talk about lyric, one must say something about beauty, something about love and sex, something about Woman and Man and their positionings, something about active agency versus malleability. This is a cluster of foundational materials with a gender cast built into the heart of lyric.
>
> *Rachel Blau DuPlessis*

*E*specially in her early poetry, Moore attempts to create a nongendered poetic by reconceiving traditionally gendered poetic elements of beauty, voice, and representativeness or universality.[1] Such a goal was entirely compatible with the feminism that became increasingly important to Moore during and following her college years. This feminism stressed individualism, in opposition to nineteenth-century assumptions that women were uniquely different from men and, as a group, essentially alike. As I argue in this chapter, a number of factors most likely converged in Moore's early decisions about the construction of her poetry—some personal, some generational, some professional, some consciously and some unconsciously ideological. The convergence of these factors, however, leads to distinctly gender-conscious and distinctly new constructions of the lyric poem. One might say that Moore devises a way to make gender a part of the structure rather than of the content of her poems.[2] Moore felt herself to be unexceptional, fully the participant in a norm of female professionalism, ambition, and experimentation, at the same time that she was conscious of her gendered position in a predominantly masculine profession. To understand the apparent contradictions of such consciousness and how it affects the construction of her poetry, we must turn to the anomalous circumstances of Moore's upbringing.

Moore took for granted women's strength and her own capacity as a woman to speak and act professionally in a way that directly contradicts stereotypes of early twentieth-century women's lives. She grew up in a tightly knit, extremely playful household consisting of her mother, Mary Warner Moore, her brother, (John) Warner, and—for most of her adolescence and young adulthood—her mother's intimate friend, Mary Norcross (Moore's father was separated from the family because of a nervous collapse before her birth).[3] In the menagerie of names this family continuously assigned each other, Marianne is never named for a stereotypically feminine creature (her mother takes these guises—Bunny, Fawn, Mouse); instead, she is most often Gator, Basilisk, Weasel, Fangs (often Hamilcar Barca or Launcelot B. Fangs, Esq.), or some other version of dog—all names that take a masculine pronoun. The masculine character of her names during these early years is underlined by the fact that Marianne's and her brother's species nomenclature were largely interchangeable and that the two siblings even used the same names; both were, at times, Weaz, Basilisk, or Bruno.[4]

The round-robin of letters that Marianne, Warner, and their mother exchanged while the two children were at college reveal the Moore love of verbal extravagance and of coded reference to experiences they have shared. In addition, through these unusual and shifting playful namings, the Moore family establishes fluid boundaries of relationship. Marianne and Warner, for example, often refer to their mother as a child for whom they must watch out. A typical exchange of letters occurs on September 24, 1905, one of Moore's first days at Bryn Mawr. Her mother opens her letter: "Dear Uncle

Fangs," and later refers to herself as "Orphan Fawn"; she closes: "Goodbye dear Uncle—I'm being very good just as you told me to be. Your Fawn." On the same day, Warner writes to "Dear brother Fangs . . . It seems expedient for you to know a thing or two about our Mouse. She has been the soul of impudence and knavery since you left"; Marianne simultaneously mails a letter to her mother that closes: "With love for his good little mouse, Uncle" (RML VII.11b.09).

After reading *The Wind in the Willows* in 1914, the Moore family switched primarily to Kenneth Grahame's animal names, making Marianne the adventurous, poem-writing "Rat," Warner either "Badger" or "Toad," and their mother the homebody "Mole." These remain the family names for several decades, although the older pet names and new names come into play, especially in Warner's letters.[5] The masculine reference to Marianne is striking throughout this correspondence. Her mother does periodically refer to her daughter as female, but not consistently—and she at times even changes pronoun reference in mid-sentence. In a fairly typical letter, referring to the poet's first interview with the editors of *The Dial*, for example, Mary Warner Moore writes,

> The time could not have been longer than half an hour that she was at the Sanctum, yet she has told me enough to fill a volume, that was said; and *they* the unpardonables that they are let *him* do every bit of the saying. (September 23, 1920; RML VI.23.23)

Subject is not a consistent guide to pronoun choice either. For example, in a letter describing one of her daughter's visits to her alma mater, Bryn Mawr, she writes that "Rat"

> was so ambition-less that he took only the pink smocked evening dress . . . I have fainted with horror several times—because of the sharpness of the rat-snout; and whereas there is occasion to bat it now and again, it doesn't get batted for I am so *thankful* to have spontaneity alive in him, and a genuine response to his *"boyhood interests."* (June 8, 1919; RML VI.23.07)

In another instance, she marks her daughter as female only to differentiate her from all other women she has known:

> Most women are themselves more in "*need*" of being loved than ever *any* man has been in need of the same, since the world began. They (women) need it so much that almost an *un* needing mate will timorously be ventured on as *an object of need*, rather than be nothing to anybody. Sissy is different from her sex. I never have seen an inkling in her of what I am admitting to in the rest of womankind. (to JWM, January 5, 1916; RML VI.22.02)

Warner rarely refers to his sister as female at any period of their correspondence, and when they are both in their late sixties he is still addressing her as "Dear Boy" (for example, March 25, 1955; RML VI.40.04).[6] Marianne also refers to herself as male beyond the context of family relationships. She writes home from college, for example, "Peggy [James] is still 'very nice, very polite, very attractive,' . . . I think we shall probably be acting like grown-ups and brothers before the end" (March 27, 1908; RML VI.14.04).

It is difficult to know to what extent this playful name-calling in letters affected actual relationships at home or the conventionally masculine bias of turn-of-the-century American families. Mary Warner Moore, for example, while referred to as a child by her children, supported them financially by teaching at a local private school, washed and mended their clothes, and performed all the other caretaking responsibilities associated with parenthood. Moreover, she clearly regarded supporting her son Warner's career in the ministry as the primary family responsibility.[7] Yet the Moore family may also to some degree have transformed its participation in the conventional promotion of men through their alternative namings to give "brother" and "Uncle" Marianne fuller support and confidence than usual. Marianne was encouraged throughout her life to be independent, outspoken, and ambitious.

Moore's overwhelming use of male characters in her poems suggests that she may have taken her private signature into her published work as well. In a poem written in 1942, for example, Moore clearly uses masculine pronouns in playful code. "The Wood-

Weasel" contains an anagram for Hildegarde Watson: "he is / deter-
mination's totem," she writes of her close friend, and "Well,—/ this
same weasel's playful and his weasel / associates are too" (CP, 127).[8]
One might also read masculine-sounding poems like "Blessed is the
Man" differently, knowing that Moore goes by a masculine pronoun
in her most intimate correspondence.

This pattern of family naming and Moore's possible extension of
it into the speakers and subjects of her poems provides rich material
for psychoanalytic speculation. My point, however, is simpler and
more pragmatic. There is undoubted masculism in the family choice
to empower Marianne by making her male rather than by recon-
structing the feminine so as to empower her as female; nonetheless,
the effect of their play seems to be an empowering self-confidence
and sense of entitlement without an apparent corresponding desire
on the daughter's part to *be* "a man." Moore does not dress, act, or
present herself as masculine (as did her contemporaries Gertrude
Stein and Willa Cather), and I see no sign that she thinks of herself
as being more like a man than a woman. Far from disguising or
obliterating her female self, she claims to have both feminine and
masculine aspects; her sense of self is fluid despite conventional
categorizations that would label various qualities of the fluidity as
disparate or oppositional.[9] Moore's apparent understanding of such
fluidity as unextraordinary depends, in turn, on broader contexts of
her development.

Moore was part of an anomalous and unique group of (mostly
white) college-educated women coming to professional maturity in
the United States between 1890 and 1920. In *Disorderly Conduct:
Visions of Gender in Victorian America*, Carroll Smith-Rosenberg differ-
entiates between two waves of the turn-of-the-century "New
Woman."[10] Those in the first wave (attending college between 1870
and 1905) were politically and economically focused in their mani-
festations of feminism and typically led woman-focused lives. The
later "New Woman" (attending college in the 1910s and 1920s) was
more sexually focused and often politically and economically more
conservative. Smith-Rosenberg attributes the rise of these genera-
tions primarily to the proliferation of women's colleges during the
1870s and 1880s. These colleges provided large numbers of women

with an environment exclusively and professionally female-focused (or, in men's colleges, accepting of women in a professional sphere) during a critical period of their development. Here women were expected to succeed at a wide variety of endeavors utterly divorced from traditional notions of "woman's sphere." As Smith-Rosenberg puts it: "To place a woman outside of a domestic setting, to train a woman to think and feel 'as a man,' to encourage her to succeed at a career, indeed to place a career before marriage, violated virtually every late-Victorian norm" (252). Those in this first generation perceived their specialness and took it as a sign of their calling to work together in the public sphere.

The demographic figures for these women are staggering. Of those attending college between 1870 and 1920, 40 to 60 percent did not marry, while only 10 percent of all American women did not (*Disorderly Conduct*, 253).[11] At Bryn Mawr, Moore's alma mater, 62 percent of the students graduating between 1889 and 1908 went on to graduate work (281). As well as openly lesbian relationships— like those between Bryn Mawr President M. Carey Thomas and, first, Mamie Gwinn and then Mary Garrett—"crushes" or "smashes" between women at women's colleges were quite common and openly spoken of by all parts of the college community. Many of these relationships developed into lifelong friendships of intense intimacy, as well as networks of professional support invaluable to this newly employed class (254). As Smith-Rosenberg's wording above and these patterns of lifelong connection imply, these women found no discrepancy in their commitment to private and public lives as women within female communities while conceiving of their education, ambition, and abilities as making them "like men."

The optimistic enthusiasm of this generation stands in marked contrast to the pessimistic ennui of their male peers. Whereas the radical shifts in social structure brought about by increasing industrialization, huge waves of southern and eastern European immigration, and (later) the devastating losses of World War I made many men fear that civilization itself was on the brink of destruction, these same conditions provided opportunities for women to act in the public and political world in roles that had not previously been available to them.[12] It is impossible to overestimate the importance of these differing responses. Women were seriously affected by the increasing poverty and crime they saw concentrated in large cities, and later by the mutilations and deaths of the Great War, but in these phenomena they also found encouragement to take action. Women from the first large classes to graduate from college became organizers or directors of settlement houses, organizers of the NAACP, and activists in innumerable other social, labor, and political causes—especially in promoting the further advancement of women. As late as 1985, Smith-Rosenberg still finds that this generation "amassed greater political power and visibility than any other group of women in American experience"—presumably including her own generation (256).

Because of the first generation's success, the second wave of New Women did not have to take the first steps in education or public professionalism; they felt themselves to be following in settled traditions and wanted to move beyond the increasingly female-dominated institutions of education and social reform. These women wanted to be powerful and autonomous not just "like" men but in the world of men. More than their predecessors, these women were apt to borrow male metaphors and images as being most appropriate for expressing their own strength. They sought, in a sense, to be free of gender, to move beyond it. As Nancy Cott puts it in *The Grounding of Modern Feminism*, "they posited a paradoxical group ideal of individuality."[13] This younger group embarked confidently on more experimental living patterns and more male-dominated professional careers than had their predecessors. For many, this in turn, paradoxically, led to more conventional gender roles.[14]

Moore comes at the end of the first wave and the beginning of the second of the New Woman, and mingles characteristics of the two groups. She graduated from Bryn Mawr in 1909, at the end of a period in which 55 percent of her alma mater's graduates did not marry and, of those who did, 54 percent still continued in professional careers and considered themselves financially independent.[15] Only 10 percent of these Bryn Mawr graduates were not employed (*Disorderly Conduct*, 281–282). Lectures and plays on feminist themes were held frequently on or near the campus, and Moore was active both in attendance and in discussions promoting feminism among her friends. In not marrying and in pursuing a professional career, Moore was solidly in the mainstream of her college peers as well as fully supported by her family. As Moore later wrote to Bryher, "my experience [at Bryn Mawr] gave me security in my determination to have what I want" (August 31, 1921; RML V.08.06). Like her younger peers, however—and perhaps as much for familial as for other reasons—Moore preferred the language of masculine generics (which she considered gender-neutral) to a feminine mode of expression.

Despite her strong friendships with men and women throughout her life, and her intense interest in the topic of marriage from around 1918 to 1923, Moore never seems to have considered a romantic/sexual partnership—except, possibly, during her college years, when she had a few intense friendships with fellow students, in particular, William James's daughter, Peggy. Such lack of interest, however, was as unremarkable as her not marrying. According to John D'Emilio and Estelle Freedman's history of sexuality in America, relatively low interest in sex was common to women of this period. In an extensive study of 1,000 married women who reached marriageable age before the First World War (that is, Moore's generation) and another study of a slightly earlier generation, more than half of the respondents of each study did not consider sex necessary for either mental or physical health, seeing it instead as necessary for reproduction and for maintaining cordial relations with their spouses.[16] The percentages sharing this attitude were no doubt even higher among women like Moore whose mothers were not sexually active; Moore's mother seems to have been celibate since her daughter's birth.[17] The most pertinent comment I have seen on this topic, however, is Richard Howard's in "Marianne Moore and the Monkey Business of Modernism," that "we have not yet devised or developed a vocabulary in which we can readily express or understand the erotics of withdrawal or recessiveness or obliquity, or the refusal of explicit sexual gesture. And consequently, I don't believe any of us can easily say: this is, or this is not, a fulfilled and rewarding sexual life" (AMM, 10).

There has been no adequate documentation to date of Moore's activity in the suffrage movement or in women's issues generally, but her ·letters make it clear that such activity was an important concern during college and the 1910s.[18] To give a single example from college, on February 14, 1909, Moore writes several pages home detailing a conversation she has had with a friend who is "on the fence" regarding suffrage and other aspects of women's rights. Among other points, Moore argues:

> If women are going to support children and perhaps unproductive adults they ought to have as much pay as men and ought to work light hours if men work eight hours and not work ten. I delivered a cruel flow on the score of men—I said the *men* are all that keep you respectable—Just because they don't *choose* to grind women down more than women *are* ground down, is not the fault of the women . . .[I said] "the clothes of every woman in N.Y a few years ago, belonged to her husband, No widow could legally be buried in the state—a widow inherited 2/3 of her husband's property—(during her life)—the cemetery lot came in the property, so the woman had 2/3 of the cemetery lot, during her life time and to get any use out of it would have to be buried before she was dead" . . .
> I said also that the eight hour day was all a question of the ballot— Elsie said she didn't see how it could be—I said, "well, in Colorado, the men had an eight hour day, the women, a ten hour day, the women got an eight hour day because they put a bill in; as voters (for state legislature). In N.Y. they did not!["] . . . I wasn't as rabid as I sound here, but I was pretty bulldoggy. I said "of course woman suffrage doesn't mean much to you, because you're petted and have money lavished on you and you wouldn't think what a slum looks like and wouldn't think of touching an infected horse-hide or dangerous machinery for anything, but a lot of girls that haven't quite your chances could see why it might help some." (RML VI.15a.03)

After graduation, Moore moved back to Carlisle, Pennsylvania. Between 1911 and 1914, she taught a range of courses (from Stenography to Commercial Law to Commercial Arithmetic) at the Carlisle Indian School—an institution she had been familiar with throughout her youth. During her teaching years, Moore was understandably extremely busy. After the department she taught in closed in 1914, however, she quickly returned to attending lectures on feminist topics and campaigning with other suffragists. For example, after an afternoon of distributing leaflets and talking to farmers at a fair, Moore wrote her brother that "today I did so much talking Hall [Cowdry] said I ought to go on the stump" (September 22, 1915; RML VI.21.10). The poet also mentions in a late interview that she wrote suffrage pieces for the Carlisle newspaper (Molesworth, *A Literary Life,* 106), and she and her mother both helped out at the polls during the first election in which women could vote.[19]

Moore's desire for gender neutrality was as typical of her feminist literary peers as the general structure of her life was for fellow college graduates: notions of gender neutrality were a common part of feminist aesthetics in the early twentieth century. Virginia Woolf's call for the ideal artist to be androgynous in *A Room of One's Own* is well known. In a 1919 lecture called "Woman and the Creative Will," Lola Ridge similarly proposed an androgynous base for all creativity, uniting qualities traditionally separated as masculine or feminine.[20] Charlotte Perkins Gilman expresses the same idea more strongly, claiming in 1911 that the true artist transcends sex and that any tendency toward self-expression rather than social expression is disfiguring: an "ingenious lack of reticence . . . is at its base essentially masculine."[21] A female or feminist artistic mode would, in contrast, focus not on self but on community or the social world. Gilman's call for a community of social- rather than self-focused art has its roots in the same cultural context as stereotyped notions of feminine selflessness but expresses the more active and positive side: for her, as for Woolf and Moore, women should not be selfless but should express themselves without the limitations of egocentric perspective.[22]

The early twentieth-century ideology of professionalism also may have affected Moore's belief in the possibility of moving beyond restrictive gender categories. In *The Grounding of Modern Feminism,* Nancy Cott argues that the woman's rights ideology of gaining political and legal equality with men to forge a "human sex" encouraged women to adopt an ideology which stressed "rationalism, scientific standards, and objectivity" (216) and insisted that professions were "sex-neutral." It was, in fact, precisely this ideology that attracted women to the professions, and there was a sharp increase of women in professional fields during this period: there, presumably, one needed only intelligence and the willingness to work hard to succeed.[23] Ideologies of professionalism, feminism, patterns of friendship at college and of affectionate play at home—all seem to push Moore in the direction of her choices not to conceive of her poetry as explicitly or essentially feminine.

Late twentieth-century critical response to this aspect of Moore's poetry, however, has not considered most of these factors. In *Women Poets and the American Sublime,* Joanne Feit Diehl analyzes with subtlety and intelligence what she sees as the psychological losses of Moore's choice to work for "poetic disengenderment" or "'transgendered' privilege."[24] Arguing that Moore displaces experience and feeling— and especially "the original mother-daughter dynamics of poetic origin"—with authorial control, Diehl sees Moore's movement toward gender neutrality as allied with "the masculine poetic tradition" (82). Moreover, while arguing for the radical gendered implications of much of her work, she finds a conciliatory move even in Moore's open invocations of the feminine: she "divorce[s] the conventionally condoned aspects of the female—maternity, modesty, gentleness— from those that threaten men: female desire, sexuality, explicit assertions of power" (47). More recently, and in longer studies of Moore, both Jeanne Heuving and Darlene Erickson argue that Moore writes deliberately in a woman's voice, to express a woman's perspective. Heuving repeats that Moore attempts the paradoxical representation of both a "universal" perspective and her woman's view; Erickson, from a more essentialized perspective, argues that Moore has a "uniquely feminine method of comprehending her world" that is both inherent and, by implication, more "real" in its invocation of the "source of human creativity" than patriarchal or "men's" methods (3, 5).[25]

Bonnie Costello's "The 'Feminine' Language of Marianne Moore" occupies an interesting place in feminist argument because it denies feminist intent on Moore's part and uses a conventional categorization of femininity while arguing that Moore inverts the values assigned to such qualities. Costello argues, for example, that "Moore's access to [her] central concern with [resisting the complacencies and] limits of language is through a conventional but redefined femininity"; "Moore's humility and restraint are not passive defenses but ways of gathering force, as a bow is pulled back in order to carry the arrow farther when it is finally released."[26] To describe Moore's "feminine" qualities without equal attention to what might be called her "masculine" ones, however, and perhaps to conceive of this determinedly independent poet at all in the exclusive terms of these categories, is to falsify the picture, and it is perhaps for this reason that Costello sees nothing "feminist" in Moore's work.[27]

While it would be foolish as well as false to suggest that Moore had no gender anxiety, that she suffered no discontent about leading a life so patently at odds with that of the majority of women of her generation (despite its similarity with that of other college graduates), or that her poetic bears no resemblance to values that are conventionally "feminine," I believe that depictions of her anxiety and her femininity have been exaggerated because of late twentieth-century critical concerns. As James Scully notes in "Line Break," "Any technique *takes place*. It entails history, raises factors of education, class, cultural access, and so on . . . There is no technique independent of the life context in which, and through which, it is realized."[28] Moore's style has seemed anomalous or conservative to many critics because they have interpreted her use of gender categories according to nineteenth-century notions of separate spheres (notions that regained much of their currency during the 1950s) or to late twentieth-century feminist theories rather than according to the complex of factors "in . . . and through which" her poetic was realized.[29] Moore's confidence in her abilities to perform the kind of gender transformational work she pursues in her poetry was both remarkably and anomalously strong. We have only begun to see a return to such confident experimentation in the work of women poets in the 1980s and 1990s.[30]

Although there is no period of concentrated focus on gender in Moore's poetry, much of her early work can be read as inscribing gender concerns. Read chronologically and including those poems later omitted from her published collections, Moore's poems from the years 1915 until 1925—when she stopped writing poetry to edit *The Dial*—reveal an ongoing analysis of ways in which power relationships and various constructions of value are affected by and oppose or reinforce widespread gender constructions.[31] This analysis helps illuminate the ways Moore structures gender politics into her poetry generally.

Before turning to these poems, it is enlightening to look at two brief comments that Moore makes about gender stereotypes in reviews.[32] In 1923, she comments that "women are regarded as belonging necessarily to either of two classes—that of the intellectual freelance or that of the eternally sleeping beauty, effortless yet effective in the indestructible limestone keep of domesticity" (CPr, 82). In 1932, she writes more skeptically:

> Some feel their own sex to be more inane than the other, some the other to be more inane than their own. Some find both inane. It is not possible to differentiate in favor of either, according to Professor Papez' collection of brains at Cornell. They are, as it were, alligators. (CPr, 283)

Power differences exist; social constructions exist. These, however, should be combated without recourse to essentialism on either side. One might even say that one goal of Moore's early verse is to persuade readers—and perhaps herself—that women may be "alligators" rather than either bluestockings or sleeping beauties.[33] This peculiar choice of metaphor, however, may also imply more; "gator" was the poet's primary family nickname during college, and the species name for all Bryn Mawr students (Warner and all Yale students were "turtles"). The poet's assertion that all people are "[alli]gators" may be one of several private ways in which Moore both claims gender neutrality and identifies that status with a female position rather than with the assumed neutrality and universality of the male one.[34]

During 1916 and 1917, Moore published several poems based on distinctions between types of behavior and/or states that might be stereotyped as feminine or masculine exclusively. The point of these poems, however, seems not to be the necessity of identifying with one or the other or establishing a gendered hierarchy of values but rather to overturn these common associations. In particular, Moore

105

divorces associations of ambition and weaponry from domination and masculinity and of beauty from merely visual attributes and femininity.[35] A slight poem called "Holes Bored in a Workbag by the Scissors" plays off a well-known contrast:

A neat, round hole in the bank of the creek
    Means a rat;
            That is to say, craft, industry, resourcefulness:
            While
These indicate the unfortunate, meek
    Habitat
            Of surgery thrust home to fabricate useless
            Voids.
                       (*Bruno's Weekly* 3 [1916], 1137)

Here Moore contrasts the desired status of the rat—for whom holes mean "craft, industry, resourcefulness"—with that of a woman who is expected to keep her workbag neat, free of "useless / Voids." While the (in family parlance, male) rat is considered by some unnamed standard of judgment to be neat, resourceful, praiseworthy, the (in cultural prescriptions, female) owner of the workbag is metonymically "unfortunate, meek." Whether by accident or through (angry?) "surgery," she "fabricate[s]" what are considered "useless / Voids." This poem may instruct critics not to interpret what Moore produces as a punctured workbag; a rat's (or Rat's) work "means" "craft, industry, resourcefulness." Or perhaps Moore contrasts a stereotyped division of rat from woman with the private joke that she can be both. Or she rewrites Anne Bradstreet's lines: "I am obnoxious to each carping tongue / Who says my hand a needle better fits" ("Prologue," 1650).

In "Feed Me, Also, River God," the speaker asks the "River God" not to "discriminate against" one with less competitive ambition for public success than the "Israelites." "Feed Me, Also . . ." the speaker cries:

lest by diminished vitality and abated
vigilance, I become food for crocodiles—for that quicksand

106

of gluttony which is legion. It is there—close at hand—
  on either side
  of me. You remember the Israelites who said in pride

and stoutness of heart: "The bricks are fallen down, we will
build with hewn stone, the sycamores are cut down, we will
            change to
cedars"? I am not ambitious to dress stones, to renew
  forts, nor to match
  my value in action, against their ability to catch

up with arrested prosperity. I am not like
them, indefatigable, but if you are a god you will
not discriminate against me. Yet—if you may fulfil
  none but prayers dressed
  as gifts in return for your gifts—disregard the request.
              (1916; P, 8)

Read as an autobiographical statement, this poem suggests that after
years of having her submissions to literary magazines rejected,
Moore sees herself as despised, outcast, a minority—like the Jews.
Yet she is not the chosen of any god, does not have the comfort of
numbers, and is not "indefatigable." The word "discriminate" and
the singularity of her bald statement "I am not like / them" suggest
that the "Israelites" of literature may be those (predominantly male)
poets already dominating her pocket of the literary world—de-
spised, perhaps, by the larger industrial, materialist world but none-
theless powerful in their chosen field. Moore may be acknowledging
her outsider status and asking for help. Yet the poem's tone is proud;
the speaker tells this god how to behave, calls attention to the god's
limitations, and states the only conditions on which she will accept
aid: "*if* you may fulfil" only prayers that wear the trapping of thanks
or exchange, even though she has not yet received anything, then
she is not interested in being helped (my emphasis). She will not
pretend that either she or this god is better than they are, and yet
insists that any god who "[is] a god" will help her nonetheless. Read
more generally as a poem about marginality, this nongendered
speaker accuses the local god of discrimination as a way of demand-
ing rightful nurturance. Yet even in this setting where one either

eats or "become[s] food for crocodiles," the speaker refuses to accept nurturance if the price is falsification. What begins with apparent despair ends with self-sufficiency. The speaker does not want to become "like / them" but to be fed on her or his own terms.[36]

The implied combat of survival in a competitive world of "arrested prosperity" is made explicit in "To Be Liked By You Would Be A Calamity":

> "Attack is more piquant than concord," but when
>   You tell me frankly that you would like to feel
>   My flesh beneath your feet,
>   I'm all abroad; I can but put my weapon up, and
>   Bow you out.
> Gesticulation—it is half the language.
>   Let unsheathed gesticulation be the steel
>   Your courtesy must meet,
>   Since in your hearing words are mute, which to my senses
>   Are a shout.
>
>   (1916; Obs, 37)

Admitting that "attack" is "piquant," this speaker nonetheless re- places violence with "unsheathed gesticulation" or a form of com- munication more effective than swordplay. The speaker regally "bow[s] out" the visitor who cannot (will not?) hear. Moore's note- books reveal the gendered conflict that inspires this poem: she quotes from a scene in Thomas Hardy's *A Pair of Blue Eyes* in which a young woman responds to a male critic's hostile review of her romance: masculine attack seems to be met by feminine expressive silence. Divorced from this explicitly gendered scene by the poet's ungendered "you" and "me," however, the poem may suggest that such labels do not assist us: there are different ways of winning, and the speaker is not apparently limited by gender or any other factor to a single one. The speaker chooses not to engage in a duel—the field of masculine honor par excellence—but instead to redefine the mode of combat, and thus demonstrates her or his superior effec- tiveness and strength. At the same time, as DuPlessis points out, by claiming the weapon of silent gesticulation in a poem of highly crafted language, the speaker reveals formidable and aggressive language skills.[37]

Like "To Be Liked By You," "In This Age of Hard Trying Nonchalance Is Good, And" distinguishes the effectiveness of different modes of communicating. Published in the same 1916 issue of *Chimaera*, "In This Age" begins with petulant and unuseful gods: "really, it is not the / business of the gods to bake clay pots. They did not / do it in this instance." Nor did they "venture the / profession of humility," instead ignoring "the polished wedge / that might have split the firmament"; and, as a consequence, it becomes "dumb." Moore implies in this mini-parable that "humility" is a "wedge" of great power, and that its proper use is decisive (firmament-splitting) yet humble speech. In response to its neglect, this wedge drops from heaven, conferring "on some poor fool" the "privilege" of storytelling—in other words, the gift of speech passes from the gods to humans, but here takes the form of fiction rather than transparent relationship to things. Like the previous speaker's "gesticulation," this fool's "tales / of what could never have been actual— / were better than the haggish, uncompanionable drawl // of certitude; his by- / play was more terrible in its effectiveness / than the fiercest frontal attack"—or, in other words, better than the dogmatic insistence of language characterizing religion and war—both spheres historically dominated by men or exclusively male.[38] Moreover, while the storyteller of this poem is male, his "weapon" is made up of "feigned inconsequence / of manner," "self-protectiveness," understatement, indirection, and "humility"—all qualities that are stereotypically feminine. A man of feminine characteristics competes with and is more effective than those who employ traditionally masculine weapons. Gender categories here are collapsed, suggesting that such categorization is beside the point. As in "Feed Me, Also, River God," Moore's concern is with power, duty, and effectiveness: if the gods (or those with traditional power) do not act appropriately, the "privilege" to do so will "fall" on marginal figures, those without traditional power—or "some poor fool." Storytellers may be more useful and more powerful than either warriors or gods.

"Roses Only" takes the stereotype of femininity as its specific theme, again linking characteristics attributed to both sexes within one.

You do not seem to realise that beauty is a liability rather than
    an asset—that in view of the fact that spirit creates form we are
                justified in supposing
    that you must have brains. For you, a symbol of the unit, stiff
                and sharp,
    conscious of surpassing by dint of native superiority and liking
                for everything
self-dependent, anything an

ambitious civilisation might produce: for you, unaided to attempt
                through sheer
    reserve, to confute presumptions resulting from observation, is
                idle. You cannot make us
    think you a delightful happen-so. But rose, if you are brilliant, it
    is not because your petals are the without-which-nothing of
                pre-eminence. You would look, minus
thorns—like a what-is-this, a mere

peculiarity. They are not proof against a worm, the elements, or
                mildew
    but what about the predatory hand? What is brilliance without
                co-ordination? Guarding the
    infinitesimal pieces of your mind, compelling audience to
    the remark that it is better to be forgotten than to be
                remembered too violently,
your thorns are the best part of you.

(1917; P, 13)

The archetypal symbol of femininity, the rose of this poem seems to stand for woman herself, and Moore fears that she has forgotten that "beauty is a liability rather than / an asset" unless it protects itself. Moreover, the poet asserts, helpless or stupid beauty is "a what-is-this, a mere // peculiarity"; only when gorgeous petals combine with "brains" and "co-ordination," only when a rose "guard[s] the / infinitesimal pieces of [her] mind" revealed in her loveliness, is she truly "brilliant." Similarly, "sheer reserve" and pride do not suffice as protection; the rose also needs "thorns." In this biting response to the "carpe diem" slogan "gather ye rosebuds while ye may," Moore reminds women that it is better to be "forgotten" than to be plucked violently. Or, as she states in a poem of 1925, "'it is better to be lonely than unhappy'" ("The Monkey Puzzler"—later republished as "The Monkey Puzzle"). Beauty is not what attracts male suitors to try to pick the rose but what is revealed when a woman uses her brains on her own behalf, and hence ceases to be a "mere peculiarity."[39]

Another poem of 1917 also links weapons with the feminine. In "Those Various Scalpels," Moore describes a woman who has transformed herself into an arsenal. The poem takes the familiar form of the love catalogue, or *blason*, but rather than having hair like gold, eyes like diamonds, lips like cherries, and so on, this woman has hair like "the tails of two / fighting-cocks head to head in stone— like sculptured / scimitars"; eyes like "flowers of ice // and / snow sown by tearing winds on the cordage of disabled / ships"; cheeks like "those rosettes / of blood on the stone floors of French chateaux"; hands like "a / bundle of lances"; and a dress that is both "a / magnificent square / cathedral of uniform / and . . . diverse appearance" and a "species of / vertical vineyard rustling in the storm / of conventional opinion" (Obs, 61–62).[40] Having disrupted all expectations of the form she imitates, Moore then asks what is the purpose of so many sharp edges: "Are they weapons or scalpels?" Like a doctor's scalpels, these constructions of appearance are "rich / instruments with which to experiment"; they confer a "hard majesty" of "sophistication which is su- / perior to opportunity." Yet everything natural or human in the figure disappears. There is nothing here but surface brilliance, self-protectiveness. This rose will never be picked, but as Moore implies in her final question, its thorns may have outgrown the flower's use for them: "why dissect destiny with instruments / which / are more highly specialized than the tissues of destiny / itself?" (P, 7). Defense is clearly necessary in the world she observes, but it too can be overdone, and Moore here directly links the made-up feminine beauty of "conventional opinion" (the donning of makeup, jewelry, and high fashion) with both armor and weapons.[41] She prefers instead the more openly hostile but less aggressive manner of "thorns."

Published in the same year as "Roses Only" and "Those Various Scalpels," "Sojourn in the Whale" appears to claim that women (represented by the Irish) may "rise" without doing battle. The poem ends with indirect dialogue between the British ("men") and Ireland ("you," a woman). Britain says:

> "There is a feminine
> temperament in direct contrast to
>
> ours which makes her do these things. Circumscribed by a
>   heritage of blindness and native
>   incompetence, she will become wise and will be forced to give
> in. Compelled by experience, she
>
> will turn back; water seeks its own level": and you
>   have smiled. "Water in motion is far
>   from level." You have seen it when obstacles happened to bar
> the path—rise automatically.
>
> (Obs, 39)

Here is the poem's conundrum. The last lines, and the woman's smile, imply that she knows more than the men who criticize her. Having "been compelled" to perform impossible deeds for centuries ("thread[ ] / the points of needles," "spin / gold thread from straw") and having not just survived but abundantly "lived and lived on every kind of shortage," she knows with absolute clarity her own endurance and strength. Yet if water rises "automatically," there is no need for thorns or weapons.

In the context of other poems, however, such a passive reading becomes implausible, and the poem's analogy between women and nature seems more problematized than problematic. According to "Roses Only," the natural woman has both intellect and "thorns"; according to "Those Various Scalpels," women are capable of aggression and weaponry far beyond that natural state; and according to all of Moore's poems, one is limited in one's effectiveness and success by one's determination and wit—not by "nature." The "rise" predicted in "Sojourn" may occur because a woman—or at least a New Woman—"automatically" responds with whatever "weapons or scalpels" she has at her command; her nature, as it were, may appear the same but has changed in its determination to respond. Unlike most of Moore's poems, this one predicts revolution. Inspired by the resurgence of Irish rebellion against British colonialism in 1916, this poem suggests the necessity or "nature" of the downtrodden to rise.[42]

Especially in "Roses Only" and "Those Various Scalpels," one sees the links between Moore's deconstruction of traditionally exclusive gender categories and her simultaneous construction of a new aesthetic for the lyric poem. "Beauty" and "weapons" are key in both categories. In "Roses Only," Moore warns women against passive, conventional beauty or self-display in a poem that is deliberately *un*lyrical. It is awkward in its very long lines, "thorny" in its complex syntax and off-rhymes. Such unlyrical form suggests that Moore is critiquing traditional aesthetics of the lyric as well as constructions of femininity. For the poem to be "brilliant," it, too, must be more than merely "beautiful." In fact it must be prickly, must warn its reader against a too aggressive appropriation of its meaning. A merely lovely poem, for Moore—at least in the context of modern life—is a "peculiarity." At the same time, the poem should not be all armor or artifice. As either weapon or scalpel—and Moore writes poems of both sorts in these early years—it must be open, not "superior," to "opportunity." As she writes in other poems, a poem should acknowledge its debts to "expediency," revel in the minutia of "unconscious fastidiousness," make place for the "raw" and "genuine." The poem, like the woman, needs to leave behind the limitations of its traditionally lovely, ideally perfect form and instead cherish its "brains," "toads," and "thorns."[43]

Similarly, "To Be Liked By You," "In These Days of Hard Trying," and "Feed Me, Also, River God" suggest links between stereotyped gender categories and the functions of poetic voice. These poems foreground a note of exasperation that is distinctly unlyrical and anti-sublime. Unlike the traditional lyric, Moore's early poetry is not universal, neither inspired nor inspiring, and not poetic in diction or tone. It is fed up with uselessness, personal animosity, and discrimination of all kinds. Hers is a public moral tone, but with a singularly emotional and private edge. The tone, in short, matches the poem's form in its prickly, complex, unlovely tones. As discussed previously, Moore typically combines the personal and impersonal, eschewing romantic transcendent, sentimentally feminine, and strictly impersonal presentation. By focusing these poems on a figure known only through its active opposition and strong feeling—variously cast as pride, "steel," and storytelling "by-play"—and at the same time divorcing the voice from conventionally masculine or feminine positioning, Moore suggests a poetic position of idiosyncratic and fluid rather than conventional and fixed gender boundaries. The speaker is not gendered, while the poetry indirectly comments on the limitations of gender stereotypes.

Repeated emphasis on Moore's "feminine" characteristics and self-protectiveness tends to obscure her equal emphasis on weaponry and at least limited capacity for offense. As she writes of the cat she admires in "Peter," "As for the disposition // invariably to affront, an animal with claws wants to have to use / them; . . . To / leap, to lengthen out, divide the air—to purloin, to pursue . . . this is life; to do less would be nothing but dishonesty" (1924; Obs, 52). In a 1923 review of H.D.'s *Hymen*, Moore directly links the feminine and weaponry in art. After finding "an apparently masculine tone" in H.D.'s writing because of her "talk of weapons and the tendency to match one's intellectual and emotional vigor with the violence of nature," Moore concludes that H.D. is nonetheless "preeminently . . . 'feminine.'" There is, Moore writes,

> a connection between weapons and beauty. Cowardice and beauty are at swords' points and in H.D.'s work, suggested by the absence of subterfuge, cowardice and the ambition to dominate by brute force, we have heroics which do not confuse transcendence with domination and which in their indestructibleness, are the core of tranquillity and of intellectual equilibrium. (CPr, 82)

114

Good weapons, as it were, do not "dominate by brute force" or confuse violence with "transcendence" but instead fight the impulse to dominate, which Moore calls "cowardice."

Moore's statements about art, as well as the unconventionalities of her forms, reflect her preference for a "beauty" that is wild, prickly, and ethical rather than iconic, aesthetic, and elite, and for a speaker who is idiosyncratic and emotional without being personal, representative, or transcendent. In "Critics and Connoisseurs," for example, the speaker unapologetically prefers "childish" behavior to ancient art: "Certain Ming / products, imperial floor coverings of coach / wheel yellow, are well enough in their way but I have seen something / that I like better—a / mere childish attempt to make an imperfectly ballasted animal stand up" (Obs, 35). "The Monkey Puzzler" proclaims of a pine tree: "This porcupine-quilled, infinitely complicated starkness— / this is beauty" (Obs, 30). "The Jerboa" prefers the simple markings and ecologically sound "Abundance" of the desert rat to the decadent artistic splendors of the Egyptians and Romans, based as they are on great differentials of wealth and on enslavement (1932; CP, 13). Moore's description of a glacier— "An Octopus // of ice"—is potentially sublime, but she juxtaposes her descriptions of its magnificence with scientific description ("pseudopodia / made of glass that will bend—a much needed invention—") and slang ("'creepy to behold'"), concluding with a preference for a "beauty" that "'stimulates / the moral vigor of its citizens'" and for the forest service's "odd oracles of cool official sarcasm" over the sublimity or "smoothness" of classical art (Obs, 83, 88, 89).

It is perhaps then no accident that Moore draws her clearest portrait of conjoined physical and spiritual beauty in a poem spoken in the voice of an elephant—an animal that she allies with the feminine although it is improbably unlike any notion of conventional female beauty. "Black Earth" is the longest poem Moore has written by 1917, first of the several animal portraits which become a trademark of her verse, and one of two animal portraits she writes in the first person (the other is "Dock Rats," which she did not republish after 1925). "Black Earth" begins, "Openly, yes . . . I do these / things which I do, which please / no one but myself." The elephant-poet speaks with utter self-acceptance and calm pride.

As I discuss at greater length in the following chapter, "Black Earth" revolves around the relation of the animal to its skin:

> The sediment of the river which
> encrusts my joints, makes me very gray but I am used
>
> to it, it may
> remain there; do away
>   with it and I am myself done away with, for the
>   patina of circumstance can but enrich what was
>
> there to begin
> with . . .
>
> (P, 10)

Constructed out of "rut / upon rut of unpreventable experience," such skin "is a manual for the peanut-tongued and the // hairy toed"—that is, for other elephants. In other words, far from conquering or demoralizing the elephant, circumstance and experience (what we might call the marks of age) make it wise, beautiful, and strong: "Black / but beautiful," she exclaims, "my back / is full of the history of power." Yet the speaker immediately checks this declaration of pride and concludes that true strength is marked by sensitivity of the spirit—"spiritual" not "external poise." Despite its thick skin, the elephant is delicately attuned to its environment; its "ears are sensitized to more than the sound of // the wind." Its skin is like a "piece of black glass" that simultaneously represents "the indestructibility of matter" and reveals the "beautiful element of unreason under it." The "patina of circumstance" creates and protects the elephant's beauty, but does not block its receptivity to the world. The elephant is emblematized as "black earth preceded by a tendril."

This elephant—like Moore's rose—combines elements that are unfeminine in conventional stereotype with those that are quite conventionally so. Its size, weight, power, indifference to a neat appearance (it rolls in river mud), and proverbially indestructible "thick skin" would seem to contrast with its "spiritual poise," its

116

ability to see and hear "more than the sound of // the wind," the paradoxically glass-like quality of its rutted skin—delicately "translucent like the atmosphere"—and its underlying "beautiful element of unreason." Reading this poem as a self-portrait, one might conclude that Moore does not need a feminine form or persona (the human "wandlike body of which one hears so much") to be satisfied with herself as the inevitable product of her own "rut / upon rut of unpreventable experience." It is only through fully "inhabit[ing]" one's own increasingly thick and wrinkled skin that one accumulates power and attains the easy openness with which she speaks here.

In "In the Days of Prismatic Color" (1919) Moore prefers an art of complexity to the purity of form possible only in a world housing "Adam . . . alone." In "The Labors of Hercules" (1921), she suggests that wisdom does not belong only to old men: one must "persuade those self-wrought Midases of brains / whose fourteen-karat ignorance aspires to rise in value . . . that one must not borrow a long white beard and tie it on" to be wise (Obs, 63). In "People's Surroundings" (1922), Moore suggests that "surroundings" like Bluebeard's castle or Utah and Texas with their "cool sirs" may be problematic—especially for a woman who will be a poet—regardless of how lovely or admirable they are in their own terms. In "Silence" (1924—a poem composed simultaneously with "Marriage"), a daughter questions the adequacy and effect of her father's words by quoting them at length—a perfect parable for an artist who uses traditional form with a difference; "Sea Unicorns and Land Unicorns" (1924) portrays a woman "as curiously wild and gentle" as the unicorn which she alone can tame (Obs, 93); and "An Octopus" (1924)—as Joanne Diehl argues, and especially in its first published version—dramatizes "the power of a female-identified nature, and the kind of strength required . . . to master the imminent threats of masculine appropriation (the intrusive climbers) and the glacier's paradoxically maternal, rapine claw" (*American Sublime*, 74). This is by no means an exhaustive list of early poems in which gender (and relationships of power as they stem from and affect constructions of gender) plays a role. I hope, however, that these examples give a sense of the pervasiveness of this concern for Moore during the period in which she is developing her own poetic powers.

The climax of Moore's exploration of the relationships between poetry, gender, and power comes in her 1923 poem "Marriage"—a tour de force of the various poetic strategies that Moore has been perfecting for the last ten or more years.[44] "Marriage" presents an extended portrait of relationships between the sexes, both of a mythical (albeit anachronistically modern) Adam and Eve, and of an anonymous "He" and "She." Far from idealizing either sex, here Moore criticizes both harshly for their failure to see beyond their own selfishness and to remember that the object of their initial desire was a "fight *to be affectionate*" rather than merely "a fight" (my emphasis; Obs, 77).[45] Nonetheless, Moore is more sympathetic to her female character than to her male, and analyzes relationships between them in ways that are notably feminist. Giving Eve precedence of place in the Eden of their mutual independence (she comes first in the poem), Moore also gives Eve linguistic ability equal to, although different from, Adam's: she is "able to write simultaneously / in three languages . . . and talk in the meantime" while he is positively "Alive with words" and "prophesie[s] correctly— / the industrious waterfall." Moore, however, also more critically notes that Adam "goes on speaking / in a formal, customary strain" of "everything convenient / to promote one's joy," suggesting the overbearing quality of his fluency. Once the poem has moved fully into the modern world, Moore further admits that Eve's "fight" against selfishness and other forms of human weakness is harder than Adam's, as she must also fight him off—that "spiked hand / that has an affection for one / and proves it to the bone, / impatient to assure you / that impatience is the mark of independence / not of bondage."[46] Although women assert "imperious humility" in the sanctioned space of the tea room, "experience attests / that men have power / and sometimes one is made to feel it" (CP, 77–78).

"Marriage" ends with a long sentence that seems to reflect in its disjunctions and complexity the multiple positionings and almost tortuous desire for fairness of the whole poem. This sentence concludes by describing a statue of Daniel Webster—representative of patriarchy as statesman and orator. A supporter of the Fugitive Slave Act, Webster attempted to preserve the political "Union" which seems here to emblematize the more private union of marriage.

Moore begins this sentence by noting the rarity of "that striking grasp of opposites" she so admires in contrast to any static or isolated perspective. Feeling, she then notes, should be similarly complex and variable—a view she characteristically implies by quoting someone who says the opposite:[47]

> "I am such a cow,
> if I had a sorrow,
> I should feel it a long time;
> I am not one of those
> who have a great sorrow
> in the morning
> and a great joy at noon;"
>   (Obs, 80)

The entire poem builds to this indirect insistence on the complexity of living affectionately, sharing a life (and I am inclined to think that much of Moore's experience of this "fight" comes from years of living with her mother), remembering that even the strongest emotions may be followed quickly by their opposite. The poem voices extraordinary suspicion and cynicism about marriage as a public and private enterprise, and perhaps for that reason ends with Daniel Webster as the only possible model for peaceful survival in its state: one must be willing to compromise even deeply held values to remain in this union. The fact that Webster's historic compromise encouraged the continuation of slavery, however, suggests that such union may not finally be desirable. The radical juxtapositions and bricolage of this poem further suggest that Moore, as poet, will not take the kind of settled stand represented by Webster's statue at the end: her shifting and multiple poetic positionings could not be more different from that icon's concrete representation of law, compromise, and public authority.

Through these early poems, Moore defines her aesthetic as something complicated, weapon-like without dominating, preeminently active, and intelligent. Rather than distinguishing between the object which inspires and the poetic subjectivity inspired by it into creating a poem of universal truths, Moore makes both object and

119

poem uninspiring and ostensibly nonpoetic, imperfect, complex. The enabling neutrality of her personal-impersonal style is positional rather than emotional—that is, she creates a distance between speaker, poet, and reader without sacrificing emotional presence. In "Roses Only," for example, Moore's speaking "we" assumes neither special knowledge (necessarily belonging to another woman) nor foreignness (which would implicitly belong to a man) but an intimate and ironic, respectful and impatient affection. In "Sojourn in the Whale," the feminine Ireland ("you") assumes fairy-tale, emblematic status as well as representing its own, women's, and any colony's allied histories of oppression under patriarchy. The poem might be read as specifically about the poet—as woman of Irish heritage—or as not about Moore at all. "Marriage" insists that the "institution" or "enterprise" the poet has taken on is of greater significance for the ways it molds, constrains, and enables relationships between the sexes than for its private relevance to any individual's experience. The poems are gendered in their representation of aesthetic and ethical dilemmas as conjoined with pragmatic gendered relations and constructions of power, but the speaker of the poems is ungendered.

In her later collections of poems, Moore omits "Holes Bored in a Workbag by the Scissors," "To Be Liked by You Would Be a Calamity," "Feed Me, Also, River God," "Roses Only," the most explicitly gendered passage of "An Octopus," and "Black Earth" (later retitled "Melancthon"). Ways to combat external and internal aggression and discrimination against the socially and politically unempowered remain important themes for Moore, but she does not again have such an outpouring of poems marking the relation of gender, or of female access to power, to these concerns.[48]

Just as Moore's confidence in her right and skill to experiment with the forms of poetry has cultural and historical as well as personal roots, so do the changes in the ways she addresses the topic of gender and its relationship to poetic form after 1930, that is, after having served for five years as senior editor of the country's most prestigious literary and arts magazine. The poet's move from Manhattan to Brooklyn and her return to part-time library work as well as to poetry suggest that she is happy to withdraw from the intensive centrality of her editing position. At the same time, the accidental and personal circumstances of her return to greater marginality in the literary world are identical in pattern to what several female poets experience or "choose" during the late 1920s and 1930s and to a sharp decline in women's involvement in professional careers.[49]

To summarize briefly, during the 1910s and 1920s there was a surge of women publishing poetry and assuming editorial positions at literary magazines. As Leavell notes, "In his autobiography, Alfred Kreymborg identifies the beginnings of modern poetry with the birth of two new magazines: *Poetry*, begun in Chicago by Harriet Monroe and Alice Corbine, and *The Little Review*, begun in New York by Margaret Anderson and Jane Heap" ("Marianne Moore and Georgia O'Keeffe," 307). In addition, Lola Ridge was the American editor of *Broom* (1921–1923) and worked with Alfred Kreymborg on *Others* (1915–1919); Elinor Wylie edited *Vanity Fair;* Moore herself was senior editor of *The Dial* from 1925 until it closed in 1929, and Alyse Gregory served as managing editor for several years during the twenties.[50] Dora Marsden and Mary Eleanor Gawthorpe founded *The New Freewoman* and edited it from 1911 to 1912, when Pound and Aldington took it over and changed its title to *The Egoist;* H.D. then edited this journal during the war (1916–1917). Sara Teasdale published the first twentieth-century anthology of poetry by women in 1917 and an enlarged edition in 1928, claiming: "The decade since 1917 has produced more good poetry by women than any other in the history of the language" (*The First Wave*, xix–xx). This phenomenon in the publishing world was widely noted as such at the time, with the predictable anxiety that poetry was being "femininized" but also with high praise. Harriet Monroe, for example, was accused in a 1920 review of being "an unwholesome influence in femininizing American poetry." On the other hand, Edmund Wilson commented that the women poets were "more rewarding than the men. Their emotion is likely to be more genuine and their literary instinct surer" (*The First Wave*, 68, xix).

In the 1930s, things changed drastically for this group of poets, because of the deaths of Wylie, Amy Lowell, Teasdale, and Monroe but also for economic and cultural reasons. The Depression's effect on all literary publishing had especially devastating effects on writers of marginal position.[51] As William Drake describes, eleven poets who had published a total of 45 volumes during the 1920s published only 16 during the 1930s; where five Pulitzer prizes for poetry were given to women during the 1920s, only one went to a woman during the 1930s. Most of the little magazines with women in editorial positions during the 1920s were defunct by the 1930s. By World War II, few of the women poets of this generation continued to write, and they did so in relative isolation from one another. Moore was among the few who did write and publish into the thirties and beyond. From having been one among several women approximately her age who were vitally active and professionally successful in publishing and editing poetry, she found herself relatively isolated.[52]

Beginning in the 1930s, Moore's poems most obviously dealing with gender revolve around mothering. In some poems she attributes maternal characteristics to male figures: for example, she calls her "Hero" (1932) "lenient," having the "feelings of a mother—a / woman or a cat" (CP, 9). In "He 'Digesteth Harde Yron'" (1941), she describes the "one remaining rebel" animal, the ostrich, as "watch[ing] his chicks with / a maternal concentration," "mothering the eggs" (CP, 99).[53] Others—"The Paper Nautilus" and "Bird-Witted"—take artist-like mothers as their primary focus. Perhaps because of her own exclusively maternal upbringing, and certainly as part of her high admiration for maternal energy and care, Moore apparently conceives of ardent parenting by either sex as "mothering." Then again, perhaps Moore intends a social comment here: while the neutral "parenting" carries some connotations of affectionate caretaking, "fathering" implies biological production. To express fully in a single verb the parent's "feelings," "concentration," and devotion, one can only choose "to mother." As in earlier poems, however, this activity may characterize either sex.

Later poems also refer to gender issues, although less frequently and typically in more propositional or more markedly personal terms. "Enough: *Jamestown, 1607–1957*" (1957), for example, retells the story of this early colony with two ironic references to the role of sexual conquest in so-called "settlement." Moore writes that British colonization in the "insidious" form of "teaching" both "enhanc[ed] Pocahontas" and "flowered of course // in marriage" (CP, 185). I find that this poem does not bear the weight of its own suggestions. Nonetheless, the ironic pun on the deflowering which has been part of every imperialist conquest and its link with education as "insidious" suggest Moore's cynical view of this love match, and of the "teaching" by which one culture dominates another. Moore's return to this subject later in the poem makes the irony more pointed: "Marriage, tobacco, and slavery, / initiated liberty," she writes, calling attention to her irony by rhyming "slavery" and "liberty" (CP, 186). The apposition of marriage with the economic and physical subjugations ushered in by the British to their new colonies makes it merely another form of capture; marriage provides no more "liberty" than an addictive weed or slavery itself.

"In Lieu of the Lyre" (1965) also begins from the premise that gender marks an enterprise from the start. Although entirely happy with her own education at Bryn Mawr, Moore presents her (apparently also female) speaker as "One debarred from enrollment at Harvard," although she "may have seen towers and been shown the Yard—" or even been invited to read her poems there.[54] The second stanza of this poem digresses into various forms of gratitude the guest (and Moore!) feels: to the *Harvard Advocate* for inviting her; to Professor Levin for his help with her translation of LaFontaine's fables; to the Vermont Stinehour Press for publishing a poem. In the third stanza, she refers to herself as "unavoidably lame," a "verbal pilgrim," and then she concludes the poem:

It occurs to the guest—if someone had confessed it in time—
that you might have preferred to the waterfall, pilgrim and hat-brim,
     a valuable axiom such as
"a force at rest is at rest because balanced by some other force,"
or "catenary and triangle together hold the span in place"
     (of a bridge),

> or a too often forgotten surely relevant thing, that Roebling cable
> was invented by John A. Roebling.
>
> These reflections, Mr. Davis,
> in lieu of the lyre.

(CP, 206–207)

"Unavoidably lame" (because of her gender, responsible for her lack of a Harvard education?), a "pilgrim" to the "Yard" of elite male education, the speaker pretends all of a sudden to think that she has brought the wrong gift. In "lieu of the" lyric poem, which she has begun, she gives "a valuable axiom" and a "relevant thing"—the kinds of nonpoetic, and non-"feminine," information Moore is famous for including in her poetry. Similarly, each stanza of this poem has a different form, as though Moore couldn't be bothered to make them match, to create a poem formally like the lyrics of the past. This poem is written not for but "in lieu of" the traditional lyre.[55]

As previously discussed, "Voracities and Verities Sometimes are Interacting" (1947) implicitly rejects conventions of gender whereby women desire all that diamonds represent. Similarly, both an early poem republished late in Moore's life ("I May, I Might, I Must") and the equally brief late "O to be a Dragon" declare an ability and a stretching after power that have great resonance for a poet who has, throughout her professional life, surmounted the barriers of tokenism and condescension. In the first poem, she asserts her ability to respond to any challenge:

> If you will tell me why the fen
> appears impassable, I then
> will tell you why I think that I
> can get across it if I try.
> (1909 and 1959; CP, 178)

In the second, she voices her desire to take on the mythical form of greatest power and divinity:

> If I, like Solomon, . . .
> could have my wish—

124

my wish . . . O to be a dragon,
a symbol of the power of Heaven—of silkworm
size or immense; at times invisible.
  Felicitous phenomenon!

                              (1957; CP, 177)

In "The Plumet Basilisk," Moore describes the dragon as a "living
fire-work," "amphibious" (1932). Perhaps, with its self-transforma-
tions, it offers a kind of androgyny as well as amphibiousness: as
dragon, Moore can be both immensely powerful in her immediate
presence and idiosyncratic, conspicuous in her (female) difference,
or "invisible"—indistinguishable from her public (male) surround-
ings.

In "Sun," another poem published both early and late in Moore's
career (first in 1916, and then as the final poem of her last single
volume of poetry in 1966), Moore specifically celebrates that which
is "not male or female." Arguing against notions of darkness, death,
and the traditionally anthropomorphized "Sun" as omnipresent pow-
ers, Moore transforms the mythologically male god of the sun,
patron of poetry, into an androgynous figure:

Hope and Fear accost him

        "No man may him hyde
        From Deth holow-eyed";
    For us, this inconvenient truth does not suffice.
    You are not male or female, but a plan
    deep-set within the heart of man.
Splendid with splendor hid you come, from your Arab abode,
a fiery topaz smothered in the hand of a great prince who rode
    before you, Sun—whom you outran,
    piercing his caravan.

        O Sun, you shall stay
        with us; holiday,
    consuming wrath, be wound in a device
    of Moorish gorgeousness, round glasses spun
    to flame as hemispheres of one
great hour-glass dwindling to a stem. Consume hostility;

125

employ your weapon in this meeting-place of surging enmity!
Insurgent feet shall not outrun
multiplied flames, O Sun.

(CP, 234)

This "Sun" is metaphorically both male and female instead of nei-
ther: as "smothered" jewel that responds to wrath by "consuming"
it, the sun seems female; as one who "pierc[es]" an enemy and as
homonym with *son*, this "plan" seems male. As the figure for poetry,
Moore's androgynous "Sun" outraces "insurgent feet"—perhaps like
the "classic multitude of feet" identified with the sun god "Apollo
Belvedere" in "In the Days of Prismatic Color." In such a reading,
both poems reject archtypally masculine form—Apollo, the Sun, the
male god of the lyre/lyric. Represented by "multiplied flames," the
sun of this poem is instead like the dragon of Costa Rica and the
lizard of Moore's "To a Chameleon": all are jewels ("a fiery topaz,"
"our Tower-of-London jewel," and "Fire laid upon / an emerald"
respectively); all consist of fire; all are associated with royalty or
divinity; and all metamorphose. The sun, like the dragon, is defined
by its multiplicity, its ability to change. This last quality may be
most central to Moore's notion of poetry: it is neither male nor
female, both "splendid" and "hid." Such a description echoes what
the poet might say of herself: as poet, as woman giving herself the
authority to speak publicly of her perceptions and beliefs, she would
create a (punning) "Moorish gorgeousness"—jewel-like, "deep-set"
in a core that is neither masculine nor feminine but allows itself
access to both conventional categories.

While recognizing imbalances of power in particular historical
circumstances and the constraints of gender categories, Moore does
not see herself, or women, as limited to any particular aspects of
perception or expression. Similarly, she makes very few broad claims
about women's position, abilities, or power. Such reluctance to
generalize necessarily weakens any public and political impact her
poetry might have in influencing controversies over women's rights
and abilities. By restricting her representations of women to a few
individualized portraits, representations of nonhuman mothers, and
various suggestive expostulations that have not typically been read

as pertaining to gender, Moore bypasses the opportunity to speak directly in a debate that she indicates in other written form is of tremendous and ongoing importance to her. As is consonant with her conceptions of clarity and of a feminist poetic, Moore instead sets out her political judgments through what she does not say, what she rejects, and through the forms of her poems themselves rather than through open analysis of the implications of her inclusions and omissions.

Largely through these forms, Moore's poetry insists on a beauty that is complicated, smart, open to experience but not vulnerable; on the right to state what one thinks without dogmatism or the egotism of narrowing personal claims; and on a continuing play against received forms of understanding in one's observations and judgments of the world. While Moore valorizes qualities stereotypically identified with the feminine and celebrates the heroism and labor of mothering, she does not create a hierarchy that raises those characteristics consistently above qualities identifed with the masculine. Instead, she combines qualities from both categories to create a fluid, composite, hence to her mind gender-neutral, ideal. These poems are concerned with gender more than with women or with the feminine as oppositional (or privileged) category, and that concern manifests itself in Moore's rejection of romantic and sentimental implicitly gendered poetic structures and in her subtle but consistent linking of fluid gender identification with her poetic of experimental form.

FIVE

"The Labors of Hercules":
Celebrating and Overcoming "Race"

The letter "a" in psalm and calm when
pronounced with the sound of "a" in candle, is very
noticeable but

why should continents of misapprehension have to be
accounted for by the
fact? Does it follow that because there are poisonous
toadstools
which resemble mushrooms, both are dangerous? In the case
of mettlesomeness which may be
mistaken for appetite, of heat which may appear to be
haste, no con-

clusions may be drawn. To have misapprehended the matter,
is to have confessed
that one has not looked far enough.

("England," P, 19)

$\mathcal{W}$hile in her personal life gender may be the most decisive
factor in Moore's attempts to redefine relationships of power, gender
is not the focus of Moore's most important or most frequent discus-
sion of prejudice or assumed inequality, particularly as that discus-
sion affects questions of subject positioning, truth claims, perspec-
tive, and history. As I have argued previously, such discussion is in
some ways central to Moore's poetry; certainly, many of her poems
make power relationships—particularly as grounded in some cultural
or historical context—their subject. Moore turns most specifically
to a thematic exploration of power relationships between and as

determined by communities, hence to public relationships of authority, and to the dangers of conventionally biased perspective, in her several poems dealing with nationality and race.

Not surprisingly, Moore's concern with race is closely allied to her more general concerns with freedom and to her intense distrust of any system, institution, or structure that prejudges individual potential or worth. Fiercely egalitarian, Moore makes it almost a crusade to celebrate excellence and value as they may be found in contexts least recognized by popular culture or general prejudice. In this sense, Moore's celebrations of unusual, small, or ornery animals (the pangolin, chameleon, jerboa, mockingbird, ox, goat); creatures or figures of popular culture (a race horse, baseball players); or people of various races and nationalities all participate in the same dynamic: she demands particularized, knowledgeable attention to and respect for that which is easily overlooked or dismissed within the value systems dominating Western education, professionalism, and spiritual/aesthetic vision.[1]

Here a representative *Dial* comment of 1926 may stand as an example: beginning the first two paragraphs, respectively, with the statements that "the civilized world is uncivilized" and that "the world of art also is assailed by a spirit of domination, gainfulness, or expediency," Moore then proceeds to compare a "Hebrew" love of decoration (as presented by De Quincey in his "Toilette of the Hebrew Lady Exhibited in Six Scenes") with modern Western "economically irresponsible detailed ornateness" as a transition toward her primary question of whether "we are stupendously naive" in trusting what appears to be genuine altruism in such a decadent, materialistic age. "When persons contribute to the support of a hospital or to a fund for eastern relief or to the support of orphans, some point out that charity is advertising and that benefactors to causes in which there may be Jewish orphans or invalids, are probably Jewish, and are in a sense giving to themselves," she notes evenhandedly, but then pointedly remarks that "in his voluntary poverty as in his conviction that 'industry must be spiritualized' Mahatma Gandhi can . . . scarcely be thought to have resorted to a clever means of enriching himself." On the one hand, "the basic selfishness of human nature, the elaborate crookedness, and the irrelevant lightness of civilization are, of course, not a myth"; there is to be no simple naiveté in Moore's celebration of what is generous, high-minded, and valuable in the world. On the other hand, some things, ideas, and actions do have distinct value: "If Phoenecian trivialities seem to find more favor with us than The Barnard Cloisters, early American furniture, or the records of The Smithsonian Institute, a lugubrious conclusion need not be drawn . . . Certain German chemical discoveries; the steam engine made in England, the telephone, the airplane, and certain noted electrical inventions of America, are not local property. To part with a valuable thing without losing it, bespeaks for this thing, a very special kind of value" (CPr, 167–169). While one might study this "Comment" at length to tease out all the implications of how Moore's punning notion of "self enrichment" supports both capitalistic dependence on the philanthropy of the wealthy and the "voluntary poverty" of a Thoreau or Gandhi, it is clear that her basis of judgment is neither narrow nor local. The decorative art of diverse times and nations, various projects of social reform and charitable giving, nonviolent protest, the founding of art museums, mechanical and electrical inventions—all contribute to one's sense of ethics, value, "human nature" in its full complexity. Similarly, in a later "Comment" on the art of fine printing, Moore finds "significance . . . in subtleties analogous to those of printing: in the Indian pictograph and in the arranged grace of such tall lower-case characters as appear on a rock in the giants', unicorns', and Dragon's lair near Mixnitz, Austria"; the combination of beauty with fine craft has appeared in numerous forms and various places (CPr, 173). Moore scrupulously insists that no single definition of value, beauty, or skill suffices, that one's context for judgment must be historically and culturally pluralistic and self-conscious.

Speaking as a white, middle-class, Protestant inhabitant of, at the time, arguably the most powerful country in the world (albeit also as a woman of Irish descent), Moore speaks in this context from a position of cultural authority. It is, perhaps, for this reason easier for her to celebrate achievements or characteristics of races and cultures different from her own than to call attention to the achievements of women; there is no risk of special pleading, defensiveness, or egotism here. And while some of Moore's poems—like "England," quoted above—do argue for the possibility of excellence within her own nation, they almost always do so within the context of a distinctly multicultural present and past, an "America" of indigenous, colonizing, and (once) enslaved peoples rather than of any single group or tradition identifiable with the poet herself. Moreover, although Moore espouses the ideals of freedom, of a nonhierarchical exchange of ideas, of intense, egalitarian scrutiny as the basis for meaningful judgment throughout her poems, she also recognizes that such ideals have far greater significance in some contexts than in others. As in the "Comment" quoted above, in her poetry she attempts to be affirmative without being naive.

More than her poems about gender, Moore's poems invoking racial specificity or about racial inequality exemplify a central tension in her work between focusing on individual idiosyncrasy or achievement and acknowledging the different experience and access to power of various groups. Race, like gender, is not emblematic for Moore; raced beings (which for Moore includes, for example, the Irish, Swedes, Italians, and Jews as well as groups denominated by "race" in the late twentieth century) do not stand for particular static qualities.[2] In categories of both self-definition and ideological categorization, Moore holds tenaciously to an idealizing belief in individual potential and equality while recognizing more pragmatically that not just "men" but white people, the upper and middle class, the well educated, and others of socially defined privilege in fact "have power / and sometimes one is made to feel it" ("Marriage").

Again, more specifically than her poems invoking gender, the poems invoking race reveal the range of attitudes constituting Moore's belief in pluralism as well as its moral and didactic edge: Moore's poems about race are those where she comes closest to entering specifically political national and international debate, and where she is most apt to take an unambiguous stand. Culminating in the late 1930s and 1940s, these poems allow particular insight into the intersections of Moore's aesthetics, her positioning as poet in relation to an audience, her general moral stance, and the place of public politics in her poetry.

The record of Moore's public actions and statements indicates an active commitment to racial equality throughout her life.[3] In her poems on race she often refers to conventions of racial prejudice, thereby placing such work in the context of contemporary controversies over race. To take the most obvious examples, Moore writes "The Labors of Hercules" (1921) "to prove to the high priests of caste / that snobbishness is a stupidity," concluding this poem about overcoming limiting preconceptions of all kinds with specific reference to racial stereotypes; one must

> convince snake-charming controversialists
> that it is one thing to change one's mind,
> another to eradicate it—that one keeps on knowing
> "that the negro is not brutal,
> that the Jew is not greedy,
> that the Oriental is not immoral,
> that the German is not a Hun."
>
> (Obs, 64)

"In Distrust of Merits" includes the statement: "'We'll / never hate black, white, red, yellow, Jew, / Gentile, Untouchable'" (CP, 137). "Virginia Britannia," the poet's longest meditation on ethnocentric colonization, calls the "Negro" "inadvertent ally and best enemy of / tyranny" (CP, 109). Typically, however, Moore's arguments against prejudicial thinking are plotted indirectly, through juxtaposed examples or a materially detailed but narratively sketchy historical scene.

Moore does not speak, as poet, from the authoritative position of personal marginality or personal experience of oppression in poems about race any more than in those about gender.[4] Although she would have had neither the inclination nor the vocabulary to articulate it, Moore's perspective is, I believe, close to the one that Gayatri Spivak articulates in various contexts. Moore does not attempt to "save," "speak for" or even "describe" "the masses" or any individual as representative of a particular race or culture. Through continuing lateral, and sometimes focal, reference to individuals of color and to non-Western or nonhegemonic cultures, Moore "render[s] visible the mechanism" of historical oppression and prejudicial thinking rather than "rendering vocal the [marginalized] individual." Simultaneously, through her prose-like, ostentatiously unpoetic, complex and difficult but also bluntly straightforward language, she attempts to "speak in such a way that the masses will not regard as bullshit," to write poetry for those who like zoos, circuses, baseball games, machines, bridges, and history as well as for those who like poetry.[5] In short, firmly believing that "others are many" and "the self is enclosed," Moore paradoxically attempts both to celebrate otherness through specific reference to race and to deny that racial categories or acculturation are finally significant.[6] The authority she attempts to construct here comes, then, not from speaking as a marginal being or for a marginalized people's needs, and not from speaking as a white Westerner, or from assumed cultural authority, but from using isolated examples and abstract generalization to specify, celebrate, and at the same time deny the importance of race. It is small wonder, given the tension inherent in such a goal, that Moore's poems about race are often problematic.

One sees a private example of this tension in Moore's first letter to Ezra Pound, in which she responds to his earlier exaggerated question—evidently posed in response to his reading of "Black Earth"—of whether she is "a jet black Ethiopian Othello-hued" (December 16, 1918). On January 9, 1919, she writes:

> I am glad to give you personal data and hope that the bare facts that I have to offer, may not cause work that I may do from time to time, utterly to fail in interest. Even if they should, it is but fair that those who speak out, should not lie in ambush. I was born in 1887 and brought up in the home of my grandfather, a clergyman of the Presbyterian church. I am Irish by descent, possibly Scotch also, but purely Celtic, was graduated from Bryn Mawr in 1909 and taught shorthand, typewriting and commercial law at the government Indian School in Carlisle, Pennsylvania, from 1911 until 1915. In 1916, my mother and I left our home in Carlisle to be with my brother—also a clergyman—in Chatham, New Jersey—but since the war, Chaplain of the battleship Rhode Island and by reason of my brother's entering

the navy, my mother and I are living at present in New York, in a small apartment. Black Earth, the poem to which I think you refer, was written about an elephant that I have, named Melanchthon; and contrary to your impression, I am altogether a blond and have red hair. (RML V.50.06)

Combining without hierarchy or even division of interest factors revealing class, religion, racial ancestry, education, employment history, family circumstances, personal appearance, and idiosyncratic detail (like owning a toy elephant), Moore uses her extraordinary specificity to veil the singular importance of any one of these factors alone. Not "white" or "American" (racist and nativist labels), Moore is instead "Irish by descent" and "blond" (with red hair). These facts are all but buried, however, in her detailed report of clergymen in the family, the size of the family apartment, how long she taught at the government Indian School, and so on. Consequently, it is hard to tell if Moore's tone is defensive (hence the detail), or ironic—thwarting Pound's desire to simplify and appropriate who she is by telling him far more than simple categorization will bear.[7] Pound's own response of February 1 includes a long poem combining more aggressive sexist and racist speculation:

You, my dear correspondent,
are a stabilized female,
I am a male who has attained the chaotic fluidities;

our mutual usefulness
is open to the gravest suspicions of non-existence, but
nevertheless, also, and notwithstanding all this,
I am glad that you are red-headed and not
woolled, dark, ethiopian.

It would have been a test case:
you dark, nubian, ethiopian: could I
have risen to it; could I,
perceiving the intelligence from a distance,
have got over the Jim Crow law;
could I have bridged the gap
from the distinguished Bengal to Ethiopia

and asserted the milk-whiteness of souls
laved in a Mithriac liquid;
or disinfected with laneline[8]

At this greater aggression of Pound's, Moore retreats from ironic, mocking, or defensive response, ignoring his (at best) bad taste in humor and familiarity, and continuing to address him formally. Moore's response here resembles that of her speaker in "To Be Liked By You Would Be A Calamity": "I can but put my weapon up, and / Bow you out"; her polite distance is a kind of "unsheathed gesticulation" (Obs, 37).

The tension between celebrating racial difference, demanding civic and intellectual equality between races, and ignoring race as finally irrelevant to questions of human worth for Moore—as for writers at this end of the twentieth century—begins with the very definition of "race." In Moore's time, such categories were most often seen as biological and fixed; even liberal or radical thinkers tended to generalize about race (including nationality and Jewishness) as genetically inherited. The German-born Jewish immigrant Horace Kallen, for example, who defined the concept of "cultural pluralism" in 1915, based his notions of ethnicity on biological descent: to use his metaphor, in the ideally harmonious "orchestra" of American ethnicities, an oboe is forever an oboe. The extreme popularity of the Eugenics movement—a pseudo-science devoted to "improving" the human race by promoting the reproduction of matched couples of the more "suitable" races—indicated how widespread such thinking was at the time.[9] On the other hand, African American writers in particular were apt to use the concept of race strategically. Alain Locke, for example, wrote of himself as an "advocate of cultural racialism as a counter-move" to a racist society; Zora Neale Hurston more controversially played with and against popular stereotypes of African Americans in "How It Feels to Be Colored Me" (1928) and in several of her stories and essays; and Nella Larsen, among others, explored the phenomenon of "passing" in her novel by that name (1929).[10] Scholars of the 1980s and 1990s also tend in this direction, as exemplified by Henry Louis Gates Jr.'s assertion that "race" is of greater significance as a "trope" than as an

135

"objective term of classification" (*"Race," Writing, and Difference,* 5).[11] For reasons having, I think, less to do with a particularly sophisticated understanding of race as an issue than with her poetic, her defense of individualism, and her strong sense of the importance of local or defined communities, Moore assumes a middle ground between these positions. While at times apparently holding to the idea of fixed racial categories (the Irish are always Irish), she is more apt to use raced beings, generalizations about various national cultures, and even historical examples of racial conflict as tropes for abstract arguments—for example, to illustrate savagery, possessiveness, or greed. Race appears as an example more often than it constitutes Moore's subject per se.

Such manipulation of politically charged subject matter is typical of this poet. Moore believes that no quality or abstraction comes alive until it receives specific shading or form: it is imprecise—which, for Moore, is to say dishonest—to write without modifying and clarifying adjectives, embedded clauses, and categorical distinctions.[12] "Be abstract / and you'll wish you'd been specific; it's a fact," she asserts in "Values in Use," warning, moreover, that the specificity must be carefully chosen: "Certainly the means must not defeat the end" (CP, 181). Her own relatively hegemonic position leads her to be "specific" almost only with regard to those whom she sees as different from herself (whites are rarely marked as such in her poems, for example), but the specificity is wide-ranging and generous. Consequently, however, there is a repeated tension—far more marked in poems about race than in those about gender—between Moore's desire to assert equality and her aesthetic and political belief in the need for detailed particulars. Such tension reveals itself in a variety of forms, which I will approach in order of increasing complexity.

In several poems that might be read as in part—or primarily—about race, Moore omits all mention of race, as though this detail were irrelevant, at the same time that the direction of her examples indicates its importance. For example, in "Tom Fool at Jamaica," "speaking of champions," Moore turns from the race horse to black musicians: "Fats Waller / with the feather touch, giraffe eyes, and that hand alighting in / Ain't Misbehavin'! Ozzie Smith and Eubie

Blake / ennoble the atmosphere" (CP, 163).[13] "Leonardo da Vinci's," which praises the Italian painter's "Saint Jerome and his lion" ends with a tribute to an Ethiopian king: "Blaze on, picture, / saint, beast; and Lion Haile Selassie, with household / lions as symbol of sovereignty" (CP, 201–202). Identifying leonine, sanctified sovereignty with Ethiopia rather than, for example, England gives a radical edge to this quiet poem of appreciation.[14] Moore's poem for the Dodgers after they won the 1955 World Series, "Hometown Piece for Messrs. Alston and Reese," begins and ends with reference to the team's black heroes, concluding: "You've got plenty: Jackie Robinson / and Campy [Roy Campanella] and big Newk [Don Newcombe], and Dodgerdom again / watching everything you do" (CP, 184). "Baseball and Writing" features Elston Howard—a black athlete who did not receive the "batting crown" one year because of what was widely believed to be a racist decision against him on technical grounds. Moore calls attention to his generosity, not his race: "Elston . . . when questioned, says, unenviously, / 'I'm very satisfied. We won.' / Shorn of the batting crown, says, 'We'; / robbed by a technicality" (CP, 221). These two poems, and the poet's frequent mention of Roy Campanella, suggest that her enthusiasm for the Dodgers may have stemmed in part from the fact that it was the first team in major league baseball to integrate, and one of the leading teams in hiring black players for several years.[15]

Moore may actually pun on the constructed notion of color in "Arthur Mitchell," written in praise of the first African American dancer in the New York City Ballet, and later founder of the first black ballet company, Dance Theater of Harlem.[16] Moore's references to Mitchell as a "gem" with "jewels of mobility" that "reveal / and veil / a peacock-tail" may refer to aspects of his costume as "Puck," in the performance she mentions in her "Notes" (CP, 220). The effect of multiple and shifting, prismatic colors may, however, also be Moore's way of prizing Mitchell's own "color," and her moral and visual appreciation of a racially mixed ballet company, as well as his "virtuosity." Also published during 1961, "Rescue with Yul Brynner," which eulogizes the Japanese-born, French-educated, naturalized American citizen and actor, refers specifically to Brynner's skin but with a deft particularity (and an ambiguity about whether it describes the man or the actor in his role as King of Siam) that defies categorical racism, just as his biography defies simple notions of nationality:

> His neat cloth hat
> has nothing like the glitter reflected on the face
> of milkweed-witch seed-brown dominating a palace
> that was nothing like the place
> where he is now.
>
> (CP, 228)

Like "Baseball and Writing," this poem focuses on generosity, in this case the discrepancy between Brynner's glamorous acting roles and his service to refugees, as recorded in Moore's epigraph: "*Appointed special consultant to the United Nations High Commissioner for Refugees, 1959– 1960*" (CP, 227).[17]

In such poems, Moore does not attribute difference or "otherness" to those she describes. These poems participate in political debate only to the extent that the reader notes their repeated reference: by referring to specific people of various races in her poems, Moore practices a kind of political recovery without political commentary or context. This is altogether in keeping with her uses of gender in her poems and indeed with her most common political strategy. Moore argues by example; she gives visibility to what she feels is ignorantly or unjustly overlooked or devalued. By including famous people of color as subjects or, as in "The Hero," by racially coding a fictional character who might otherwise be regarded as "universal" (hence implicitly Anglo-Saxon), Moore brings the ethnic diversity of her (and our) world into view. On the other hand, unless the reader happens to be familiar with the names Elston Howard, Haile Selassie, Arthur Mitchell, the effect of such a quiet strategy is lost.

Poems that deal more directly with racial difference show a different kind of strength and limitation. In "The Jerboa," for example, Moore's use of African nomads as a model in this poem for her (primarily white) readers sends contrasting signals. On the one hand, she celebrates nomadic Africans as being like the desert rat, who serves as the hero of her poem and a clear model for humanity,

138

as the pangolin, elephant, ostrich, and other animals do in other poems. The nomadic "blacks," like other unmaterialistic and unimperialistic communities which Western culture regards as "poor," provide a model of morality, health, and satisfaction for those who live in middle- and upper-class exploitative decadence. The very simplicity of the contrast, however, weakens the political impact of the claim. Moore rejects all negative content of stereotypes for "that choice race" without altering the structure of such stereotypes itself. The poem presents "the blacks" as *other* at the same time that it argues for the values of the unmaterialistic life she uses them to represent. By calling African "blacks" a "choice race" characterized by their "elegance," Moore exoticizes their difference from European whites in a way that constitutes romantic racialism—while also countering the more popular racist perception of Africans as primitive.

To put this more specifically, reference to "blacks" as a "choice race" constitutes what Aldon L. Nielsen calls a "frozen metaphor" of race—one of those phrases embedded in "white discourse about blackness" that mark the discourse as hegemonic and racist.[18] Understanding Moore's reversal of values in "The Jerboa" requires that one assume the hegemonic white perspective that regards Africans and those of African descent as distinctly "other" and therefore, by the structure of such opposition, inferior to whites. The liberal move of then idealizing the *other*ness by marking it as admirable or even as a model for colonizers (including the Egyptians) merely alters the surface of the presupposition. More problematic, to return to an earlier example, is the noncontextualized attribution of animal characteristics ("giraffe eyes") to Fats Waller in "Tom Fool," despite the poet's obvious admiration for this musician and her frequent use of animal characteristics to describe people. The language of such poems reveals the author's participation through discourse in the very racism that she rejects. As Nielsen writes, "Racism exists as a discursive structure within our culture . . . thus whites who have never had any contact with blacks in their lives may still exhibit an essentially racist mode of thought, one which privileges them while demoting an invisible other to a secondary status" (*Reading Race*, 3). Moore inevitably participates in this discourse given her race and upbringing at the turn of the century. Nonetheless, her liberal politics in this area and her self-consciousness about all characterizations of individuals mediate against her frequent or extreme adoption of the language of racism.

The first decades of the twentieth century were a time of heightened racial awareness in the United States in part because of extreme increases in southern European and Asian immigration and the movement of many rural southern blacks to (especially northern) cities.[19] As a consequence, many white writers of this period experimented with racial metaphors or racially marked subjects, in addition to the increasing number and increasing prominence of African American writers doing so.[20] More particularly, and as Nielsen's study describes, the white modernist poets who were Moore's peers were fascinated with racial otherness and invoked it in a variety of ways in their verse.[21] Unlike some of her peers, Moore does not use darkness to stand for loss or death or sexuality in her poems, and she does not employ blacks or members of other racial groups for local color in her descriptions. Instead, she is apt to assign blackness or other such racially coded concepts positive and personal value. For example, in "Sun" she puns on her own name, and the properties of her poetry, with the phrase "Moorish gorgeousness" (CP, 234). John Slatin claims that "dark" and "black" are words that typically stand in code for the properties of Moore's poems (in conjunction with "complexity," "obliqueness," and the "opaque"; SR, 6).[22] Although "black" and "white" are among her most frequently used words, her 32 uses of "black," 12 of "dark," and 50 of "white" in her poems almost all occur in the context of botanical or natural historical detail, and the two extremes are often linked with each other or with other colors in descriptions.[23]

That Moore was not captivated by, and did not fetishize, racial otherness is indicated by the unusual breadth of racial/national reference in her poems, and the even greater breadth of her reviews—extending to poetry, culture, and myths of Jewish ("Hebrew"), African, African American, Native American, and several Asian and European peoples. Among others, for example, Moore reviewed William Topkins's *Universal Indian Sign Language of the Plains Indians of North America* (1926; CPr, 248); *Spanish Folk-songs of New*

Mexico (1927; CPr, 250); *Guide-Posts to Chinese Painting* (1928; CPr, 255); *Min-Yo: Folk Songs of Japan* (1928; CPr, 255); *The Ukiyoye Primitives* by Yone Noguchi (1933; CPr, 308–310); and the Philippine poet Jose Garcia Villa's *Have Come, Am Here* (1942; CPr, 369–372). More often, she combines reference to several cultures and historical epochs casually as part of her discussion of issues not apparently linked with national or international issues of race and culture—as in the "Comment" concerning materialism in the arts and contemporary society, discussed above. Moore's imagination seeks metonymic links between, and seeks to break down, hegemonic and hierarchical dichotomies—racial as well as those between women and men, imagination and fact, animal and human, or poetry and "business documents." Her mind works toward connection, a broadly conceived sameness that allows full play to particular differences of external marks or cultural trappings. In several poems, consequently, the poet uses race to praise what she sees as general human strengths made unusually visible in certain historical moments or groups: the Swedes are a race of the swift, generous, and clean ("A Carriage from Sweden"); the Irish are enchanted, proud, poetical, and "dissatisfied" ("Spencer's Ireland"). In such poems, race is less a matter of radical *otherness* than a useful lexicon for delineating human characteristics in specific historical and social contexts.

In the poems themselves, much of the tension between, on the one hand, didactic response to immediate political events and an emphasis on pluralism and, on the other, a firm belief in the equality of spirit among all people, takes the form of philosophical discussion about the importance of outer trappings, the skin or other elements of the physical (including history), to the spirit. The most extended example of this debate appears in the early poem "Black Earth" (1918). The fact that Moore initially wrote this poem as a dramatic monologue also implies the importance of this question for Moore as poet: she seems to question how much her own physical circumstances—her "skin"—affect her spiritual vision.

In "Black Earth," "I" is a black elephant of indeterminate sex. Although Moore must have been surprised at Pound's biographical reading of this poem, she could not have been entirely naive about her choice of a first-person speaker.[24] Moreover, the poem's opening assertion sounds very much like what Moore might actually have said about her own writing of verse, as well as containing a possible self-reference in "alligator"—recalling her family name ("gator") and the Bryn Mawr species. Like other Bryn Mawr "gators" and this elephant, Moore writes to "please" herself:

Openly, yes,
with the naturalness
    of the hippopotamus or the alligator
    when it climbs out on the bank to experience the

sun, I do these
things which I do, which please
    no one but myself. Now I breathe and now I am sub-
    merged; the blemishes stand up and shout when the object

in view was a
renaissance; shall I say
    the contrary? The sediment of the river which
    encrusts my joints, makes me very gray but I am used

to it, it may
remain there; do away
    with it and I am myself done away with, for the
    patina of circumstance can but enrich what was

there to begin
with. This elephant skin
    which I inhabit, fibred over like the shell of
    the coco-nut, this piece of black glass through which no light

can filter—cut
into checkers by rut
    upon rut of unpreventable experience—
    it is a manual for the peanut-tongued and the

hairy toed. Black
but beautiful, my back
    is full of the history of power. Of power? What
    is powerful and what is not? My soul shall never

be cut into
by a wooden spear; through-
    out childhood to the present time, the unity of
    life and death has been expressed by the circumference

described by my
trunk; nevertheless, I
    perceive feats of strength to be inexplicable after
    all; and I am on my guard; external poise, it

has its centre
well nurtured—we know
    where—in pride, but spiritual poise, it has its centre where?
    My ears are sensitized to more than the sound of

the wind. I see
and I hear, unlike the
    wandlike body of which one hears so much, which was made
    to see and not to see; to hear and not to hear;

that tree trunk without
roots, accustomed to shout
    its own thoughts to itself like a shell, maintained intact
    by who knows what strange pressure of the atmosphere; that

spiritual
brother to the coral
    plant, absorbed into which, the equable sapphire light
    becomes a nebulous green. The I of each is to

the I of each,
a kind of fretful speech
    which sets a limit on itself; the elephant is?
    Black earth preceded by a tendril? It is to that

phenomenon
the above formation,
    translucent like the atmosphere—a cortex merely—
    that on which darts cannot strike decisively the first

time, a substance
needful as an instance

of the indestructibility of matter; it
has looked at the electricity and at the earth-

quake and is still
here; the name means thick. Will
depth be depth, thick skin be thick, to one who can see no
beautiful element of unreason under it?

(P, 10–11)

As discussed in the previous chapter, "Black Earth" appears to distinguish the internal from the external, or "soul" from "skin," making a factor like race utterly irrelevant to moral and intellectual being. Contrasting external and internal poise, the elephant brags that (unlike its skin) its soul "shall never // be cut into / by a wooden spear." On the other hand, it is only by the elephant's skin that we know it, and the externals of skin and size dominate the poem. Repeatedly, the elephant describes itself: with skin like a "piece of black glass through which no light // can filter," it is like the speaker of the Song of Songs—"Black / but beautiful"[25]—"Black earth preceded by a tendril."

This repeatedly "black" or "very grey" and beautiful skin provides a text for its soul's history by being "cut / into checkers by rut / upon rut of unpreventable experience," hence providing "a manual" for others to live by. "Do away / with" the skin and its "patina of circumstance" and, the speaker exclaims, "I am myself done away with." The indivisibility of these aspects of life is manifested in the mythology the elephant claims for its body's shape: "the unity of / life and death has been expressed by the circumference // described by my / trunk." Like soul and skin, life and death are united by what this body expresses. In a further pun on unities and body, one might even venture that the elephant's body manifests itself as a poem, a text in which expressions of experience and philosophy may be read.[26]

The link between Moore's speaker and that of the Song of Songs underscores the conjunction of poet/speaker and poem/body in "Black Earth."[27] The massive elephant is the lover (speaker) and the beloved (text), the source of power and "a cortex merely"; the skin or page of her or his text is "translucent like the atmosphere," revealing the vicissitudes of "unpreventable experience," and yet it manifests the "indestructibility of matter." Skin is not the same as spirit, but spirit expires with the loss of that outer legible page of experience and difference just as the outer "manual" takes its worth from the knowledge that it contains an unseen mystery. As Moore states in the poem's final lines, understanding even the depth and thickness of skin depends on seeing the "beautiful element of unreason under it." The poet as individual is not contained in her poems, but without them she, as poet, does not exist.

Although all species are limited in their understanding ("The I of each is to // the I of each, / a kind of fretful speech / which sets a limit on itself"), Moore implies that there is a difference between human and elephantine limitation. A "tree trunk without roots"—in punning contrast to the elephant's "black earth" and therefore fully rooted "trunk"—the self-obsessed human being "shout[s] / its own thoughts to itself like a shell." The elephant instead reaches out through its form: it "is? / Black earth preceded by a tendril?" Yet even here the double question marks of the phrase suggest that the elephant may only tentatively explore what is beyond its massive solidity.

Although it is a far leap from the philosophical debate of this poem to the politics of race, it is instructive to read Moore's poem through the lens provided by Hortense Spillers's distinctions between body and flesh in "Mama's Baby, Papa's Maybe: An American Grammar Book."[28] Body, especially in its rootless, "wandlike" form, may be seen as representing the positioning of selfhood assumed to be physical but in fact ideological; human bodies, for example, are conceived of unrealistically as "white" or "black" or "yellow." As Spillers puts it, under the hegemony of "'ethnicity'. . . the body, in its material and abstract phase [becomes] a resource of metaphor" (66). Flesh, in contrast, is the unmetaphorical substance through and within which we live.[29] In Spillers's "American Grammar," it is the flesh of slaves that may be thought of as "primary narrative . . . its seared, divided, ripped-apartness, riveted to the ship's hole, fallen, or 'escaped' overboard"; "flesh is the concentration of 'ethnicity' that contemporary critical discourses neither acknowlege nor discourse away" (67). To return to Moore's terms, while one may generalize about bodies as "black, white, red, yellow," flesh is constituted by a multitude of shades—the "milkweed-witch seed-brown" of Yul Brynner or the pointedly composite "very grey" sediment creating "blemishes" on the elephant's multitextured "black" skin. The speaker of "Black Earth" easily separates him or herself from the body whenever thinking of the soul, yet repeatedly returns to "this . . . skin / which I inhabit" as the expression, the record, the source of that "element of unreason" that, at the philosophical level, seems distinguishable from it. As "patina" or in the abstract language of art and culture, "circumstance" can be stripped away from "what was there to begin with," but for the person living in history—which is to say living in the flesh—such stripping brings cultural as well as physical death.

Unlike Spillers's essay, which argues for acknowledgment of the crucial experience of (black) flesh, Moore repeatedly tests the relation of flesh to metaphorical body to soul, thereby repeatedly erasing and then revivifying the particulars of the flesh which determine and live its experience. In their utterly different formats, however—Spillers's in slave history, Moore's in Christian/philosophical discourse—both conclude that the "I" who acts with "open[ness]" can do so only by maintaining (in Moore's words) external and internal power and "poise"; for both there is no such thing as a freedom that is only of the soul, or in the realm of interpretation.

This black elephant represents the subject position par excellence, the text that writes itself "openly . . [to] please / no one but myself," a manual for all others of its kind and yet the ultimate hieroglyph, affording insight only to readers who can "see" the "beautiful element of unreason under" and supporting the text of its skin. That text, in turn, is the combined result of biology, soul, culture, "experience," and "circumstance"—breaking down the boundaries of what one denominates as "self." While merely calling an elephant "black" does not constitute the creation of a racially marked character, the elements of self-portraiture in the poem do make the elephant seem emblematic of something beyond itself, and certainly writing out this dialogue between body, soul, and experience through a black body gives a very different edge to its conviction of independence and power than the same poem spoken by a white body would have.

146

Moore's only poem to interpret color emblematically, "The Buffalo," begins "Black in blazonry means / prudence; and niger, unpropitious. Might / hematite- / black, compactly incurved horns on bison / have significance?" Rather than answer this question, however, Moore turns to a catalogue of types and colors of oxen, concluding with the "Indian buffalo, / albino- / footed" as meeting "human notions best." Moore then immediately again calls attention to this animal's color by negative comparison:

> No white
> Christian heathen, way-
> laid by the Buddha,
>
> serves him so well as the
> buffalo—as mettlesome as if check-
> reined—free neck
> stretching out, and snake tail in a half-twist
> on the flank; nor will so
> cheerfully assist
> the Sage sitting with
>
> feet at the same side, to
> dismount at the shrine . . .
>
> (CP, 28)

Serving "Sage"/god Buddha as well as humanity "best," this ox is distinctly not like the "white / Christian heathen" although white-footed. While again, this clearly is not a poem about racial difference, in it Moore indicates no preference for either the white, Christian, or American qualities one might predict from one of her heritage, instead celebrating a "mettlesome," "free," "fierc[e]," Indian buffalo that "need not fear comparison / with bison / . . . indeed with any / of ox ancestry," implied to be black by the opening lines and its white feet.

Like "Black Earth," and indeed like much of Moore's poetry, poems with a distinctly African American or Native American subject focus on interdependent physical and spiritual states of being. Detailed description of context, the "skin," as it were, leads directly to or stands partially in place of description of moral and internal qualities. In "The Jerboa," both "the blacks" and their counterpart, the lengthily described "sand-brown jumping-rat," enjoy freedom from domination and from domineering over others, and therefore, the poet implies, also enjoy "excellence . . . wit . . . happiness . . . rest . . . joy . . . [and] *Abundance*" (CP, 10–15). In contrast, the slaveholding Egyptians and Romans seem spiritually impoverished by their own hierarchies of culture and wealth. "These people liked small things," she states in one of the poem's few fully line-encompassed sentences—as though calling attention to the meanness of their vision as well as their taste in art.

In "The Jerboa," Moore uses the rat as moral exemplum, referring comparatively to humans merely to ensure that she has made her point. The jerboa's strength lies in its residing outside the boundaries of struggle over property and power, including the struggle to define. Because it is valued neither as divine object (like the beetle or "Pharaoh's . . . mongoose") nor as chattel—and therefore neither idealized nor despised—this rat (unlike any African or other people) enjoys an absolute freedom from the oppression of human interpretation, with its nearly inevitable hierarchizing. One sees, moreover, its boundarylessness in the composite quality of its description. While the wealthy receive no description of themselves as people— as though they exist physically only through their multiple possessions—the rat's portrait is intricately detailed and complex. Rather than impose itself on its surroundings, the rat "honors the sand by assuming its color"; it is "sand-brown" but also "black and / white" and "buff-brown," with markings "fish-shaped and silvered to steel by the force / of the large desert moon." Just as it has no single color, the jerboa cannot be described with reference only to itself. It launches itself "as if on wings," "hops like the fawn-breast, but has / chipmunk contours" and a "bird head"; it is like Jacob ("part terrestial, / and part celestial"), like a Chippendale table leg when "propped on hind legs, and tail as third toe," and like the uneven scale of "the Bedouin flute" in its movement—leaping "with kangaroo speed."

By comparing African "blacks" with what is, in the vision of this poem, an extraordinarily mutable animal, Moore may suggest that to see anyone as simply "black" (or "white") or as resembling only itself is to see too narrowly, to restrict oneself to the Roman/Egyptian impoverished world of "small things," artifice, and enslavement.[30] As Ursula Le Guin writes:

> If you deny any affinity with another person or kind of person, if you declare it to be wholly different from yourself—as men have done to women, and class has done to class, and nation has done to nation—you may hate it, or deify it; but in either case you have denied its spiritual equality, and its human reality. You have made it into a thing, to which the only possible relationship is a power relationship. And thus you have fatally impoverished your own reality. You have, in fact, alienated yourself.[31]

Rather, however, than engage in the delicate task of delineating the world of nomadic Africans in such cross-cultural, pluralistic detail, Moore describes the jerboa—letting the fine shadings of that portrait stand for what the other might have produced. The jerboa and Africans, then, trope each other, both representing an idealized nonpossessive attitude toward property and other people. Without the Africans, the poem's point would have not have been as clear; without the animal subject, Moore would have had to risk much greater romantic racialism or ethnocentricism—as she does later in her career in her portraits of Europeans.

"Enough: *Jamestown, 1607–1957*" explores historical context rather than physical appearance in broaching relationships between race, gender, and colonial power. This cryptic poem presents a history of the first attempt to colonize North America, concluding in mid-poem that "Marriage, tobacco, and slavery, / initiated liberty." Starting the poem with the 1607 colonists' dying hopes and "doomed communism" as a system of economic support, Moore next turns to the Pocahontas story, implying by this sequence that the colonists turn to usurpation of others' rights when they fail to support themselves cooperatively.

Captain Dale became kidnapper—
the master—lawless when the spur

was desperation, even though
his victim had let her victim go—

Captain John Smith. Poor Powhatan
was forced to make peace, embittered man.

Then teaching—insidious recourse—
enhancing Pocahontas, flowered of course

in marriage. John Rolfe fell in love
with her and she—in rank above

what she became—renounced her name
yet found her status not too tame.

The contradictions of this middle section of the poem are multiple: teaching is "insidious" but "enhanc[es]" the "victim" Indian princess; Powhatan is "forced" to make peace, but his daughter's education "flowered of course // in marriage"—a sentence ironically implying that the sequence leading to this second legal contract is both natural and inevitable. Yet both contracts have to do with imperialistic altering of power relations. Although Moore implies that Pocahontas, unlike her father, finds at least minimal satisfaction—her new life is "not too tame"—the word "tame" suggests the more ominous "tamed" so strongly that it is hard not to regret her change as much as that of her "poor" royal father.

The central question of this history lesson comes near its end and is never answered:

Marriage, tobacco, and slavery,
initiated liberty

when the Deliverance brought seed
of that now controversial weed—

a blameless plant-Red-Ridinghood.
Blameless, *but who knows what is good?*

The victims of a search for gold
cast yellow soil into the hold.

With nothing but the feeble tower
to mark the site that did not flower,

could the most ardent have been sure
that they had done what would endure?

It was *enough;* it is enough
if present faith mend partial proof.
                    (CP, 185–187; emphasis mine)

The "site" of Jamestown does not "flower" as the earlier "insidious" teaching did, and yet the continent was colonized; tobacco is "blameless" like a fairy-tale good girl, yet smoking is bad for the health (as Moore was well aware) and the cultivation of tobacco and other cash crops provided the excuse for slavery in North America; the colonists are "ardent" teachers, conquerors, and lovers yet "victims" of their own (or their monarch's) greed. There is nothing in this poem to make us respect or like these early colonists and much to make us dislike them—yet Moore questions whether their history of treachery, genocide, and enslavement may in fact, ultimately, be "good" and states that what "they had done . . . was enough" in a way that gives a positive cast to that ambiguous and potentially ironic judgment. Moreover, "if" we maintain "present faith" in their enterprise, their legacy is still "enough"—although this final conditional conjunction once again begs the question by seeming both to require "faith" of the reader and to demonstrate how tenuous the proof is of the colonists' "good[ness]."[32]

The contradictions of "Enough"—no doubt engendered by the tensions between, on the one hand, the specific patriotic occasion for which the poem was written and Moore's general patriotism and, on the other, the cruel history it recites—do not mar "Virginia Britannia" (1935). In this earlier poem, Moore more successfully contrasts the extraordinary beauty of the landscape with the ugly history of colonization, concluding that:

> Like strangler figs choking
> a banyan, not an explorer, no imperialist,

not one of us, in taking what we
pleased—in colonizing as the
saying is—has been a synonym for mercy.
(CP, 110)

The progression of names Moore equates with each of "us" through apposition (strangler figs, explorer, imperialist) reveals the strength of her judgment and the depth of her understatement: "colonizing" is slow murder.[33]

"Virginia Britannia" asks who or what is savage in this context of murderous greed, and repeatedly prevents the reader from falling back on the easy answers of jingoistic history for response. Describing in detail John Smith's hodgepodge European heraldry, for example, Moore wryly understates: "We-re-wo- / co-mo-co's fur crown could be no / odder than we were," later repeating that "The redskin with the deer- / fur crown, famous for his cruelty, is not all brawn / and animality" (CP, 107, 110). The corrective negative here and in the line above ("not one of us . . . has been a synonym for mercy") points to the hypocrisy of those who held (or hold) the view the poet corrects. Contrary to received opinion or legend, the "kind tyranny" of the new republic is not kind at all. Declaring "Don't tread on me" on its flag while paradoxically "establishing the Negro" in its territory to tread upon, this land that proclaims "liberty" is guilty of terrible human crimes. Moore, however, sees the seeds of tyranny's downfall in the slavery which embodied one of its worst exploitations of power: although "inadvertent ally" in enslaved service, "the Negro" is also "best enemy of / tyranny" (CP, 109).

As in "Black Earth," Moore concludes this poem by turning away from all racial distinctions to mark savagery as a quality of the soul, not of culture, power, or education. The true savages of this land, according to her conclusion, are those who are blind to their own strangeness, to the humanity of others, and to the land they claim as their own but which they do not allow to inspire them. As Moore also suggests in "New York," another poem about colonization, savages are those who claim possession—whether of people or of land—for materialistic and self-serving ends.[34] In three drafts of the final lines of "Virginia Britannia," Moore stresses the difference between true savages and so-called savages by denoting the former as "pale," in obvious contrast to American Indians and African Americans (RML 1:04:73). Yet by omitting this racial marker in her final version, Moore reiterates her continuous claim that savagery is not a matter of skin color—dark or pale.

"The Hero" presents a doubled vision of race, one of a black man and the other of a (presumably) white woman. The poem may also contain a self-portrait that is both ironic and revealing in the boundaries it obscures and crosses. The "decorous frock-coated Negro" tour guide at Mount Vernon provides the centerpiece of the poem; the "sightseeing hobo" of a tourist appears secondarily. Moore insists early in the poem that her hero (unlike the "fearless" tourist) *is* afraid of all the same things the rest of us are ("deviating head-stones / and uncertainty . . . suffering and not / saying so," and bat shrieks), and she devotes most of the penultimate stanza to him:

> The decorous frock-coated Negro
> by the grotto
>
> answers the fearless sightseeing hobo
>   who asks the man she's with, what's this,
>   what's that, where's Martha
>   buried, "Gen-ral Washington
>   there; his lady, here"; speaking
>   as if in a play—not seeing her; with a
>   sense of human dignity
> and reverence for mystery, standing like the shadow
> of the willow.

This man has all the qualities Moore most admires—gentleness, "human dignity," "reverence for mystery," maternal leniency (mentioned earlier in the poem), and the ability to block out inessential sights ("not seeing" the tourist).

For these reasons, regardless of how unlikely a figure he would cut in the annals of white patriarchal history briefly catalogued earlier in the poem, this Negro fits the bill of hero. Moreover, the last stanza of the poem, in marking the hero "he" for the first time, implicitly links heroism with this man:

Moses would not be grandson to Pharaoh.
  It is not what I eat that is
  my natural meat,
  the hero says. He's not out
  seeing a sight but the rock
  crystal thing to see—the startling El Greco
  brimming with inner light—that
covets nothing that it has let go. This then you may know
as the hero.

(Selected Poems, 19)

Like Moses, this descendant of former slaves "would not be grand-son" to a great patriarch who has enslaved his people but instead finds his "natural meat" or sustenance beyond the contingencies of his daily situation. He looks without covetousness or rancor past the mansion of the former slave-owning President (whom he still metaphorically serves) and past the white woman's insistent questioning to "inner light."

The tourist, in contrast, is all wrong: "fearless" and "sight-seeing," she is the gadfly to be ignored, the irritating circumstance to rise above rather than the hero herself.[35] And yet it is difficult not to see Moore in this figure, with her distinctly masculine way of life (as hobo), her untiring interest in the mundane and popular, her factual questions and her desire to see sights slightly off the beaten track that give unaccented attention to women—asking, for example, "Where's Martha / buried" rather than for George's grave. It is as if Moore confutes archetypes of white Western heroism with one anti-hero in her maternal man and with another in her brash female tourist.

Following this line of thought, the conditional of the poem's last line sounds louder: "you *may* know" the dignified and maternally lenient, black male as "the hero," or again "you *may* know" the persistently questioning, gender-crossing female, white hobo as "the hero" (my emphasis). You may, in fact, define heroism in a number of ways, according to your circumstances or those of the observed subject—as the rhyming of Negro, hobo, and hero suggests. In particular, different qualities may signify heroism in a lower-class, employed black man and in a financially indigent but independent, footloose white woman. "*The* hero" as a distinctive singular being, then, does not exist.

"Rescue with Yul Brynner" is unusual among Moore's poems for its combination of racial and historical specificity with outright mythologizing. As mentioned previously, she gives unique particularity to Brynner's skin-color—the "milkweed-witch seed-brown"; here, too, she heroizes her subject in direct contrast to the "I" of the poem. "Like a grasshopper that did not / know it missed the mower, a pygmy citizen; / a case, I'd say, of too slow a grower," the speaker once listened "with detachment" to the "displaced but not deterred" Budapest Symphony that should instead have roused her to appropriate action, as thousands of refugees fled from the bloody Soviet repression of Hungary in 1956. The poem then praises in part by mythologizing and in part by self-blame. The multilingual Brynner is "Magic bird with multiple tongue— / five tongues," a greater "king" outside the movies than in his most famous role, "twin of an enchantress," "tale-spinner— / of fairy tales that can come true"; "he flew among / the damned, found each camp / where hope had slowly died" while the music-loving "I" sits at home.

> There were thirty million; there are thirteen still—
> healthy to begin with, kept waiting till they're ill.
> History judges.
>
> (CP, 227)

And so does Moore. Among other things, she judges Brynner's race both peripheral to his generosity and yet important, perhaps less to his identity than as a way of marking racial presence in a crucially international, interracial, and multilingual world.

Although there are differences in stress between Moore's poems on ethnic minorities of the United States and her poems on European nationalities, the two sets of poems are related and come together in Moore's poems of the 1930s and 1940s, when her concern for European Jews brought her didacticism more fully to the fore than any topic before or since. While "The Jerboa," "Virginia Britannia," and "Enough: *Jamestown, 1607–1957*" use racial difference to explore questions of power and to rewrite the history embedded in a cultural and physical landscape, Moore's poems about European nations typically take one of two forms: either they are primarily ahistorical, focusing on legendary or mythologized aspects of identity, or they are abstract, not focused on race but including openly didactic statements against prejudice. Poems of the first type, even more than Moore's poems that mention individuals of color without calling attention to race as a theme, respond only indirectly to the politics of race. Moreover, those that focus exclusively on links between the United States and European nations might be seen as supporting the ethnocentrism of much American racism. Poems of the second type make their political stance clear.

"Spenser's Ireland" (1941) would seem to be Moore's most specific poem about race since here she refers to the poem's "I" as "Irish," and since the poet's own multiple public and private references to her Irish heritage imply the identity of that speaker with herself. Yet the speaker knows Ireland only through reading and myth. The poem begins with its title: "Spenser's Ireland // has not altered;— / a place as kind as it is green, / the greenest place I've never seen. / Every name is a tune." Mythical elements predominate even in the primary didactic statement of this poem, which occurs at its center:

> Outwitting
> the fairies, befriending the furies,
> whoever again
> and again says, "I'll never give in," never sees
>
> that you're not free
> until you've been made captive by
> supreme belief,—credulity
> you say?
>
> (CP, 113)

Typically for Moore, this didactic statement couches itself as a conditional description, contains a double negative (never . . . not free), and ends with a question that undercuts the speaker's stance— all aspects modifying the absolutism of its claim. Presumably, stub-

bornly independent people (all Irish?) do not know that their free-
dom lies in supreme belief, hence their "obduracy," continuous
fighting, and dissatisfaction.[36] In a more directly conditional query,
the speaker previously asks

> If in Ireland
>   they play the harp backward at need,
>   and gather at midday the seed
> of the fern, eluding
> their "giants all covered with iron," might
>   there be fern seed for unlearn-
> ing obduracy and for reinstating
> the enchantment?
>
>   (CP, 112)

But it isn't clear why the condition is necessary or who the recipient
of the reinstating should be—today's Irish recovering their lost
heritage? the rest of the world learning from mythically "[un]altered"
Ireland? Moreover, she implies that even this heritage may be a
mixed blessing. "Hindered characters / seldom have mothers / in
Irish stories," Moore states, "but they all have grandmothers"; she
then follows this generalization about loss by quoting a hopelessly
bigoted ancestor:

> It was Irish;
>   a match not a marriage was made
>   when my great great grandmother'd said
> with native genuis for
> disunion, "Although your suitor be
>   perfection, one objection
> is enough; he is not
> Irish."
>
>   (CP, 112–113)

Irish heroes may need both to escape or "unlearn" such closed-
minded "native genius for disunion" at the same time that they
reclaim a heritage of almost magically skilled craft and kindness.

As racial portrait, this is myth-making par excellence. Moore's knowledge of earlier extreme discrimination against the Irish in the United States may contribute to her strong allegiance to that part of her heritage, but it does not enter the poem.[37] Similarly, Moore's concern for the political and religious factionalization of Ireland and its continuing semi-colonial status appears nowhere in this poem, as it does in the earlier "Sojourn in the Whale." Instead, she identifies her speaker with a country of garrulously cantankerous individuals who live a life of antithesis to the rational materialism and selfishness characterizing the United States.[38]

Nonetheless, the final lines of "Spenser's Ireland" emphasize the distance between the speaker and Ireland, even as they assert identity: "The Irish say your trouble is their / trouble and your / joy their joy? I wish / I could believe it; / I am troubled, I'm dissatisfied, I'm Irish" (CP, 114). By rhyming "I'm Irish" with "I wish," by denoting the Irish "they" (rather than "we"), and by stating that she can't believe what "the Irish" do, Moore allies her speaker with the earlier skeptical "you" ("credulity you say?") rather than with the Irish themselves. The poet's acknowledged borrowing from Don Byrne's "Ireland: The Rock Whence I Was Hewn" in the 1927 *National Geographic Magazine* for much of the description of her poem further dislodges any claim to authority through identity (see "Notes," CP, 280). This is an intertextually constructed portrait, not a racially or culturally "inherited" one.

As with "Enough: *Jamestown*," I do not find that this poem accounts for all its own implications and detail—perhaps in this case because the poet has restricted herself to the mythological and personal, yet places the poem in a temporal context and thereby hints both at the country's history of strife and at its neutrality during a "world" war against fascism. "Sojourn in the Whale" more successfully combines the mythological, political, personal, and didactic in its representation of Ireland. The poem begins:

Trying to open locked doors with a sword, threading
    the points of needles, planting shade trees
        upside down; swallowed by the opaqueness of one whom the seas
love better than they love you, Ireland—

you have lived and lived on every kind of shortage.
  You have been compelled by hags to spin
  gold thread from straw and have heard men say: "There is a
                                                    feminine
temperament in direct contrast to

ours which makes her do these things.

                                                    (Obs, 39)

Here the Irish, like Moore's later "paper nautilus," are "hindered to succeed" (CP, 121). "Compelled" to perform impossible tasks, to make do with "shortage," to listen to "men" (or Britain, in the poem's fable) call her "blind" and "incompeten[t]," and authoritatively predict her failure, Ireland (like women) knows its own strength. In opposition to what the British say, "'Water in motion is far / from level.' You have seen it when obstacles happened to bar / the path— rise automatically." This romanticizing poem affectionately accepts a past of hardship and enchantment while predicting revolution. "Spenser's Ireland"—with its ambivalence toward mythologizing, its pragmatic description of Irish industry and character, and its invocation of personal relationship to racial stereotype—is potentially the more interesting poem, but does not come to terms with its own complex dissatisfaction.[39]

Moore uses nationalist cultural myth to particularize characteristics she admires in other poems as well. In "England" (1920) for example, she repeatedly links a country with a spiritual or psychological quality it typifies through parataxis or apposition: England's own "baby rivers and little towns, each with its abbey or its cathedral . . .—the / criterion of suitability and convenience"; "Greece with its goat and gourds, the nest of modified illusions"; "the East with its snails, its emotional // shorthand and jade cockroaches, its rock crystal and its imperturbability"; leading finally to America's redundant defining lack, "where there are no proof readers, no silkworms, no digressions":

the wild man's land; grass-less, links-less, language-less country—in
                                which letters are written

> not in Spanish, not in Greek, not in Latin, not in shorthand,
> but in plain American which cats and dogs can read!

The rest of this poem, however, instructs the reader what to make of those apparently innate native qualities (or lack thereof).

> To have misapprehended the matter is to have confessed
> that one has not looked far enough. The sublimated wisdom
> of China, Egyptian discernment, the cataclysmic torrent of emo-
> tion compressed
>   in the verbs of the Hebrew language . . .
>
>   the flower and fruit of all that noted superi-
> ority—should one not have stumbled upon it in America, must
>   one imagine
>   that it is not there? It has never been confined to one locality.
>   (P, 19)

This poem uses stereotypes to conclude that although national differences are "very noticeable" they should not lead to "continents of misapprehension"—the geographical metaphor suggesting the local foundation of much racism. "No con- // clusions may be drawn" about characteristics that the outsider may misinterpret out of knowledge stemming from some different "continent," or, that is, out of ignorance: "to have misapprehended the matter is to have confessed / that one has not looked far enough." In this defense of possible American excellence, Moore warns that no culture or people should be judged merely by what an observer (or reader) may have "stumbled upon."

In other poems about race as nationality, Moore similarly celebrates human characteristics as epitomized by a particular nation, although not, finally, as exclusive to it. "Light is Speech," for example, redundantly links the "light" of "flaming justice" and freedom with the French, by apposition identifying the adjectives *French, free,* and *frank.* The poem concludes: "The word France means / enfranchisement; means one who can / 'animate whoever thinks of her.'" Whether this 1941 poem is in fact a sorrowful reproach to France for capitulating to Germany, as Slatin argues (SR, 255), or a romanticized portrait of a besieged country that gave the United States its symbol of freedom ("Bartholdi's / Liberty holding up her / torch beside the port"), the point of its definition seems to be to stimulate the French and non-French into action (CP, 97). France, or frank speech, or freedom itself, by definition "animate[s]" others. It is others, then, as much as the French, who construct the "France" that animates them. In "The Web One Weaves of Italy" Moore exults over the variety of "quiet excitement" available in "this modern *mythologica / esopica*" or land of fables, at first concluding that the result is "quite different from what goes on / at the Sorbonne" or in France—"but not entirely" (CP, 164). Further thought will always reveal similarity where at first there appeared to be only difference.

In a 1956 poem, Moore tells us that "Style"—the title of the poem—revives in Escudero's skating, and in the gracful movement of other "Iberian-American" champions—the jai alai and tennis champion Etchebaster, the dancer Soledad, the guitar player Rosario Escudero, and finally El Greco. These artists are linked solely by nationality, yet the poem does not suggest that style is the province of Spain alone. After all, the performers Moore names are of hybrid nationality (Spanish-American), and Pierre Etchebaster was jai alai champion of France (hence Spanish-American-French?). Moreover, their precursor in Spain was also of composite nationality: El Greco is Spanish for "the Greek," a label describing an artist born in Crete and trained in Italy. In "Granite and Steel," similarly, the "German ingenuity" and "tenacity" of the Brooklyn bridge is "as if inverted by French perspicacity" and by allusion Mediterranean (a "Caged Circe of steel and stone") while, of course, quintessentially American: designed by a German immigrant, the bridge, together with the (gift of the French) Statue of Liberty, "enfranchis[es]" the bay (CP, 205). In a draft of this poem, Moore experiments with an even broader, and more specific, mingling of nations: "French perspicacity / American stone. / German tenacitye" [sic], adding in the margin "Spanish actuality" (RML 1.02.12).[40]

In her war poems of the early 1940s, Moore brings together the themes of her poems on national race with those on racial difference in the United States. Appalled by the racially defined nationalistic fervor in Europe, Moore generalizes the horror of that hatred to the racism of her own country. Poems that begin as descriptions of particular countries and people end with reminders that no race or racism stands alone.

Like "England" and, by implication, "Spenser's Ireland," "A Carriage from Sweden" (1944) proceeds by contrast with the United States. The poem begins "They say there is a sweeter air / where it was made, than we have here" and contrasts Brooklyn's "freckled / integrity" with its "vein // of resined straightness from north-wind / hardened Sweden's once-opposed-to- / compromise archipelago / of rocks," concluding with an appeal to George Washington and Gustavus Adolphus to "forgive our decay." In contrast to such decay, the carriage is preserved as "a fine thing!" of "unannoying / romance!" and representative of the Swedes:

> And how beautiful, she
>   with the natural stoop of the
> snowy egret, gray-eyed and straight-haired,
> for whom it should come to the door—
>
> of whom it reminds me. The split
>   pine fair hair, steady gannet-clear
>   eyes and the pine-needled-path deer-
> swift step; that is Sweden, land of the
> free and the soil for a spruce-tree—
>
> vertical though a seedling—all
>   needles: from a green trunk, green shelf
>   on shelf fanning out by itself.
> The deft white-stockinged dance in thick-soled
> shoes! Denmark's sanctuaried Jews!
>   (CP, 131–132)

Here all aspects of the country merge: racial or physical genotype (blonde, light-eyed); geography (rocky, pine-covered terrain); quaint customs (traditional dances and shoes); and recent political history (Sweden's offer of sanctuary to Danish Jews). And, the poem implies, together they make of Sweden a more faithful "land of the free" than the United States—which perhaps risks forfeiting its right to this title by refusing such refuge.[41] Although, like "Spenser's

Ireland," "A Carriage from Sweden" remains primarily mythical rather than historical, here Moore indicates that current events vindicate her description.

"'Keeping Their World Large'" is also a relatively simple poem, mourning the losses of the war ("That forest of white crosses! / My eyes won't close to it"). "I should like to see" the simple things of Italy, Moore writes, but then immediately follows her list of tourist attractions by listing things impossible to see anywhere and associated with war: "A noiseless piano, an / innocent war, the heart that can act against itself." In Italy, the dead are everywhere: "each unlike and all alike . . . / so many—stumbling, falling, multiplied / till bodies lay as ground to walk on—" (CP, 145). Through Moore's typical indirection of conditional clauses and questions, this poem insists hopefully that death not be "in vain"—neither Christ's nor that of the many soldiers "whose spirits and whose bodies / all too literally were our shield." More obviously than the other poems about national race, this poem refuses to distinguish one kind of body from another. "Each unlike and all alike," those who fight are leveled to one condition horribly by death and gloriously by their self-sacrifice—as the allusion to Christ suggests.

Although "'Keeping Their World Large'" begins as a poem about Italy, it ends as a poem about all war—including those fought domestically or internally, against "fat living and self-pity." As she states in "In Distrust of Merits": "There never was a war that was / not inward; I must / fight till I have conquered in myself what / causes war" (CP, 138). Yet the "I" of this passage also misleads. Always the educator in her poems, Moore attempts especially during the war years to speak to the historical moment. In drafted notes for "In Distrust of Merits," Moore writes "(may) humbly but with—confidence (may as one.) Say OUR"—as though reprimanding herself for both objectivity and singularity (RML I.02.30).[42] More specifically a few years earlier, after reading an essay "by Reinhold Niebuhr on Germany's condition as a race—in persecuting & being subject to Hitler," she writes her brother that "intolerance is at work in us all, in *all* countries,—that we ourselves 'persecute' Jews & Negroes & submit to wrongful tyranny. Or at least feel 'superior' in sundry ways" (November 19, 1939; RML VI.35.12). The "I" of "In

Distrust of Merits" blends into the "our," "we," and "us" that pre-dominate in the poem, allowing Moore both a field for highlighting self-doubt and the construction of a larger authority. As Susan Schweik points out, Moore here is "exploring . . . the possibility of assuming the voice of a collective 'we,' a pronoun which would function . . . to articulate a nation, or the whole world," while expressing the convictions of an individual (an "I") in her own highly singular style (*A Gulf So Deeply Cut,* 37). This is as close as Moore comes to taking on the voice and stance of universalizing poet, although even here she undercuts this stance through parenthetical questions and asides.

Like many of her generation, Moore believed in the possibility of a justified war. Nonetheless, her poems of the 1940s reveal a profound discomfort with the knowledge that one side wins because of physical rather than moral force, and with any kind of nationalism that promotes divisiveness or hatred.[43] As in "'Keeping Their World Large'," where Moore hypothesizes that "'If Christ and the apostles died in vain, / I'll die in vain with them' / against this way of victory" (CP, 145), in the earlier poem she writes:

> If these great patient
> dyings—all these agonies
>   and wound bearings and bloodshed—
> can teach us how to live, these
>   dyings were not wasted.

Although Moore promotes trust, love, and tolerance of difference in this poem, "how to live" is defined most strongly by what it is we must no longer, "never" do:

> trust begets power and faith is
> an affectionate thing. We
>   vow, we make this promise
>
> to the fighting—it's a promise—"We'll
>   never hate black, white, red, yellow, Jew,
> Gentile, Untouchable."
>
> (CP, 138, 137)

164

Whether producing and produced by slavery, colonization, religiously based systems of caste, or nationalistic fervor, hatred promotes death and the "disease, My / Self."[44] Trust begets the only kind of power she will give her faith to.

As the focus of "In Distrust of Merits" shows, Moore conceives of selfhood and humanity morally in ways that preclude extensive focus on the race or gender of particular selves. As I have said before, however, and as her war poems in particular show, Moore is too firmly grounded in history and her own experience to promote a pretense of purely spiritual or racially neutered existence. Fiction or not, it means something to exclaim: "I'm Irish." The point is not to imagine that no one is "black, white, red, yellow, Jew" or to ignore race, but to care about such facts only through the modes of trust and compassion.

Race, then, for Moore focuses important questions about self-definition and about pluralism as a moral stance in a multiracial world. Prejudice, xenophobia, selfishness, materialism, greed, cynical distrust of others—these for Moore are the enemies of an ethical (for her, democratic or "free") community of individuals against which wars, internal and international, should be fought. For her, such abstractions—and their contrasting qualities: love, trust, tolerance, willingness to compromise, skill at some activity or art, generosity—constitute selfhood more importantly than aspects of physical being. Such a belief goes hand in hand for Moore with that of the mutableness of the self, but perhaps more clearly in a Progressivist moral than a Kristevan sense: the self may change in that it may gain faith, learn skills, win against at least some of its own weaknesses. As she says of the mind in "The Mind Is an Enchanting Thing," "it's / not a Herod's oath that cannot change" (CP, 135). The "superiority" of "England" can be found in any nation and learned by any individual. At the same time, differences of race, gender, and other categories identified with selfhood powerfully influence an individual's and a group's possibilities for such achievement.

In this sense, Moore's poems on race and nationality bear some resemblance to her animal poems. Each creature has proclivities, habits, characteristics of skin (armored, thick, feathered, blemished, beautifully translucent) that determine how that creature will behave. A pangolin is not better or worse than an elephant or a desert rat (or the poem-writing Rat herself). Unlike animals, however, notions of race may assume innumerable forms; there is no static or essentialized black woman or man, or Jew, or American, any more than there is a fixed Woman and Man. Pluralism demands difference—yet Moore has witnessed for decades that ideas of difference may lead to catastrophic violence. As she says in "In Distrust of Merits" following her hopeful "vow" to end racial hatred, "We are / not competent to / make our vows" (CP, 137). Or, to return to "Black Earth": "The I of each is to // the I of each, / a kind of fretful speech / which sets a limit on itself." It is hard to step far enough outside one's own body or idiosyncratic and materially and culturally constructed proclivities to hear or see accurately any other "I," let alone to value a model that leads to personal change. Perhaps poems are for her analogous to the elephant's trunk, a "tendril" firmly rooted in an individual's cultural and historical, grounding "earth" but attempting to reach beyond it.

As a comparison of the 1918 "Black Earth" with the 1943 "In Distrust of Merits" or the more private and affectionate 1947 "Voracities and Verities Sometimes are Interacting" shows, Moore's youthful conviction that one may live unconflictedly within one's own thick or thin skin markedly diminishes with the repeated global crises of the century. Although underlying satisfaction with the self or "love" of others may still be "undying," one no longer proclaims it "Openly . . . with the naturalness / of the hippopotamus or the alligator" but instead asks for "pardon." It may be in part for this reason that she turns in her later years to poems that are both more abstract and more conversational, more occasional—poems that claim less in the way of individual particularity and in taking ethical stands yet are more openly didactic, less ambiguous in their presentation, and generate a stronger sense of community.

SIX

Quotation, Community, and Correspondences

> Of things purporting to be transitory, letters can be seriously a pleasure and as permanently a monument as anything which has been devised. With John Donne one "makes account that this writing of letters when it is with any seriousness, is a kind of extasie, and a departure and secession and suspension of the soul, which doth then communicate itself to two bodies." One can safely affirm at any rate that a writer of letters is not one of those who know much and understand little.
>
> (CPr, 182)

> Only use gives possession.
>
> (MMR, 105)

$\mathcal{M}$oore seems from very early on to have conceived of her poetry in the related forms of appreciative (if also, at times, contentious) and nonhierarchical exchange—between poet and tradition, poet and subject, poet and reader. Poetry, in this sense, resembles letter writing—as Moore suggests at the end of "Bowls," "he who gives quickly gives twice / in nothing so much as in a letter" (Obs, 70). Such correspondence takes structural form in Moore's lifelong use of quotation within her poems and is, I believe, loosely theorized by her explanation of this practice as a "hybrid method of composition" (CP, 262). Moreover, this principle takes thematic form in

Moore's turn in her later poetry to the love poem, or poem of singular appreciation.[1]

This shift in Moore's later work toward the more personal, popular, occasional, and openly appreciative may have occurred because her personal life changed so dramatically during the 1940s and early 1950s—first, because World War II pushed Moore toward a more public and didactic stance in her poetry than any other event of her life; second, because her mother died in 1947; and third, because the several prizes she won following the publication of her *Collected Poems* in 1951 made her a national celebrity. Not coincidentally, between 1946 and 1954 Moore took on her longest and most ambitious poetic project—the translation of the *Fables of La Fontaine.* This change in Moore's choice of themes and projects is typically described as stemming from her greater acceptance of conventional values and greater desire to establish universal and stable truths; I instead see it as stemming from Moore's increasingly felt desire to represent the individual as functioning within a community.[2] The later poems manifest with particular clarity priorities of longstanding importance to Moore.

Because Moore's poems of the 1950s and 1960s (and sometimes the 1940s) are almost invariably read in the context of an eccentric and gendered public persona that Moore cultivated during these decades, discussion of her late work must begin with that context.[3] In "Something Inescapably Typical: Questions about Gender in the Late Work of Williams and Moore," the most perceptive work to date on Moore's older age, John Slatin argues that Moore is demonstrably gender-conscious in her choices about self-presentation and publication and that it is specifically the gendered aspect of her choices that has most distanced her from high serious regard.[4] Starting in the 1950s, Moore published in magazines that would have been unheard of as forums for a male poet of her stature: the *Bryn Mawr Alumnae Bulletin, World Week, Vogue, Harper's Bazaar, House and Garden, Seventeen, Women's Wear Daily,* and the women's section of the *New York Times.* As Slatin points out, such publishing created problems of interpretation for a critical audience ideologically trained to assume that no work of value will appear in such venues—an ideology that tars most feminists as well as traditional critics:

168

We read from the standpoint of a system of value which takes it for granted . . . that a piece appearing in, say, the *Nation* or the *Times Book Review* is more "serious" as literature or criticism than something in *Harper's Bazaar* or *Women's Wear Daily* or *Seventeen*. We—I—have tended to dismiss the latter out of hand . . . So that even in these pieces, where Moore writes on subjects (fashion, jewelry, morality, women writers) in which women are *supposed* to be competent—and where she writes, moreover, specifically *for* women—her project is doomed . . . *because* her subjects are women's subjects and *because* her readers are women. (The supposed "triviality" of her subject matter is "confirmed," of course, by the "triviality" of the magazines in which her work appears.) ("Something Inescapably Typical," 98)

Although only a small part of her publication during these years addressed such an audience or issues, its effect—together with that of a persona leaning toward stereotypes of the eccentric older woman—was to make Moore more a public celebrity than a poet of noted intellectual and moral stature.[5] This phenomenon underlines the wisdom of Moore's early decision to structure gender concerns into her poems through an ostentatiously nongendered poetic.

But Moore's situation had changed. Once she had won the Pulitzer and the Bollingen prizes, the National Book Award, and the Gold Medal of the National Institute of Arts and Letters (between 1951 and 1953—followed by the Poetry Society of America's Gold Medal for Distinguished Achievement, the Edward MacDowell Medal, the U.S. National Medal for Literature, and the Chevalier de l'Ordre des Arts et des Lettres award in France), Moore could no longer position herself as outside the literary establishment.[6] Yet there was no established role for a distinguished female poet comparable, for example, to the tradition of authoritative cultural critic so well suited to Eliot in his later years. As Slatin asks,

What *public* language could a woman poet speak in the '50s? . . . there was no (literary) discourse she could use, no subject matter she could treat, no position she could take, no forum she could speak in, that was not already marginal . . . the impression of inadvertent self-caricature that Moore so often gives in her later work is itself the (almost?) inevitable consequence of her effort to solve the problem of how to speak publically as a woman. (95).

Moore played the poet in one of the few ways the American public could imagine an older woman doing so.

Inevitably, Moore's acceptance—for the first time in her life—of the public role of poet also planted her solidly in the mire of changing cultural constructions of what a "woman" was during the 1950s and 1960s. By speaking through conventional venues for women and on some conventionally feminine issues, Moore inadvertently supported a regressive image of womanhood that stood in direct contrast to the role she otherwise and for decades had attempted to construct for herself. Similarly, Moore's early twentieth-century notions of feminism and female community collided outright with mid-century notions of the same. In attempting to carry out some version of her own principles and to keep herself current with her audience, Moore placed herself in a difficult position for being taken seriously by either late twentieth-century feminists or the critical establishment.

Most damaging has been the assumption that Moore's late exaggerated modesty—or, to use her word, "humility"—represents "deep feelings of insecurity" and of "constitutional inability to do anything right," as Eileen Moran has argued on the basis of Moore's correspondence with Hildegarde Watson.[7] I would argue, in contrast, that while such behavior may express personal needs, it also significantly resonates with the politics of her poetic: self-effacing behavior marks a place where need or feeling, role-playing, moral convictions, and aesthetic theory or politics intersect for Moore in complex ways. As this intersection suggests, it is not surprising that Moore exhibited all the characteristics of her later years in earlier decades, but less frequently and in less extreme ways.

Moore was highly productive during her later years: after the age of sixty, when living alone for the first time in her life and in the midst of a busy schedule of correspondence, readings, and lectures, Moore translated La Fontaine's *Fables* (and three fairy tales) and published an impressive number of poems and essays. When poems were rejected—as some still were, even after her plethora of prizes—Moore did not sink into depression or stop writing, but revised her work (again) and sent it off to another journal.

In short, Moore's remarkable modesty did not stem from an inability to work but had other sources or motives. For example, in her private correspondence, particularly with Hildegarde Watson, Louise Crane, and other very close women friends, Moore seems to engage in a kind of role-playing in which she "needs" encouragement and the friend "needs" to provide it. This pattern is striking in the Watson-Moore correspondence. "Higgie" is the "lover," praiser, devoted one, writing letters of extravagant support to Marianne, the "beloved," who responds by saying how "childish" she is and how she (and her mother—before 1947) depend on her friend. To give a few brief examples, Watson writes:

> Marianne dear, What joy your letter gave me not only in some expressions you used for me. I so much needed that you should tell me you liked me to be somewhere and [word unclear] if I were not . . . (July 1934; RML V.70.01)

> One cannot say I love you Marianne. Love is not said like that. It must be placed and situated and sublimated and shaped like sound running through intervals never losing the light of right expression. And yet I long to show you truly in a way of words feeling without the means—and sincerely—more & more admiration . . . (July 27, 1937; RML V.70.02)

> Dearest Marianne, My heart trembles in knowing you. You did speak of some increase of friendship. Mine only is an infinitesimal expansion admitting "mehr licht" the better to understand your brightness. (January 3, 1949; RML V.70.04?)

Although Moore responds affectionately, she does not express the same romantic intensity, tending instead toward the practical and comic: for example, she calls herself "demented with work . . . a kind of Coney Island fun fair victim" (August 19, 1957; Moran, "Portrait of the Artist," 132) or, earlier, reports: "I go thrashing along like a farm tractor of the old-fashioned kind, determined not to come to a halt; that is the most that can be said of me" (October 25, 1933; RML V.70.01). Watson even comments indirectly on her own role in this exchange: "It had been natural from a child for me to take care of others instinctively . . . or so it seems" (August 23, 1953; RML V.70.05). Although this pattern can be seen in the early correspondence between these friends, it becomes more marked during the late 1940s and 1950s (most of Moran's examples are taken from the 1950s).

Moore at times assumes a similar tone in professional letters and activities, as well as in poems. For example, in 1943 Moore asks an editor of *The New Republic* to decide whether to publish a prose- or "verse-form" of "Elephants"—both of which she submitted to him (MMN V.2:11–13); similarly, she instructs Lawrence Scott to "change the verse as you like" in printing her poem "Occasionem Cognosce" (private correspondence to Scott, April 6, 1963). In the poem "In Lieu of the Lyre," Moore refers to herself (or the speaker who resembles her) as "unavoidably lame," a "verbal pilgrim" (CP, 206). Elizabeth Bishop recounts another public instance of extreme modesty and eccentricity: at the age of seventy-six, Moore enrolled in a poetry workshop and (to the dismay of Louise Bogan, the teacher) participated unselfconsciously in the class, taking copious notes, asking questions, and discussing matters of technique and style with the other students.[8]

That Moore would at least occasionally take the role of the dependent with friends is not surprising.[9] Given her long adult relationship of mutual dependence with her mother, it may have had an easy fit—especially after her mother's death. As discussed in Chapter 4, Moore's practice of role-playing extended beyond the family and no doubt took a much broader range of forms than assigning animal names to friends. In addition, it would be astonishing if a serious poet did not have recurring, at least minor, crises of confidence that she shared with her friends. Moore notes that such feeling increases after her mother's death, often lamenting the lack of her previous editor/collaborator and at one point writing in a notebook, "The thing must be admitted, I don't care for the books that were not worked on by her."[10] Yet surely any writer would acknowledge these as the most normal of feelings while in the midst of some creative venture.

Moreover, while some of this behavior is indeed eccentric, and her dependence on reassurance is great, it is crucial to remember that Moore's convictions also determine such behavior. First, Moore's commitment to a nonhierarchical, responsive poetic demands that she reject whatever would elevate the poet as singular and "great"; she is not above a brother's, editor's, or friend's advice—and indeed welcomes it. Moore's moral convictions take identical form: as she states in "In Distrust of Merits," all must fight "the disease, My / Self." Similarly, Moore remarks in "Humility, Concentration, and Gusto" that "humility, indeed, is armor, for it realizes that it is impossible to be original, in the sense of doing something that has never been thought of before" (1949; CPr, 420–421); acknowledging dependence on others constitutes honesty, not particular modesty or self-effacement.[11] As Sandra Gilbert argues in "Marianne Moore as Female Female Impersonator," adamant modesty—like Moore's frequent late remarks about her "frightful" appearance—may also provide Moore a culturally approved way to emphasize her resemblance to one type of ordinary woman (comic spinster) rather than standing alone as the century's only broadly acclaimed woman poet. Apologizing, or unusually modest self-presentation, seems to become a "habit" for Moore—both an unconscious behavior pattern and something like a piece of clothing. She doesn't regard it as false or as a disguise (clothes are not a disguise—they are what one wears to be polite, a customary gesture), but it remains peripheral to her energy and a principle of, not a hurdle for, her writing.

Moore's expression of dependence and appreciation as a principle of her poetic may best be examined through the metaphor of letter writing—a private communication in constructed, publicly conveyed form. Moore in fact uses letter writing as a model for poetic production in an early poem: "Bowls"

on the green
with lignum vitae balls and ivory markers,
the pins planted in wild duck formation,
and quickly dispersed:
by this survival of ancient punctilio
in the manner of Chinese lacquer carving,

173

layer after layer exposed by certainty of touch and unhurried
    incision
so that only so much color shall be revealed as is necessary to the
    picture
I learn that we are precisians—
not citizens of Pompeii arrested in action
as a cross section of one's correspondence would seem to imply.
Renouncing a policy of boorish indifference
to everything that has been said since the days of Matilda,
I shall purchase an Etymological Dictionary of Modern English
that I may understand what is written
and like the ant and the spider
returning from time to time to headquarters,
shall answer the question
as to "why I like winter better than I like summer"
and acknowledge that it does not make me sick
to look modern playwrights and poets and novelists straight in the
    face—
that I feel just the same;
and I shall write to the publisher of the magazine
which will "appear the first day of the month
and disappear before one has had time to buy it
unless one takes proper precaution,"
and make an effort to please—
since he who gives quickly gives twice
in nothing so much as in a letter.

                                                        (Obs, 70)

Typically read as an incoherent assertion of Moore's interest in the
precise, this poem coherently focuses on the concept of response.[12]
Cause follows effect: the speaker observes lacquer carving on a
bowling game and consequently resolves to pay more attention to
the historical "layer upon layer" of meaning in words, answer even
trivial questions of personal preference, acknowledge her links with
other poets, write to publishers, and attempt to please—both
through answering mail promptly and because doing so constitutes
a doubly generous gift.

These resolutions suggest that the process of response has a value apart from what is said. Indeed, responsiveness to what one has observed makes one a "precisian"—or "precisionist" as she puts it in a later version.[13] Art stands at one end of a continuum; there is only a difference of degree between *corresponding* with friends and *responding* to beauty in the details of a game, or in ancient or contemporary art. By this logic, one who stands outside the continuum, or does not respond, is spiritually dead, "arrested in action." Unlike Emily Dickinson's "This is my letter to the world / That never wrote to me," this poem presents poetry as writing *back*.[14] In her interview with Donald Hall, Moore even specifies an interactive motive for her writing: "I think each time I write that it may be the last time; then I'm charmed by something and seem to have to say something. Everything I have written is the result of reading or of interest in people, I'm sure of that" (MMR, 256). Moore "ha[s]" to speak back to what she encounters, if only as evidence that she is not a citizen of Pompeii, and writing a letter epitomizes the combination of necessary response and reaching an audience. In "Pigeons," she marks as "fine words" the epistolary formula "'So please write me and believe that I / am yours very truly'" (*Poetry* XLVII, 2; 1935). Moore considers a letter as permanent "a monument as anything which has been devised" (CPr, 182).

The most literal link between letter writing and Moore's poetry, or between the various kinds of response that constitute a poem, lies in her use of quotation—in particular her quotation of letters, conversation, and ephemeral, popular writing like that found in magazines or advertising. Through such quotation and the accompanying documentation of her "Notes," Moore presents a range of voices in her work as having authority and presence apart from her own. Like all makers of mosaic or collage, Moore constructs the poem, but its pieces come from a larger collaborating world or community.[15] Moore even refers to her method of quoting as a "mosaic" in "Idiosyncrasy and Technique": "Odd as it may seem that a few words of overwhelming urgency should be a mosaic of quotations, why paraphrase what for maximum impact should be quoted verbatim?" (CPr, 512). Moore repeats such statements frequently:

'Why the many quotation marks?' . . . When a thing has been said so well that it could not be said better, why paraphrase it? Hence my writing is, if not a cabinet of fossils, a kind of collection of flies in amber. (MMR, xv)

If I wanted to say something and somebody else had said it ideally, then I'd take it but give the person credit for it. That's all there is to it. If you are charmed by an author, I think it's a very strange and invalid imagination that doesn't long to share it. (interview with Hall; MMR, 260)

Speaking from the perspective of one who shares as well as one who borrows, in her essay "Dress and Kindred Subjects," published in *Women's Wear Daily*, Moore writes, "Life is happiest, I am sure, when it is in some sense contributory, not wholly self-centered" (CPr, 600). Or she tells Hall that a poem "start[s]" for her when "a felicitous phrase springs to mind"—a comment that obscures the distinction between creation and memory, as it is often already constructed phrases that "spring to mind" (MMR, 259).

Quotation functions minimally in "Bowls" and is, in *The Complete Poems*, without annotation; its two quoted phrases are: "why I like winter better than I like summer?" and "appear the first day of the month / and disappear before one has had time to buy it / unless one takes proper precaution."[16] Nonetheless, "Bowls" typifies Moore's use of quotation. The poem begins by describing an instance of what might be called artistic quotation: an unpretentious game ensures the "survival of ancient punctilio" by repeating features of its craft. By renouncing "a policy of boorish indifference" to all work of the past in response to observing this game, the speaker rejects popular indifference to art but also artistic indifference to popular ephemera, like games; she democratically rejects indifference to "what has been said" in all its varieties. Further debunking a hierarchy that raises art over craft or other kinds of "saying," Moore then concludes that it is writing a *letter* that gives "twice" the pleasure in "an effort to please." Quotation functions as the ultimately equalizing or democratic structure in Moore's poems: here she both acknowledges that others' words contribute to her thought and verse as importantly as (or more than) her own, and she uses precisely the same mechanism to mark ephemeral and canonical or elite sources.

Quotation is probably the most frequently discussed aspect of Moore's verse, and certainly one of its most prominent.[17] Margaret Holley estimates that Moore uses marked quotation in half of the poems written before 1918, two-thirds of the poems of the twenties, thirties, and war years, and three-fourths of the poems written thereafter; "there is no increase in the quantity of the material quoted; the practice simply appears in an increasing number of her poems, suggesting that it grows to be a more and more reliable, even habitual strategy" (PMM, 39). As has been well established, Moore's use of quotation is both clearly related to several other kinds of modernist experimentation with form (collage, bricolage, cubism, perhaps even dadaism—as well as actual uses of quotation by other poets), and distinctly different from that of her peers.[18] The primary differences are easily reviewed. Moore's quotations are almost exclusively in English, unlike the ostentatious multilingualism of Pound's *Cantos* or Eliot's *The Waste Land.* Like Williams (although far earlier and more radically) and again unlike Pound and Eliot, Moore quotes more noncanonical than canonical, or even literary, sources—favoring newspapers, popular journalism, advertising, conversation, and private letters. Her quoting gives no elevation to her verse; it does not place the author in the context of a major tradition.[19] To the extent that she does invoke canonical authors and texts, it is typically to disrupt their authority rather than to assume it. Moreover, as Lynn Keller indicates by calling Moore's quotation mosaic rather than collage-like, Moore at times fragments what she quotes so extremely that the quoted words or phrases carry little weight, and are not memorable, on their own; these fragments are integrated into a single portrait or argument rather than maintaining their individual integrity—at the same time that they call attention to themselves typographically as quoted.[20] Similarly, and unlike her peers, although Moore shows egalitarian respect for all previous uses of the word (quoting remarks overheard as well as famous literary texts), she shows equally egalitarian disregard for maintaining the precise form of the original wording, often altering what she has found to suit her purposes. Moore also employs

177

quotation marks idiosyncratically—sometimes using them for her own words and sometimes omitting them for borrowed material.[21] And Moore accompanies her quotations with an apparatus distinctly her own.

From the publication of *Observations* on (1924), Moore annotates her quotations in a series of endnotes. Like the quotations themselves, these "Notes" refer as often to popular and unpoetic as to traditionally literary sources: for example, "People's Surroundings" quotes Thomas Humphry Ward's *English Poets,* an advertisement from the *New York Times,* the description of a Persian object exhibited at the Bush Terminal Building in 1919, Anatole France, Reverend J. W. Darr, and the *Horary Astrology.*[22] "Four Quartz Crystal Clocks" quotes at length from a Bell Telephone leaflet; several poems quote sermons or lectures Moore has heard as well as newspapers. These notes are also inconsistent: some give information not mentioned in the poem; some poems containing quotations have no explanatory notes; and a few annotations are wrong.[23] For *Observations,* Moore compiled not only "Notes" but an extensive "Index" including entries like "Edmund Burke," "business documents," "cockroaches," "emotionally sensitive," and "Congress, Act of." Obviously, this index is idiosyncratic; not all phrases or nouns are indexed. Moore indeed values precision, but that is not the hallmark of her annotations.

Like her quotation generally, Moore's notes and the index she compiled for *Observations* directly contradict any notion of the poem as natural or inspired form, instead both reflecting and almost parodying critical response to poetry. On the one hand, the documentary quality adhering to the paraphernalia of quotation, endnotes, and index suggests that Moore's poems result from hard work, not revelation or the wisdom of experience. Moore places herself on a level with scholars by annotating her sources and debts. On the other hand, the inclusions seem at times so arbitrary that the notes are better read as part of the poem's "imaginary garden" than as factual information illuminating it.

Critics tend to agree that Moore's quotation, as Holley puts it, "paradoxically both emphasizes and disregards the sense of a source, and thus of an 'owner,' of texts," creating "a double relation to the tradition from which the fragment was lifted. The conservative tendency of preservation is set in tension with the progressive tendency of dismantling and renewal" (PMM, 15, 16). Similarly, Celeste Goodridge comments that "this highlighting of the fragment accounts for the nonlinear movement and the multiplicity of perspectives in her critical discourse."[24] Lynn Keller argues that Moore uses quotation and allusion to engage previous cultural contexts and arguments while making room for her own distinct perspective by creating a new (often feminist) context for the quoted material ("'For inferior who is free?'"). And yet especially at its most heteroglossic, Moore's quotation also underlines her own extensive and impressive authorial control.[25]

Moore's use of quotation epitomizes the structures of contradiction that I have argued are central to her poetic: controlled but relinquishing singular control; acknowledging but dismantling the traditional authority of literary intertextuality; engaging literary and popular "texts" in open communication but manipulating both to construct her own analysis and views. Here the previously examined contrasts of the personal and impersonal and the written and spoken elements of Moore's poetic "voice" come fully to the fore. Most paradoxical and disruptive, however, is the quotation and annotation of casual speech or common written sources. This practice most radically overturns boundaries between poetry and ordinary language (not just prose), between vernacular speech and the crafted written word, and between the poet as transforming genius and as collector of the accidentally overheard. Hence, this aspect of Moore's quotation presents in clearest form the politics of exchange and dependence in her general practice.

Many of the unacknowledged quotations in Moore's poems stem from remarks of her mother and brother or friends, made in conversation or in letters. For example, both the beginning and the end of "In the Days of Prismatic Color" originate in conversation.[26] At the end of "New York" Moore quotes Henry James's phrase "'accessibility to experience,'" as quoted by her mother to Warner in a letter which the poet read (PMM, 44). On the bottom of a typescript for the early, unpublished poem "I Tell You No Lie," Moore reproduces an anonymous conversation that provided her with the title of the poem, in this case making the whole conversation and not just a reference to it the acknowledging footnote. Similarly, the late poem "Blessed Is the Man" is drafted on pages that include a long transcription in dialect between "Reuben Todd" and "Captain Newman"; when asked what his name is, Todd responds "Reuben Todd Bless by God"—a phrase Moore repeats twice, ending the dialogue with phrases that may link the poem with this dialogue: "Devout respect for the subject innocent bewildered innocent" (RML I.01.20).

In a more dramatic example of unmarked borrowing, Moore's references to armored animals could be quoted from and as easily portray her mother, or the whole Moore family, as herself.[27] All at some point refer to themselves as "basilisks" or armored animals and use the metaphor of armor. For example, Mary Warner Moore writes to her son: "I have no armor to buckle to me yet"; or later, that they'll meet the year "unarmored"; and a year later that "armor was laid aside."[28] Quoting her family and friends or using their manner of speech in her poems makes them, for at least the knowledgeable reader, less the product of individual genius than of group effort, suggesting what might be an almost unimaginable percentage of borrowed material in the poems, although probably even among her friends and family no one reader would be able to identify all the borrowed phrases.[29] Indeed, in 1935 Moore acknowledges: "in my immediate family there is one 'who thinks in a particular way'; and I should like to add that where there is an effect of thought or pith in these pages, the thinking and often the actual phrases are hers."[30] More broadly, in her "Note on the Notes" in *Complete Poems*, Moore writes that "in anything I have written, there have been lines in which the chief interest is borrowed, and I have not yet been able to outgrow this hybrid method of composition" (CP, 262). Not just her "pith," "thinking," "interest[s]," and words are borrowed, but Moore's method itself is "hybrid," the product of more than one source.

Moore's poem "Silence" reveals most clearly the politics of form that may inhere in quoting, and speech-act theory provides perhaps the clearest description of its functions, for while the words Moore quotes may be identical to those previously used, the speech-act is inevitably different. To repeat J. G. A. Pocock's dictum, words constitute not just actions but "acts of power toward persons."[31] In a poem consisting, except for two and a half lines, entirely of quotation and depicting the relationship between a daughter and a father, it is particularly crucial to understand how speech-acts are performed on others, and where negotiations of power enter into the performance(s):[32]

> My father used to say,
> "Superior people never make long visits,
> have to be shown Longfellow's grave
> nor the glass flowers at Harvard.
> Self-reliant like the cat—
> that takes its prey to privacy,
> the mouse's limp tail hanging like a shoelace from its mouth—
> they sometimes enjoy solitude,
> and can be robbed of speech
> by speech which has delighted them.
> The deepest feeling always shows itself in silence;
> not in silence, but restraint."
> Nor was he insincere in saying, "'Make my house your inn'."
> Inns are not residences.
>
> (Obs, 82)

This poem has long been read as a sincere appreciation of a father's dictum that "superior people" may be known by their independence and "restraint"—and in her Notes Moore reports that the appreciation is a daughter's (Miss A. M. Homans). Recently, however, various critics have read the poem differently. Jeanne Heuving argues that the daughter quotes her father's words ironically to show both his dominating will-to-power and her subversion of it: "Inns are not residences," the poem ends—which is to say, that even if a literal, or a poetic, daughter rests within the house of a father, she does not and perhaps cannot spiritually or practically "live" there (*Omissions Are Not Accidents*, 117–120). Slatin sees the daughter using silence with what Moore in "Marriage" calls "'criminal ingenuity,' to circumvent the father's authority and appropriate it to herself" as restrained speaker (SR, 151).[33] Charles Altieri observes that "Silence" concludes Moore's *Selected Poems* and hence suggests "that everything in the book contributes to, and is modified by, this dialectical assertion of her female strength." This assertion, in turn, depends on a controlled manipulation of the very "restraint" that the father assumes epitomizes his word and that the daughter acknowledges as exemplifying her very different values: "Should [the daughter] either overestimate her power or underestimate the task [of fixing her father and freeing herself], she is likely to trap herself in poses of hatred and obsessive resistance that only confirm his victory . . . One in her situation must refrain from any self-staging."[34]

A return to speech-act theory strengthens such readings. By structuring the poem as representing a two-way process of communication, Moore reveals and establishes her moral insistence on the possibility of response: anyone can talk back, as it were, and the most responsible rhetorical and poetic stance is to abet that possibility. By emphasizing the imperfect character of her verse—those characteristics that distinguish it from traditional poetry, or the perfect(ed) literary icon—Moore seems to encourage readerly intervention or response, and hence a *structure* of freedom. Again, as J. G. A. Pocock suggests, because we do not initiate and cannot monopolize the language we use, we neither fully control its power nor prevent others from sharing it: "In performing a verbalized act of power, I enter upon a polity of shared power"—even if that power is shared unequally, and against the will of the institutionally more empowered speaker ("Verbalizing a Political Act," 31).

Using this vocabulary, one could say that "Silence" quotes a father performing an act of power upon his daughter, in a way that presupposes her silent, or restrained, obedience. The daughter responds however by repeating this father's words at length, in a new performative act that undermines, if it does not transform, the power structure assumed. She changes the father's pronouncement—which apparently was intended to prevent the freedom of a two-way process of communication—into an opportunity for response. Moreover, her statement implies that now *he* is the one incapable of response: one of the few nonquoted lines reads, "my father *used* to say"—suggesting that he can no longer repeat this behavior (emphasis mine). She manipulates the father's words so as to structure a "polity of shared power" rather than a relationship of "power over."

That she does not simply reverse the situation so that she now assumes "power over" the father is revealed, as Altieri implies, by the fact that her response does not voice simple resistance: she accepts the father's words and his concept of restraint. What she rejects is his elitist and controlling uses of language which assume that behavioral "superiority" and all other power relationships are stable—hence that response can be prevented. And by rejecting his concept of language even while using every one of his words, she suggests that response to her own speech-act is welcome. The poem offers a concise paradigm for feminist analysis of any daughter's relationship to patriarchal or phallic language.

More to the point of my discussion of quotation, however, is the poet Moore's use of the daughter's quotation of the father—which again constitutes a separate speech-act and performance of power from either the father's or the daughter's. By structuring this poem as a monologue, without dramatic context, Moore implies that it addresses a general audience. And in this context, the poem's text at first seems to function analogously to the father's words: as an unexplained directive to the reader about how "superior people" act, or read poems. The politics of the daughter's speech-act within the poem and of Moore's poetry generally, however, suggest a more complex relationship. Again language theory may be useful. In *The Poem as Utterance*, R. A. York hypothesizes that a poem may "re-verse[ ] the usual polarity of language, in which presupposition . . . act[s] as an inconspicuous background for a dynamic speech act" by instead making the reader work to understand not just the content of its words but the conditions of the utterance, the presuppositions, that make them appropriate.[35] In "Silence," Moore indeed leaves the conditions for both the fictionalized utterance (the daughter's to the father) and the poetic utterance (hers to the reader) a matter of interpretation—that is, she constructs the poem as a speech-act that functions as the opposite of a command.

Pocock refers to the *inherent* uncontrollability of language. Annotated quotation provides a stunning instance of Moore's more radical because *chosen* relinquishment of the claim to originary control of her words: here, the poet doubly documents (through quotation marks and through notes) that she borrows from others.[36] Moore, in such a reading, functions simultaneously as father and daughter—as she perhaps does in all her quoting. As poet, she is structurally the father—even as woman—and therefore, as I have argued, resorts to a variety of formal strategies and themes to undermine that structure of (patriarchal) authorial authority. Through that undermining, she is also structurally the daughter, debunking the notions that any text is "superior" to others (using quotation to place overheard speech on the same level as literature) and that any speech-act unilaterally prevents the possibility of response or alternative political structuring—including her later revisions of her own words.[37] As daughter, the poet marks the uncontrollability of language that has allowed her own response. As discussed earlier, Moore indeed prefers the unlovely, the not fully controlled—the "mere childish attempt to make an imperfectly bal- / lasted animal stand up"; she has a "very special fondness for writing that is obscure, that does not quite succeed" (CP, 38; CPr, 435). Such imperfection—born of "ardor, of diligence, and of refusing to be false"—gives freedom of both expression and response (CPr, 437).

Moore's densest use of quotation appears in her poems of the twenties—for example, "Marriage," "An Octopus," "Novices," "Sea Unicorns and Land Unicorns"—and Patricia C. Willis provides the fullest examination of such density in her essay on "An Octopus." Although the mosaic of quotation in "An Octopus" bears little superficial resemblance to the epigrammatic utterance of "Silence," quotation functions similarly in these poems. In her Notes, Moore acknowledges quoting from a remark she overheard at the circus, the *Illustrated London News*, *London Graphic*, John Ruskin, and W. D. Wilcox's *The Rockies of Canada*. For the most part these sources are not individually relevant to the commentary of the poem, nor does the poem subvert the performance act constituted by the original statement of each source. Yet, as a whole, they reflect and enact the poem's praise for a mind that responds with passion to the "invigorating pleasures" of a "menagerie of styles."[38] To make this point—

and arguing characteristically from an obverse or negative portrayal of her own position—Moore devotes nearly a third of her poem to explaining why the (in many ways admirable) "Greeks" cannot appreciate such a menagerie:

> "Emotionally sensitive, their hearts were hard";
> their wisdom was remote
> from that of these odd oracles of cool official sarcasm,
> upon this game preserve
> where "guns, nets, seines, traps and explosives,
> hired vehicles, gambling and intoxicants are prohibited,
> disobedient persons being summarily removed
> and not allowed to return without permission in writing."
>
> (Obs, 88–89)

"The Greeks liked smoothness, distrusting what was back / of what could not be clearly seen," Moore comments wryly—suggesting, among other things, that they would not have liked her poem, with its far from "smooth" associative leaps, complex syntax, and lack of a transparent thematic center—or at first even subject, since the "octopus" of the title stands for a glacier on Mount Ranier. Moore rejects "smoothness," "benevolent conclusiveness," and classical (the cultural fathers') "wisdom" in favor of practical difficulties, a "capacity for fact," a landscape with "merits of equal importance" for a wide range of plants and animals, and the ostentatiously unliterary tones of "cool official sarcasm."

I do not mean to suggest that each instance of quotation in this poem (or any single one) directly criticizes Greek wisdom or patriarchy. Rather, the mosaic of quotation resembles the glacier's "menagerie of styles" which Moore calls "American" and which clearly resembles—if it does not in fact represent—her own style.[39]

> Instructed none knows how, to climb the mountain,
> by "business men who as totemic scenery of Canada,
> require for recreation,
> three hundred and sixty-five holidays in the year,["]
> these conspicuously spotted little horses are peculiar;

hard to discern among the birch trees, ferns, and lily pads,
avalanche lilies, Indian paintbrushes,
bears' ears and kittentails,
and miniature cavalcades of chlorophylless fungi
magnified in profile on the mossbeds like moonstones in the water;
the cavalcade of calico competing
with the original American "menagerie of styles"
among the white flowers of the rhodendron surmounting rigid
    leaves
upon which moisture works its alchemy,
transmuting verdure into onyx.

                                        (Obs, 86–87)

To the extent that this poem takes poetry as its subject, it claims as its chosen style the multivocal resonance emblematized by inter-mingled animal, bird, and natural noises and concretized textually by the several human voices explicitly differentiated through quotation marks: that is, Moore constructs what she then circularly labels "original[ly] American," making her verse appear to follow in a tradition that it has created. Also, as in "Silence," the lack of "smoothness" of this verse, the "clumsi[ness]" she attributes to her own naming (while marking its American background as typified by "Neatness of finish!" and "Relentless accuracy") again opens acknowledged space for critical intervention and exploration. By beginning the concluding sentence with a question—"Is tree the word for these strange things / 'flat on the ground like vines';"—Moore even requests such response. And it is possible on many levels: one might visit Mount Ranier and compare her observations with one's own; or read the multiple sources the poet has cited and alluded to, comparing her performance of this material and their directions as acts of power with those of the original authors; or weigh the multiple voices of the poem against each other to determine the acts of power among them, if in fact there is a controlling voice in the poem rather than the claimed egalitarian menagerie; or write back—quoting selectively from Moore's poem as she quotes from the work of others.

A very late poem, "'Reminiscent of a Wave at the Curl,'" reflects yet another use of quotation:

On a kind of Christmas Day—
big flakes blurring everything—
cat-power matching momentum,
each kitten having capsized the other,
      one kitten fell;
the other's hind leg planted hard
on the eye that had guided the onslaught—
ears laid back, both tails lashing—
a cynic might have said,
"Sir Francis Bacon defined it:
'Foreign war is like the heat of exercise;
civil war is like the heat of a fever.'"

Not at all. The expert would say,
      "Rather hard on the fur."
               (1969; CP, 244)

The poem's sole Note reads "Kittens owned by Mr. and Mrs. Richard Thoma." The poem begins with a quotation in its title and then quotes what two fictional sources—"a cynic" and "the expert"—might have said about the kitten's fall. Especially since the conversation is imagined, it is not clear why Moore presents anything but the lines from Bacon as quoted; indeed, the poem was first published as "Like a Wave at the Curl"—without marked quotation in the title. Such marking does, however, call attention to differences among the poem's voices. While the title and the cynic use a distancing formal diction and do not refer directly to kittens, the final speaker's dry colloquialism is utterly practical. "The expert" reminds the reader that the poem does not deal with the sea, Christmas, heroism, or war of any kind, but—cats. Similarly, and although the other voices may be more interesting as well as more elegant than the expert's remark about fur, by labeling this speaker "*the* expert," Moore highlights the value of his or her pragmatic response.

187

This poem blurs the boundaries between quotation and dialogue. As Elizabeth Gregory notes, because quotation marks serve to indicate both quotation and dialogue, all of Moore's quotation has the effect of dialogue (unpublished manuscript). The number of voices involved in such dialogue, however, may far exceed two: for example, in this poem one hears the speaker, the cynic, Bacon, the expert, and perhaps also the poet. In contrast to the implied dialogue of "Silence," the power relationships among these voices are not clear. While Bacon's words are the most eloquent and canonical, hence doubly authoritative, the speaker's deflating "Not at all" and the structure that gives the expert the last word apparently equalize their value. The point here may be, then, not to read the poem as any kind of "battle"—between kittens, levels of speech, or observers— but to respond to all situations with appropriateness: kitten play is "hard on the fur." Their activity is "'Reminiscent of a Wave at the Curl'"—something the title encourages us to *remember*, not just regard as a poetic trope; the kittens and their observers have reached a peak from which they fall, not as heroes or in tragedy, but just so—like a wave—only to rise, or play, or disagree again. By indicating in her note that these kittens do not belong to her, the poet may also be saying that she is not "the expert" on their behavior; but then none of the voices in the poem may be hers. Hers is the dialogic meta-voice, the combined describing, witnessing, and disagreeing structured in the poem, and hence both the most authoritative position and no position at all.

The contrast of Bacon's elegant and the expert's pragmatic speech in this poem encapsulates the general effect of Moore's quotation to undermine hierarchical distinctions between different kinds of voice. In particular, her annotated quotation may reject the distinction between "idle talk" and a "profound" language of high philosophical or poetically intuitive understanding. According to Patricia Meyer Spacks's *Gossip*, both Heidegger and Kierkegaard focus on subject matter or content in their analysis of language, and hence understand abundant talk, especially that concerned with mundane matters (a kitten playing—as opposed to war), to be at best trivial and at worst obstructive to real understanding. Spacks, in contrast, argues that gossip uses superficial content to establish or extend "a form of intimate relationship"—that is, it uses language as a means for interaction rather than as significant because of what is said.[40] This "serious" use of gossip

> provides a resource for the subordinated . . . a crucial means of self-expression, a crucial form of solidarity . . . the relationship [it] expresses and sustains matters more than the information it promulgates; and in the sustaining of that relationship, interpretation counts more than the facts or pseudo-facts on which it works. (5–6)

Gossip epitomizes what speech-act theory attributes only to illocutionary language, functioning as a kind of meta-illocutionary performance, indefinitely extendable and varied.[41]

Moore's quotation of conversation, advertisement, and other casual, non-elite language structurally resembles Spacks's serious gossip: such language seems more significant structurally (as quoted material) than literally within the poem.[42] Through such practice, Moore represents her poetic act as a borrowing of ideas, a process through which the poem emerges as the result of multiple contributions rather than because of any individual's wisdom or genius. That this is in part a fiction does not reduce its importance. And such interaction is not entirely fictitious; Moore does rely on other people's phrasing and information. More important than its truth value, however, is that this partial fiction promotes a concept of poet as crafter rather than artist; she selects and arranges rather than creating from whole cloth. For Moore these are worthy activities. In 1927, she wrote of "the *science* of assorting and the *art* of investing an assortment with dignity," concluding that "the selective nomenclature—the chameleon's eye if we may call it so—of the connoisseur, expresses a genius for differences" or "analogous dissimilarities" (CPr, 182, 183; emphasis mine). As Linda Leavell mentions, Moore also underlined the following sentence in an article about Alfred Stieglitz: "The esthetic basis of all art is selection" (*Prismatic Color*, 125). As artist and scientist, she selects "analogous dissimilarities" to construct a poem, calling attention structurally to the rich and multiple sources of her materials but nonetheless revealing the "distinct unity . . . of the mind which brought the assembled integers together" (CPr, 183). Quotation for Moore is a metapoetic act, calling attention to itself as a process of selection, as the basis of an egalitarian yet discriminating poetic.[43]

Moore's art might be said to resemble gossip, then, not in using colloquial rhythms, not in its subject matter, but in considering nothing too trivial to be grist for its mill and in valuing the *process* of interaction represented by the speech-act of the poem, and initiated by the quoted speech-acts to which the poem responds, equally with the poem as icon or significant performance in itself.[44] Slatin suggests, and Darlene Erickson develops, a similar metaphor for such annotated quotation—namely that of "the female ritual of visiting" (SR, 154; *Illusion is More Precise than Precision,* chap. 3). Tess Gallagher refers to Moore's "team spirit"; "she preferred the responsibility of conversation to the responsibility of an orator."[45] Again, Moore's verse that includes quotation is metapoetic. It constitutes speech-act as performance; it is an *ironized* authorial act of power toward, and attempting to include, its audience. Moore translates one of La Fontaine's *Fables* as beginning, "Only use gives possession"; through her use of others' words she demonstrates her possession/power over them while at the same time offering them to us for both use and possession (but only possession if also "use"). All the words of Moore's poems are *hers* but only in the shared ritual or fiction with which we say "my" guest or "my" visitor, that is, by which we claim presence as (temporary and partial) ownership.

I would like, finally, to argue that there may be a sociolinguistic and cultural-biographical basis to Moore's sense of her poetry as a broadly (not just mother-daughter or familial) collaborative process, as well as the metapoetic one explored above.[46] According to a variety of empirical studies, the use of apparently trivial conversational exchange as a way of developing or maintaining intimacy in a relationship (sometimes denigrated as "gossip") is typically more characteristic of women than of men and particularly characterizes exchanges between or among women.[47] These studies indicate that conversational exchange among all-male groups tends to involve turn-taking: one man has the floor and keeps it competitively through linguistic or humorous display until he has finished or another takes the floor and maintains his turn. Interruptions are ignored or taken as a sign of the interrupter's lack of interest in or competition with the speaker's performance. Conversation among women, in contrast, tends to have less distinct turn-taking and greater numbers of interruptions, some of which may redirect the topic under discussion—with the assumption commonly held that no one speaker is in control or should determine the discussion's course. Clearly, women's speech-acts, like men's, constitute acts of power toward or over others, and women, like men, are at times competitive, manipulative, and hostile in their speech. Nonetheless, they seem—at least in some instances, and among themselves—to practice a kind of speech-interaction suggestive of the bricolage or mosaic structures of a Moore poem, and culturally reflecting the emphatically interactional focus of gossip. Moore's inclusion of multiple voices to explore a line of thought through the fiction of a process of exchange rather than through the reasoned pursuit of a controlling authorial voice may be seen as a more culturally feminine than masculine mode.

Empirical research on the *apprehension* of women's language suggests that Moore's verse also utilizes both extremes of language popularly stereotyped as female: silence and excess. Here I distinguish between how empirical studies indicate women speak and what people attribute to them because of cultural constructions of how "women" speak.[48] Certainly other Moore critics see this paradox in Moore's language use and link it to gender. For example, Bonnie Costello in writing of Moore's "feminine" language states that "once natural reticence gives way to speech it paradoxically causes an overflow of words" ("'Feminine' Language," 96). As Costello quotes, Geoffrey Hartman too comments that "While [Moore's] message eludes us through understatement, the poem itself remains teasingly alive through the overstatement of its many tactics" (97).[49] Like women generally, Moore is perceived as saying both too little and too much to be easily comprehensible. Yet clearly neither her "omissions" nor her excesses "are accidents."

I am suggesting, then, that Moore's use of quotation in particular and other aspects of language generally may be linked culturally and through their metapoetics to modes of communication typically regarded as feminine in American culture. Moore does not write a

191

women's language, does not address her poems to women (as a rule), and would have had no use for the concept of an *écriture féminine*. However, she is demonstrably conscious of gender constructions and alert to the power of language as speech-act. Moreover, Moore may be aware that a kind of communication typical of the female community in which she has taken an active part at least since her years at Bryn Mawr provides an alternative to the autonomous, authorial poetic stance she consistently rejects. Moore constructs what she regards as an ungendered poetic by combining experimentation with formal poetic structures traditionally denominated as masculine (meter, rhyme, intertextual literary allusion) and experimentation with traditionally nonpoetic, culturally "feminine" aspects of language use (substitution of multivocality for an authoritative voice; inclusion of trivial, apparently irrelevant, information; excessive detail and excessive restraint; overemphasis on the mundane through marked quotations from the private sphere; and a didactic tone without accompanying transparent clarity). Moore does not construct a "female" poetic nor an idealization of women. This is where the importance of the other side of the tension in her work becomes crucial: through her quotation, Moore calls attention to dependence, her "hybrid" method of composition, but also to the written, constructed, powerful, and singular elements of her poetry. She knows that no one else writes like this, and that she is in control of the shape of the poem, no matter how many voices go into making it—all the while insisting that the language is not (only) hers, that only "use gives possession."

On the biographical side, Moore's transformative four years at Bryn Mawr and her experience of working among a vital, anomalous, and phenomenal group of female poets and editors during the late 1910s and 1920s (as well as within the larger, extremely lively shared male and female modernist circles in New York City) may have established for her a concept of poetic community that lingered long after this community itself dissolved.[50] William Drake somewhat idealistically describes the women poets first publishing between 1910 and 1925 as having a different general conception of their careers and of the act of writing than their male contemporaries did: "To a far greater extent than men, women perceived the arts in the context of community, of education, uplift, and personal fulfillment"; not altogether consciously and despite enormous political and aesthetic disagreements among them, he argues, they saw themselves as a group.[51]

Moore's later support of Elizabeth Bishop—from encouraging her, to making (sometimes misguided) editorial suggestions on drafts of particular poems, to reviewing, promoting, and even offering to type her manuscripts—is well known.[52] Less well known is that Moore offered advice, encouragement, and practical assistance to several other younger women, and to her peers.[53] For example, among countless small acts of assistance and encouragement, she reviewed and promoted the work of Bryher and H.D.; typed manuscripts for Lola Ridge; and polished and edited the memoirs of the sculptor Malvina Hoffman.[54] Moore unarguably benefited from this community as well. She owed the publication of her first book of poems to the financial support and editorial efforts of H.D. and Bryher, and Bryher assisted in her later publication of The Pangolin. Katherine Jones helped Moore with her (never published) novel during the 1940s and later with her translation of La Fontaine—as did Hoffman; Louise Crane performed secretarial duties for Moore briefly during the 1950s; and several writers and friends offered encouragement through reviews and private letters.[55] As Moore writes to Alyse Gregory, and similarly to other friends, "Your chivalry to my [poem] stirs me to the soul. I can scarcely trust that news that somebody likes my 'poems,' but your kindness to them and your suggesting that I go on has had a part in keeping me alert and in my dashing into print again" (October 17, 1932; RML V.23.05). An early draft of her important essay "Humility, Concentration, and Gusto" suggests that Moore even considered introducing her own poetic principles by reference to other women's work: "It is a misuse of opportunity, it seems to me, to be discussing principles of PERSUASION when persuasiveness is objectified on all sides, in the current exhibition of Amer. Women Writers" (RML II.2.26).

Throughout her life but especially after moving to Brooklyn in 1929, Moore also maintained an extraordinarily active and broad correspondence, including among her regular correspondents the poets and writers H.D., Bryher, Bishop, Edith Sitwell, and Alyse

Gregory, as well as women active in music and the visual or plastic arts—for example, Watson (a concert pianist), Crane (an important patron of music), and Hoffman (a sculptor).[56] Perhaps most remarkable, however, is the number of intensely devoted correspondences she carries on for decades—with Watson, Crane, and Jones (and, later, Marcia Chamberlain)—as well as deeply affectionate ones with H.D., Bryher, Bishop, Gregory, Hoffman, and Frances Brown (to mention her female correspondents only). Moore's life in her later years is as full of the responsibilities and sharing of intense friendship as of literary activity and production. For example, not only does she nurse sick and dying friends (her mother, Mary Norcross, Marcia Chamberlain), but she travels with college friends Frances and Norvelle Brown (with whom she maintained contact since her graduation from Bryn Mawr in 1909) to Italy and Greece in 1962, to England and Ireland in 1964, and to Florida in 1965; she spends summers with Jones and Chamberlain, and later with Hoffman, in Maine; sends frequent small gifts to several friends; and makes a continual "effort to please" through letter writing.

In the only serious critical work so far on this topic, Cyrena Pondrom insightfully describes the importance of the female culture of exchange—as emblematized by gift-giving—to Moore's career, and particularly as it influences the pattern of correspondence between Moore, H.D., and Bryher preceding and following their publication of Moore's *Poems*. According to Pondrom's analysis, it is quite typical of such exchanges that Moore first encourages and then allows a gift (like *Poems*) to be given, but shows only disbelief when it finally appears.[57] Later, Moore gave similar "gifts"—particularly during the war years when she helped H.D. correspond with Bryher (who was in Europe working with the Jewish underground) and when she helped H.D. publish in the States. Both practically and morally, as Pondrom writes, "For a lifetime, each had assured the other that she was not alone in her uncompromising effort to articulate a woman's vision of form and experience." Moore writes to H.D. in 1956, "A blessing is it not, that the mind has wings—that the page is the person. Could I live if it were not so?"[58]

It may also be that Moore turns with such determination to the project of translating La Fontaine's *Fables* during the final illness and after the death of her mother because it is by definition and necessity a collaborative one—both in the sense that the poet must work continuously with a predecessor text and in her frequent turning to French and translation "advisors," particularly Harry Levin at Harvard and Ezra Pound. Again, this is a position Moore seems to be comfortable with, and the process of such long-term collaborative work may have helped her over the transition of having to write poetry without the possibility of turning for immediate comment to her mother.[59] Similarly, Moore's translation of Maria Edgeworth's novel *The Absentees* into a play during the 1950s may have appealed to her because of the intertextuality of the project and the interactive immediacy of dramatic dialogue.

These issues may culminate in Moore's repeated choice of love as a topic in her later poetry, and I will conclude both this chapter and my discussion of Moore by turning to these late poems.[60] Moore devoted the primary energy of her approximately last fifteen years of writing verse to appreciation—perhaps because she found it appropriate to her public role, perhaps out of a broad gratefulness at having survived the grief over her mother's death and at signs that her world had survived a catastrophic war, and perhaps for more theoretical reasons.

Structurally, these poems constitute as radical a critique of one mode of lyric poetry as any of the more obviously rebellious constructions of her earlier years. In the interest of a poetic of exchange, one that establishes a "polity of shared power" through acknowledging its own imperfections rather than establishing a relationship of "power over," Moore writes a type of love poem that breaks the traditional mode in several ways. These poems do not idealize a beloved. In fact, they often use quotation to disrupt any clear distinction of lover from beloved, thereby also disrupting the traditional power differential between active speaker/lover and silent, subservient, passive beloved.[61] As in her other poems, Moore highlights qualities of imperfection and uncontrollability—both by including the expression of clearly unromantic irritation, grumpiness, and even diatribe and through the standard lack of smoothness in her form. Moreover, the lack of reference to heterosexual or even a two-person relationship suggests the extent to which she rewrites this genre. Moore constructs a love poem of "unannoying / romance" (CP, 131)—anticipated by her earlier portrait of Handel in "The Frigate Pelican" as an "impassioned" man who "never was known to have fallen in love" (1934; CP, 25). Moore's poems are not about being "in love" but about unsentimentalized loving.

Like "Voracities and Verities Sometimes are Interacting" (also published in 1947), "A Face" moves from highly Latinate diction and unexplained exasperation to a simple and moving declaration of love:

> "I am not treacherous, callous, jealous, superstitious,
> supercilious, venomous, or absolutely hideous":
> > studying and studying its expression,
> > exasperated desperation
> > > though at no real impasse,
> > > would gladly break the mirror;
>
> when love of order, ardor, uncircuitous simplicity
> with an expression of inquiry, are all one needs to be!
> > Certain faces, a few, one or two—or one
> > face photographed by recollection—
> > > to my mind, to my sight,
> > > must remain a delight.
>
> (1947; CP, 141)

In this poem, as in the other, Moore gives no clue as to the identity or gender of the beloved: the unannotated quotation portraying someone "studying and studying *its* expression" (my emphasis) does not belong clearly to any role, speaker, or gender (although the stereotype of women as obsessed with appearance might suggest female gender for either or both parties). A similar ambiguity characterizes the beginning of stanza 2, where the phrase "are all one needs to be!" is truncated: these are characteristics one needs—to be beautiful? loved? happy? human? or perhaps a poet? The poem plays, then, between two ambiguous sets of identities—the speaker's and that of the face (s)he loves, and the speaker's and the poet's. Although in a traditional love poem the (male) poet actively extols the charms of the (female, passive, inspiring) beloved, here it is not

196

clear who speaks, who is exasperated, who should be characterized by "love of order, ardor" and so on. The poem presents quoted but unclaimed—hence peculiarly both intimate and impersonal—insecurities about being lovable in the form of exasperation that knows itself to be "at no real impasse."

At the same time, the poem comments on itself. In definitely circuitous fashion, it claims that "uncircuitous simplicity," not beauty, makes itself loved—that is, it both debunks beauty as a basis for loving or praise (perhaps—as in "Roses Only"—both feminine and aesthetic beauty) and ostentatiously does not provide the "simplicity" it would substitute in beauty's place. The last lines of the poem, in contrast, begin evasively ("certain faces, a few, one or two—or one / face") but then state in clear, metered, rhymed verse, unquoted "delight"—at the same time using its rhyme to continue the ironic meta-commentary established earlier in the poem. The rhymes of the first stanza are all "feminine"—polysyllabic and unaccented—except for the final couplet: reference to "break[ing] the mirror" breaks the rhyme scheme. In the second stanza, the first two rhyme pairs link a monosyllabic function word with the least accented syllable of a polysyllabic word—creating "weak" rhymes ("simplicity"/"be" and "one"/"recollection"). The final couplet, in contrast, rhymes an aurally and semantically strong noun ("sight") with the accented syllable of a two-syllable noun ("delight")—thus for the first time in the poem approaching a "masculine" rhyme while the two syllables of "delight" keep it technically "feminine." Even the lovely cadence of the final statement that "one face / photographed by recollection—/ to my mind, to my sight / must remain a delight" may play on the traditional gendering of poetic form.[62]

"By Disposition of Angels" also deliberately obfuscates the gender and identity of its beloved. The poem's second and final stanza reads:

Star that does not ask me if I see it?
Fir that would not wish me to uproot it?
Speech that does not ask me if I hear it?
    Mysteries expound mysteries.

197

Steadier than steady, star dazzling me, live and elate,
   no need to say, how like some we have known; too like her,
   too like him, and a-quiver forever.

                             (1948; CP, 142)

This poem claims there is "no need to say" what it implies, and then fusses—"too like her, / too like him"—before returning to a brief (feminine) internal- and end-rhyming cadence (like her/a-quiver/forever). Containing six questions in its fourteen lines, "By Disposition of Angels" is cantankerous. The miraculousness of this beloved presence, however, lies in its steadfast self-sufficiency: unlike a demanding lover, this loved one remains "a-quiver forever"—perhaps even without the speaker's continued sight or hearing. Reference to "angels" and a "star" imply that the beloved is dead. But this person, or star, is nonetheless "live" and only "Mysteries expound" its "mystery"—that is, it is not fixed even in eternity. Moreover, as it is both "too like her" and "too like him," the star seems to represent "some" rather than a single one loved person. The authority of the speaker is balanced by the mystery and independence of those(?) the speaker loves.

"Efforts of Affection" (1948) is impatiently concise in listing examples of "love's extraordinary-ordinary stubbornness"—ranging from the story of Jubal and Jabal to La Fontaine's *Fables* to plants named for sentimental obsessions but far surpassing them in appeal. "How welcome," the speaker concludes:

vermin-proof and pilfer-proof integration
in which unself-righteousness humbles inspection.

"You know I'm not a saint!" Sainted obsession.
The bleeding-heart's—that strange rubber fern's attraction

puts perfume to shame.
Unsheared sprays of elephant-ears
do not make a selfish end look like a noble one.
Truly as the sun
can rot or mend, love can make one
bestial or make a beast a man.
    Thus wholeness—

wholesomeness? say efforts of affection—
attain integration too tough for infraction.
(CP, 147)

Love is praised here not because it is "perfumed" or "noble" or even ennobling (it is as likely to "make one / bestial" as perform the opposite transformation), but because its "efforts" finally "attain" a unit or community too "tough" to be violated. This poem does not identify such "efforts" with coupledom but with (a word Moore repeats) "integration." Especially with its abstraction and heavily Latinate diction, this reads like an anti-love poem. As Moore writes a few years later in "Armor's Undermining Modesty" (1950):

> No wonder we hate poetry,
> and stars and harps and the new moon. If tributes cannot
> be implicit,
>
> give me diatribes and the fragrance of iodine,
> the cork oak acorn grown in Spain;
> the pale-ale-eyed impersonal look
> which the sales-placard gives the bock beer buck.
>
> (CP, 151)

Moore writes about love with the "fragrance of iodine," providing thereby a poetry we do not need to "hate."

As the "bock beer buck" of "Armor's Undermining Modesty" anticipates, after the late 1940s Moore turns to nature and to the popular, ephemeral world epitomized by advertising for her subjects. "Apparition of Splendor" celebrates the porcupine; in "Then the Ermine" she is "charmed" by a bat—and in both these poems by the "Foiled explosiveness" of Dürer's art (CP, 158–161). Other poems praise public figures, or a combination of animals and people—for example, "Tom Fool at Jamaica," which attributes "submerged magnificence" to a race horse, jockey, and other "champions" (CP, 162–163); "The Staff of Aesculapius," in its heralding of what truly seem to be miracles of modern medicine—vaccines, surgery to cut back cancer, "lung resection," and so on (CP, 165); "Style" with its celebration of other "champion[s]"—a figure skater, a tennis player,

199

and a dancer (CP, 169); "Logic and 'The Magic Flute'" with its double praise of Mozart's opera and the "first telecolor-trove" (CP, 172); the baseball poems; the musician "Melchior Vulpius"; the open praise of "W.S. Landor," "Arthur Mitchell," "Rescue with Yul Brynner," and "The Arctic Ox (Or Goat)," which even calls itself "an advertisement" (CP, 195).

It is not that Moore ceases to be ironic, critical, acerbically witty in these poems, but that such tones do not dominate. In fact, in some poems they are relegated to the Notes—for example, in "The Staff of Aesculapius," Moore acknowledges the institutionalization brought about by modern medical practice and even "apologizes" for her own praise in the note: "Dr. Grace of Grace's Clinic, Brooklyn, deplores the need for hospitals and says that I imply it, but the intervention of hospital service for myself and others I cherish, in need of trained skill, apologizes for my allegiance" (CP, 287). Similarly, "Tom Fool at Jamaica" presents two texts of parallel material—the poem's one and a half pages and then three and a half pages of notes, including the following: a drawing given to Moore by Louise Crane, made by a six-year-old and sold at a benefit for Republican Spain; a poem by the French poet Madame Boufflers; Moore's deploring of gambling and admission that she "had never seen a race" in the context of three newspaper articles about horse-racing; and a series of brief notes on black musicians. Reading the notes as part of the poem, as part of the conversation or collaboration that results in the poetic text and hence as necessary to understanding its presuppositions, demands that we discover the "analagous dis-similarities" between gratitude for a gift, opposition to fascism, reference to a predecessor woman poet, black musicians, and a "champion" race horse as described by sports writers and his jockey.

"For February 14th" literally enacts ongoing conversation: as its single note reveals, Moore quotes in the first stanza from a poem written for her by Marguerite Harris:[63]

> Saint Valentine,
> although late, would "some interested law
> impelled to plod in the poem's cause"
> be permitted a line?

This poem concludes by debunking the gift-giving gratitude of the poem's middle three stanzas with an impatient exclamation and a question:

> But questioning is the mark
>
> of a pest! Why think
> only of animals in connection
> with the ark or the wine Noah drank?
> but that the ark did not sink.
>   (1959; CP, 198)

Beginning with the offer of culturally commodified, exoticized gifts—each a memorial to colonization in some form ("Might you have liked a stone / from a De Beers Consolidated [diamond] Mine?" a "saber-thronged thistle / of Palestine . . .?" a vine called "'alexander's armillary / sphere' . . .?" a bird preserved by the ark so its "descendants might serve as presents?"), Moore turns instead to a cause for gratitude so broad it cannot be represented by a commodity: "that the ark did not sink"; that we are alive; that the world has survived (yet another) catastrophe. Perhaps a love poem to the world more than to Marguerite Harris or any other "Saint Valentine," this poem leaves all critique of colonization, commodification, and militarism unspoken. It may be that, as in "By Disposition of Angels," Moore believes there is "no need to say" such things because they are so obviously true, and she has already said them. Or it may be that she does not even imply serious criticism. The turn at the end of this poem resembles that of "Marriage" to Daniel Webster, or of "Virginia Britannia" to the sunset, or of "To a Steam Roller" to butterflies—but the basis for serious critique is better developed in those poems before the turn to a relatively affirmative ending than in this late poem.

While it is obvious why critics would focus on the appreciative mode of so many of Moore's last poems, if one reads them as continuous with her early work in constructing a critique of the traditional lyric (here the love poem), a different conclusion comes to the fore. Poems celebrating love, grace, technological advancement, skill in popular sports, music and other arts, patriotic occasions and traditional holidays are community-building. Their negatives ("'I am not treacherous . . .'", "though at no real impasse," "'You know I am not a Saint!'", "No wonder we hate poetry," "that the ark did not sink") emphasize a lack of distinguishing difference, or "integration" and survival. That the negatives continue is significant. The world has not changed, nor has Moore's astute assessment of it. Yet given the forces arrayed against the possibility of enduring mutual affection (mortality, war, illness, responsibilities to work, and the fact that even in the best of times affection requires continuous "effort"), it is not unreasonable that Moore in her older age seeks to stress simply that the possibility exists—that the cup is half full instead of half empty, that "the ark did not sink," that the mind is "not a Herod's oath that cannot change," that although history may repeat itself, or discover even more unimaginable horrors, it will not necessarily do so. As Moore writes in "Love in America—," at the age of seventy-nine, "It's a Midas of tenderness; / from the heart . . . identifying itself with / pioneer unperfunctoriness // without brazenness or / bigness of overgrown / undergrown shallowness." This poet of emphatic and repeated negatives ends one of her last poems with a negative construction underlined by affirmation:

Whatever it is, let it be without
    affectation.

Yes, yes, yes, *yes*.
                    (CP, 240)

Moore was a phenomenally productive and successful poet throughout a century in which that role, for a woman, was constantly embattled. She created for herself a poetic stance, a public style, and a personal life that enabled her to write poetry and pursue a markedly independent and vital career for almost sixty years. This poetic stance, moreover, reflected and enabled her moral and tactical "humility" as well as her clearly felt authority to speak in public. That she spoke differently at various times only appears obvious in the context of even a rudimentary history of the almost ninety years through which she lived. And that she spoke with a self-confidence as woman and poet that is just beginning to be understood is also not surprising, given that the educational advantages and sense of thriving female community in the professional world that she enjoyed during her youth have only recently been reestablished (this time on a broader basis) in the United States; similarly, only recently has a substantial body of theory and criticism appeared that is devoted to understanding the historical, material, and psychological contexts affecting women writers. That Moore's poetry will become increasingly important to this theory and criticism seems to me inevitable, given the brilliance of her production and its profound structural concern with issues of gender, race, and other forms of social hierarchy.

SEVEN

Questioning Authority in the
Late Twentieth Century

In my book
inclusions are not accidents

Alice Fulton

$\mathcal{M}$y reading of Moore in the preceding chapters maps the patterns I see developed during the six decades in which she wrote poetry. In this chapter, I use that reading to mark similar patterns in other personal and impersonal, didactic and pluralistic, experimental, nonhierarchical, multivocal bodies of poetry. My use of Moore's work as a touchstone for the poetry of more recent female poets does not constitute a "tradition" or line of influence among women writing poetry; some of the poets I discuss, for example, have been far more obviously influenced by male predecessors and peers—or by other female poets—than by Moore. Neither does it reflect my sense of which poets have been most important to the development of poetry in this century, or which ones most resemble Moore in their thematic choices or in singular elements of style. Instead, I want to indicate through a series of brief sketches the extent to which concerns that are central to Moore's poetic recur in the works of other women writing in this century. In doing so, I will highlight convergences between Moore's poetry and that of other poets both to illuminate the projects of those later poets and to underscore the usefulness of Moore's career and poetic for understanding more recent poetry.[1] To give as full a sense of the range of that usefulness as possible, I have chosen to discuss poets of various generations, personal backgrounds, and political and sexual orientation, as well as poets who have made differing uses of traditional poetic forms. These discussions, in turn, show different degrees and kinds of convergence with Moore's poetic and poetry.

Moore's work strikingly resembles that of other modernists in much of its experimentation, and even in some of the peculiarities of its form. However, Moore also clearly departs from earlier poetic models in her authoritatively impersonal yet personally grounded poetic, her acknowledgment of both the necessity and the limits of personal perspective. As explored at length earlier, Moore's extensive use of quotation to create a multivocal yet ostentatiously constructed poetic base and her combination of scientific fact and abstraction with idiosyncratic and illocutionary effects reveal and develop this aspect of her poetic. Her insistence that achievement, ethical behavior, personal worth, and historical importance be judged unprejudicially, in conscious opposition to racist and masculist hierarchizing—an insistence she constructs through style and through explicit and implied subject matter or theme—also contributes to this anti-authoritarian poetic base. Such insistence is key to Moore's feminism (as defined by her world and context)—as is her departure from what she understands as the poet's masculist egotism. The result is a poetic that radically restructures aesthetic values— promoting pragmatic, obviously imperfect rather than inspired or iconic form; idiosyncratic and exuberant pronouncement in a verse without a characterized or even gendered speaker; and an openly invitational, albeit challenging, rather than a mastering relationship to the reader. Moore constructs a new kind of lyric poem.

As a key element of this construction, Moore strikingly undercuts the high seriousness or sublimity associated with romantic vision and witness, and with poetic genius more generally. While poems like "An Octopus" and "Virginia Britannia" evoke an awesome, powerful beauty in nature that supersedes the human, the dominant note even in these poems, and throughout her poetry, is what Marie Borroff has called "solemnity-retardant."[2] Her mixed scientific and colloquial diction, repeated assertive and self-corrective illocutionary effects, and the comic effect of her metonymic tendency to describe all things as though they are made up or partake of elements utterly distinct from themselves (remember the highly praised jerboa, which resembles Jacob, a flute, a bird, a chipmunk, sand, something that rolls on wheel castors, and a chair!)—all these and other effects of her verse combine to inhibit solemnity and undercut the notion that either nature or human perception is sublime. In a statement that perfectly underscores the principles of her poetic, she concludes the early poem "Dock Rats" by exclaiming that "shipping is the / most interesting thing in the world"—not magnificent or leading to any kind of transcendence but "interesting," the focus of her "inquisitive intensity."[3] These qualities of ethically powerful but also witty anti-solemnity, and this movement toward an oppositional, indirectly politicized, and feminist authority, are central to Moore's verse. These same qualities, variously articulated, reappear among later twentieth-century poets who explore questions of authority similar to Moore's.

More than a century of popular feminist movements, nearly three decades of widely distributed feminist poetry, theory, and literary criticism, and several decades of widespread civil rights activism have politicized self-representation and language use in ways that make a higher level of articulate self-consciousness than Moore's about such issues nearly inevitable. The formulations for conceiving of identity, and hence of authority, particularly in its sexual aspects, have changed dramatically since the formative years of Moore's youth. As I have argued, however, Moore avoids the language of sexual identity and desire in response to the conventions of an earlier discourse and to her political determination to center her poems outside a singular, concrete self, rather than from prudery or lack of interest; consequently, Moore's poetry may be politically and aesthetically analogous to poetry that appears quite different from it. In differing ways and degrees, widely diverse poets such as Gwendolyn Brooks, Adrienne Rich, Heather McHugh, Cynthia Macdonald, Susan Howe, M. Nourbese Philip, and Alice Fulton share with Moore the conviction that gender, race, class, sexuality, and other aspects of identity (as currently defined in social discourse) have powerful historical roots and pragmatic effects, yet are nonetheless fundamentally arbitrary. Like Moore, these poets seek to undermine the structures supporting the stereotypes of such social constructions—including gender-inflected categorizations of poet and reader—with the relations of mastery they imply. These poets emphasize the possibility of nonhierarchical but also nonsimplified relationships between a writer who is a woman, poetic tradition(s), and readers.

In her own time, Moore's work resonates most closely with that of Mina Loy (1882–1966)—another of the poets (like Lola Ridge) associated with the *Others* group.[4] These resonances are persuasively outlined by Carolyn Burke in "Getting Spliced: Modernism and Sexual Difference" and by Rachel Blau DuPlessis in "'Corpses of Poesy': Some Modern Poets and Some Gender Ideologies of Lyric."[5] As Ezra Pound noted in 1918 in a joint notice of these two women's poetry, Loy—like Moore—writes a markedly metalinguistic and intertextual poetry. Pound, in fact—as Burke demonstrates—used his analysis of the poetry of Moore and Loy to develop the concept of "logopoeia," a concept that became critical to the development of his own poetic and of masculist modernism. Burke argues, however, that Loy's and Moore's poems contain not just what Pound called a "poetry that is akin to nothing but language, which is a dance of the intelligence among words and ideas" but a poetry of gendered awareness and radical decentering of authorial perspective ("Getting Spliced," 99, 116). Loy, for example, writes of the moon in "Lunar Baedeker" as "Pocked with personification / the fossil virgin of the skies"—a formulation as evocative and challenging as it is humorous.[6] Like Moore's rose in "Roses Only," Loy's moon reveals that human perception has long been both gendered and ideological. More generally, Loy's disjunctive syntax, quick juxtaposition of historical and cultural allusions and contexts, and multiple perspectives create the same kind of decentered authority as Moore's. For example, the first section of "Love Songs to Joannes" begins and ends with:

Spawn of Fantasies
Silting the appraisable
Pig Cupid
His rosy snout
Rooting erotic garbage

"Once upon a time"
Pulls a weed

. . . . .

I must live in my lantern
Trimming subliminal flicker
Virginal   to the bellows
Of Experience
    Coloured glass[7]

With satiric humor, a sharp critique of gendered power structures, shifting representations of a poem's speaker, and a dense poetic surface, Loy's poetic provides a significant companion to Moore's, making more obvious the political features of her verse.

Lorine Niedecker (1905–1970) constructs a poetic voice so spare that it approaches the impersonal qualities of Moore's, even while foregrounding its lyric "I." Niedecker in fact refers to herself in a 1965 letter to Cid Corman as "a weak sister of Marianne Moore"; she continues, "I appreciate, I don't criticize, and I quote like she does but all without her acumen," and in other letters she refers to Moore with interest and admiration.[8] There is also a highly compressed pragmatism in Niedecker's work that makes the surface of her poetry dense and wry, like Moore's. For example, the sequence "Lake Superior" begins:

In every part of every living thing
is stuff that once was rock

In blood the minerals
of the rock

Iron the common element of earth
in rocks and freighters

Sault Sainte Marie—big boats
coal-black and iron-ore-red
topped with what white castlework

The waters working together
    internationally
Gulls playing both sides

Radisson:
'a laborinth of pleasure'
this world of the Lake

Long hair, long gun

Fingernails pulled out
by Mohawks[9]

Like Loy and Moore, Niedecker writes an unbeautiful poetry, a verse that calls attention to its rough edges, its idiosyncrasy, its (typically understated) gendered perception that shifts the balance of what is noted, rhymed, juxtaposed. Like Moore, Niedecker indicates how others neither present, nor often remembered (in the poem above, for example, Pierre Radisson—a French-Canadian explorer—and the Mohawks) shape the landscape of her own perception and poem. On the other hand, Niedecker more often writes a poetry that circles around experiences which may be identified with the poet herself than Moore does, and her poetic line has much closer affinities to Zukofsky's radical juxtapositions than to Moore's prosaic inclusiveness.

While several African American women writing poetry during the Harlem Renaissance share certain aesthetic, political, and social concerns with Moore, Gwendolyn Brooks (1917–) is the first to engage in a poetic that resembles hers. From her earliest publication on, Brooks's verse links modernist formal experimentation to Harlem Renaissance experimentation with the looser forms of the blues and of black vernacular. As a consequence, Brooks's voice—like Moore's—balances strikingly between speech-like and abstract, obviously constructed forms.[10] Similarly, Brooks addresses a wide range of philosophical and social concerns while rejecting categorical distinctions and binary understandings of identity, morality, or people's lives. For example, her modified sonnet sequence "Gay Chaps at the Bar" understatedly announces that its primary topic is the particular experience of black men in World War II ("we" "Knew white speech," she writes in the first poem), but several of the poems take more general themes—a lust for faith ("the full jewel wile of mighty light"), relationships with those who have already died ("For

I am rightful fellow of their band. / My best allegiances are to the dead"), loss of the capacity for simple pleasures, and how "identity" is maintained in the face of mass action and death. Moreover, two of these poems may not speak in male voice at all: "looking," in which "you" ponder what words or act to give a soldier as he leaves, and "love note / I: surely," which might belong to either a soldier or his lover. "Gay Chaps at the Bar," like the later sequence "In the Mecca" (1968) and to some extent like all Brooks's volumes of poetry, is a multivoiced work, a poem that integrates the concerns of several speakers and perspectives. Brooks speaks with authority in her verse, with directness, judgment, and moral force, but the source of that authority is oblique, dispersed amid a community and among several elements and voices.[11]

Alliteration, rhyme, word play, fragmentation of phrases, metaphorical exuberance, and shifting metrical and rhythmic patterns provide the tonal backdrop for Brooks's unusual combination of philosophical formulations with concrete description and the dramas of daily urban life involving racism, poverty, sexism, and war. This combination takes extraordinary form, for example, in "The Sundays of Satin-Legs Smith," where Brooks describes with Moore-like detail Satin-Legs' clothing and the complex cultural forces that shape his life. The poem begins very formally and in the abstract—"Inamoratas, with an approbation, / Bestowed his title. Blessed his inclination"—but moves quickly to "cabbage and pigtails":

> Down these sore avenues
> Comes no Saint-Saëns, no piquant elusive Grieg,
> And not Tschaikovsky's wayward eloquence
> And not the shapely tender drift of Brahms.
> But could he love them? Since a man must bring
> To music what his mother spanked him for
> When he was two: bits of forgotten hate,
> Devotion: whether or not his mattress hurts:
> The little dream his father humored: the thing
> His sister did for money: what he ate
> For breakfast—and for dinner twenty years
> Ago last autumn: all his skipped desserts.
> (*Blacks*, 45–46)

The poem moves in and out of rhyme, in and out of Latinate or poetic diction and reference ("the shapely tender drift of Brahms" in contrast to his sister's implied prostitution), and in and out of direct address to a reader and conventional grammar—note, for example, the repeated colons, as though each item stems grammatically from what precedes it in a domino effect echoing her theme. In the ambitious longer sequence *Annie Allen*, Brooks similarly marks her links with and difference from high art and cultural traditions of greatness, particularly in "The Anniad" (*Blacks*, 97–112), which uses its title parodically to underline the discrepancies between a daydreaming black girl's development into disillusioned womanhood and the adventures of heroes in the *Aeneid* and *Iliad*.

Brooks, like Moore, reveals and thematizes her identity and experiences without essentializing them or depending on them for the authority of her own presentation. Not until the late 1960s does she turn to a black nationalist style and a specifically black aesthetic ideology—and even here the focus is not on herself as black poet.[12] Similarly, although women have been central subjects of Brooks's poems from her earliest publications, she makes no claims to an authority of female experience. Brooks's poetry is more apt to tell a story, stems more obviously from a particular community, and is more centered in the perspective of a dramatized speaker or character than Moore's. Yet it strongly resembles Moore's in its borrowing from but also structural critique of the implications of conventional poetic form (remarkable, for example, in "The Mother"), its shifting authorial or speaking presence, and its combination of abstract vocabulary with a generous inclusion of pragmatic and colloquial detail. In short, Brooks, like Moore, writes a poetry of highly constructed oppositionality.[13]

Far more than Niedecker or any of the poets I discuss here, Elizabeth Bishop (1911–1979) openly acknowledged Moore's influence, and critics of both poets accept that influence as a given. In recent years, however, her poetry has increasingly been read as manifesting, albeit in restrained form, a personally revelatory poetic in direct contrast to Moore's. Despite her own complaint that "you just wish they'd keep some of those things to themselves," Bishop's verse is now widely interpreted as indirectly revealing her own struggles with alcoholism, asthma, and depression, and her discomfort with public knowledge of, or reference to, her lesbian relationships.[14] Bishop's poetry indeed resembles Moore's in its tendencies toward understatement, concern with detail, and play within (for Bishop, far more rarely against) traditional forms. Both poets also construct their acute critiques of power relationships, imperialism, and oppression through descriptions of nature and history, or some other topic providing ostensible distance: think of Moore's "The Jerboa," "Virginia Britannia," and "The Plumet Basilisk" and Bishop's "Cootchie," "The Roosters," and "Brazil, January 1, 1502." Yet Bishop writes a syntactically uncomplex poetry of the lyric "I," often not foregrounding the self or a particular perceiver but clearly writing around such an emotional center. Even when her verse contains no reference to a particular moment of her experience, she writes what is much more traditionally a poem of self-expression or lyric voice than anything in Moore's oeuvre.

Adrienne Rich (1929–) stands at the opposite extreme from Bishop in her acknowledgment of Moore as a predecessor—not only disclaiming influence but repudiating Moore as a constraining rather than liberating example of the woman as poet.[15] Nonetheless, Moore's poetic of understated oppositionality may interestingly illuminate the grounding assumptions of Rich's more openly confrontational and polarizing poetic stances. More than any other poet of this century, with the possible exception of Moore, Rich has developed a poetic of communal voice—what she has called "a common language"—manipulating quotation, biography, autobiography, a prose-like syntax, and various kinds of stylistic and topical disjunction to keep her poetic open. Like Moore, Rich moves with ease between extensive documenting of concrete detail and a plethora of suggestive contexts—national, international, economic, personal, philosophical. While hers is a voice of didactic and personal urgency, of immediate and strongly felt desire to communicate with her readers, the surface of her poetry often withholds the kind of transparency or simplicity that her polemical aspects would seem to promise. Moreover, although her poetry foregrounds personal voice—her own and that of the historical women she recreates as speakers—the frequent "Notes" sections concluding her books (as in *Your Native Land, Your Life, Time's Power,* and *The Atlas of a Difficult World*), as well as the factual detail of many of her sequences, testify to Rich's conviction that "Poetry never stood a chance / of standing outside history," of being either transcendentally or simply personal.[16] Like Moore, Rich believes profoundly in the limitations of language, choice, and circumstance; like Moore, Rich does not allow this belief to stand in the way of her writing occasional poems—that is, poems of response to particular moments or circumstances—or of her constructing a poetic of oppositional authority as decisively and powerfully articulated as Moore's own.[17] It may also be a sign of the times as much as one of poetic principle that, in her older age, Rich turns increasingly to global crises rather than to poems of appreciation: any euphoria that Moore (and the nation) enjoyed during the 1950s and 1960s based on the end of World War II, a booming economy, and vast (apparent) changes in civil rights has long since disappeared by the 1990s.

As we move into the poetry of the 1970s, 1980s, and 1990s, with these decades' increasing number of volumes written by women, patterns of resemblance to Moore's poetic occur more frequently and are more striking—perhaps in part because these poets could look back to Moore as an important predecessor but also because the writers of these later decades are more apt to have enjoyed educational and familial support for their professional ambitions similar to Moore's than were women coming of age in the middle of the century. These writers may begin with a more confident assumption of personal authority and hence approach the construction of alternate modes of poetic authority differently from many of their immediate predecessors.[18] Also like Moore, these writers have come of age during a period in which clear patterns of voice and representation are associated with feminist poetry—patterns that run counter to those developed by Moore in her poetic. Late twentieth-century feminist poetry tends to resemble Rich's in being openly political, anti-romantic, and anti-sentimental. At the same time, this poetry resembles early twentieth-century sentimental poetry in stressing (auto)biographical experience, bared emotions, subject matter explicitly linked with women's lives, and personal voice. This vein of poetry has been celebrated as a powerful tradition in its own right in Alicia Ostriker's *Stealing the Language*.[19] It has also received more attention from feminist critics than any other poetry, and the writers who have developed some of its primary tones are now well known: for example, Anne Sexton, Sylvia Plath, Adrienne Rich, Lucille Clifton, Judy Grahn, and Audre Lorde. In contrast to this celebratedly feminist poetry, the poetry I turn to in the rest of this chapter moves away from a poetic of experience and personal female voice through a variety of Moore-like experiments with impersonal, multivocal, colloquial, highly artificial, and ungrammatical traditional and nontraditional forms.

Heather McHugh (1948–) writes a poetry of striking tonal similarity to Moore's, especially in its combination of an understated first person "I" with repeated questions, parenthetical asides, self-corrections, and other illocutionary structures. Like Moore, McHugh alternates between a dense, complex, relatively formal and abstract syntax and diction, and a blunt, concrete one. She creates a speaker of immediate presence but not dominantly of voice. McHugh does include more revelatory information about her speaker's relation to a poetic subject than Moore does. For example, she writes a sequence of poems in *Shades* about the death of a beloved friend, concluding the poem "By Faith Not Sight" with the extremely personal question "Now that he's dead / where can I live?"[20] Neither this poem nor the sequence is framed, however, as a personal lament. Both, instead, begin and are dominated throughout by an exploration of what it means to love in the context of mortality, and more particularly of AIDS. While this friend's death is suggested in the previous poem of the sequence, it is first presented with unmistakable clarity five stanzas into "By Faith Not Sight," and there it is introduced so briefly and occurs between questions of such syntactic and philosophical complexity that it provides as much a temporary respite of emotional clarity as a key to the poem:

> All the little
> strata of the world—the
> audible and visible

of frequencies, the
findable and thinkable
of facts—could they
be fashioned

by and for
our expert self-
importances? Somebody
I adored has died

into unbearability.
But where is that?
Is where a narrow
inquiry? We aren't

our lives, or anything we made
in man or camera's image—where
is where itself? Who's
who? The issue's not

rhetorical:

(Shades, 10–11)

With a lovely balance resembling that of Moore's own love poems, McHugh keeps "the issue" of love propositional and speculative as well as a matter of passion. Maintaining a similar balance, McHugh's poem "Earmarks" combines Moore-like scientific description with foregrounded but unauthoritative personal presence. This poem describes both flowers in a time-lapse film, blooming "in ways we find too suddenly / familiar," and "the solid calcium we laid / beneath the new electron microscope" as a prelude to the speaker's conclusion of conviction and doubt: "each unity turns out to be / a part, each part appears from / somewhere else the sum . . . Upon / the universe of animals I swear / I mean I think I mean / I pray we are a stripe" (46).

Although McHugh's poems do not as distinctly engage questions of social concern as Moore's, they do contain similar suggestions of deliberate positioning in regard to the politics of representation and the lyric tradition. For example, like Moore, and even when writing

215

of sexual relationships, McHugh tends to make her speakers ungendered. In "Not a Sin" she writes, "It's not a virtue either, really, this / rubbing and rubbing against / someone, yourself / a someone too, until / someone must burst or yell"; or in "Thought of Night," she claims "Love mends / the broken language—we are each // first persons (though I know / I mustn't speak for two)" (57, 69). McHugh also turns repeatedly to questions of how and whether diverse things, phenomena, and people are connected with each other: "Do we see // a line where there is none? We draw / up sides, forgetting how in cells // division made things whole. To me / I'm complete, but I'm partial to you" ("Thought of Night," 69). While McHugh is not markedly experimental in her free verse forms, not given to multivocality of any kind, and much closer to creating a traditional lyric voice than is Moore (one poem refers to "We lyricists"—31), her poetry nonetheless has the tough, compressed challenge of Moore's in its combination of scientific, inquisitive, broadly speculative, and personal tones. Like Moore's, this is a poetry that challenges conventional stances of personal and poetic authority through word play and rhyme, wit, pointed fascination with the forms and conventions of language, and intensive questioning.

Combining the multiple voices of Rich's poetry with the density and compression of McHugh's, Cynthia Macdonald (1932–) creates a chorus of voices in her poetry. Although she constructs this chorus cumulatively through the speakers and descriptions of individual poems more often than within a single poem, she also experiments with direct multivocality. For example, her 27-page poem "Burying the Babies" contains dozens of quotations—including an elephant joke, passages from a 1902 advice book, and other poets' poetry—and both "The Stained-Glass Man" and "The Precise Shape of a Wave" are structured explicitly as two-way exchanges.[21] The voices within these poems and from poem to poem distinctively establish a plurality of vision that illuminates the limitations and prejudice of normative perception through its inclusion of widely variant or marginal speakers. For example, Macdonald writes about or in the voices of a "Stained Glass Man," a "Stained Glass Woman," a "Kilgore Rangerette" turned bag-lady, the "World's Biggest Man," a "Lady [baseball] Pitcher," victims of incest or of deathly diet remedies, a "Holy Man" fluent in three Native American languages who survives an unsuccessful attempt to walk unscathed through fire, and so on. As Macdonald puts it, "I'm very much interested in the collisions of different kinds of voices and speech."[22]

Poems like "How to Order a Freak" and "Celebrating the Freak" indicate that Macdonald's depiction of the outsized, excessive, failed, marginal, or "freakish" stems not from bizarre fascination or fetishism but from a profound understanding of the way social categorization defines and determines degrees of human worth, and how intertwined economics, international politics, and personal prejudices are with such categorization. The former poem, for example, satirically advises that "Boat women require discipline," and suggests through its more frequent listing of female than male categories that the "freak" is defined in part by her or his economic dependence on those with power, those who may "choose" a "freak" or person not integrated into normative power structures to provide intimate service: "The betrayed woman to serve you blowfish / On her platter" (83). "Celebrating the Freak" states more openly, in a suggestive two-column type, that "the freak is   the other":

The freak leaves us	bereft, forcing a little
Mutilation somewhere	to set things right
	(*Living Wills*, 96)

And because "it" can "Alarm[ ] . . . Astound[ ] . . . Amaz[e]" us, the freak is also "precious"—the mirror-image that assures a self-righteous "us" that *we* are not freaks. As with many of Moore's poems not about gender but suggesting feminist analysis, this poem seems directly responsive to contemporary understandings of sexism and racism. "Freaks" are "other" by definition but inseparable from "us." Macdonald's multivocality, then, is one of information and contextualization (involving research and eclectic reading), and of community-building in the broadest sense.[23]

Macdonald's poetry also employs surface density and contextual multiplicity similarly to Moore's. Her poems combine puns and other forms of word-play, internal and end-rhyme, repetitions (including a powerful modified villanelle—"The Sounding Cataract"), a teasing play around the pentameter line in poems like "The Precise Shape of a Wave" or "A Past-Due Notice," and experimental stanza forms and typographical marking of multiple voices or positions. This poetry carries conviction and moral force, but keeps its readers juggling a language of forceful presence and multiple contexts. "The Dangers of Looking Back," for example, begins with an epigraph from *Ancient Hawaii: The Volcano Museum*, calling attention to class and gender prejudices: *"Men and women could not share the same table and many foods were forbidden to the women and common people under penalty of death."* The poem then balances capitalized and typographically high-lighted (or marginalized—depending on one's interpretation) phrases describing a volcano with descriptions of the speaker's mother's two husbands, and of the (nongendered) speaker's own relationship with her or his lover:

> The volcano has snow on top, concealing
> What is beneath
> >   Festooned Stalactite of Basalt
>
> . . . . .
>
> >   Mass of Driblet
> Both men my mother married liked
> Their toast burned, would
> >   Gas Driblet tube
> Send it back to the toaster for blackening:
> Charcoal, buttered with preserve.
> >   Festooned Paho-e-ho-e
> We are walking an arrested lava sea, crunching
> Waves under foot:they are black, break
> With the sound of burnt toast . . .
> >   (*Living Wills*, 109)

Macdonald's poetry, like Moore's, contains densely layered, histori-cally, factually, and personally grounded representations of an event, situation, or thing. While this poem, like many of Macdonald's, tells a story of relationships, its focus is neither self-expression nor an authority of experience. The poem instead calls attention to ques-tions regarding the abuse of power and how one is, at times, complicit with it, but may also, without despair, survive it and oppose it.

The poetry of Macdonald and McHugh bears clear resemblance to Moore's. That of Susan Howe (1937–) sounds and looks strikingly different. Whereas even Moore's poetry of greatest abstraction and densest syntax contains repeated illocutionary effects and colloquial phrases and, typically, focuses itself on the articulation of some didactic claim, Susan Howe's poetry tests the far edges of communicability. On the other hand, Howe's poetry evokes traditions of American history and literature through repeated quotation and allusion resembling Moore's, and the two poets are similarly absorbed by questions of form, especially by the implications of particular rhetorical and poetic structures within the multiple contexts of literary and popular discourse. Like Moore, Howe seeks to redefine a poet's relation to both the present community and the literary past. In Howe's work this tension reveals itself in her sometimes quite lengthy quotations and in her use of a particular historical moment or event to center a poem more than in a manipulation of traditional forms or a Moore-like mosaic of topically unrelated quotations. Also like Moore, Howe includes several disparate fields of knowledge in her poems—for example, naming a collection *Singularities* after hearing a lecture on mathematical modeling, or including an Irish postage stamp among several literary quotations in her *Defenestration of Prague*, a poem "about" a seventeenth-century Czech religious conflict as it elucidates more recent religious conflict in Ireland.[24]

Even more than Moore, or poets like Brooks and Macdonald, Howe revels in the physicality of poetry, the play of word-sounds. For example, a section of "Articulation of Sound Forms in Time" begins with a couplet that echoes "evergreen season" with "maiden" in a slant-rhyme and then ends with the lines:

In forest splinter companion

essential simplicity of Thought
wedged back playmate of Remote

Hares call on Pan
To rhyme with reason revels run
                    (*Singularities*, 24)

Here Howe's use of the word "rhyme" highlights the syllabic and consonantal sound play patterning her couplets and her irregular rhymes within lines and between couplets (companion/reason/run). The word "rhyme" and sound play both, in turn, call attention to the companionship Howe sees established by any poet "Singing into the draft." Like words that rhyme, images and concepts are brought together in this poetry—in this passage specifically, the "Mother and maiden," Hares with Pan, and "essential simplicity" with revel or play. Howe suggests that such "singing" always entails a "companion" or "rhyme"—that the poet does not sing alone.

Howe begins this poem with a prose narrative account of "The Falls Fight" colonial massacre of the men, women, and children of a "Nipmunk, Squakeag, Pokomtuck, or Mahican camp" and the retaliation of Indian survivors and friends. This narrative concludes with the highly abstract claim, "I assume Hope Atherton's excursion for an emblem foreshadowing a Poet's abolished limitations in our demythologized fantasy of Manifest Destiny" (3–4). The poem's Part 2 begins with archaic and disjunctive but highly suggestive passages ("Prest try to set after grandmother / revived by and laid down left ly"; 6) leading quickly to list-like successions of words from (or suggestive of) Latin, Romance, Greek, Anglo-Saxon, and Native American languages: "velc cello viable toil / quench conch uncannunc / drumm amonoosuck ythian // scow aback din" and so on (10).[25] Including a crossed-out line, lines spaced "too closely" (by normative print standards), two pages that repeat each other exactly except that the words in the middle of the page appear in exactly the opposite order and are capitalized, these passages call attention to language as such, to the mechanical process of constructing a poem, to the surface of a page in ways most likely inconceivable to Moore—although Moore admired similar strategies of Gertrude Stein's. Here, in other words, is a multivocality at the level of word root and typography; Howe marks language itself as the place of communal amalgamation rather than constructing or manipulating a community of speakers or voices.

As in Moore's verse, in Howe's there is no accessible narrative of personal experience, no ready moral, no obvious link of obscure, detailed, difficult subject matter to contemporary political situations or struggles.[26] As with Moore, however, Howe does embed and analyze such concerns through the forms of her verse. As DuPlessis suggests in the only statement I know linking these two poets, the question they both ask is "'how to write'": "How to gather authority without authoritarian power; how to indicate clarities without the limitation of certainties; how to give and receive pleasure without rhetorical or generic proscriptions; how to indicate one's volume without squatting hibernations of mass."[27] Howe illuminates the necessity of balancing complexity with clarity in commenting on gendered or feminist aspects of her poetry: about "Articulation of Sound Forms in Time" she notes that "it would have been easy to end on the second to last poem as I have done in readings of it and which makes it more overtly feminist." But making the poem "more overtly" feminist than it already is would be "too easy": "there are no answers and life is hard" (quoted in Perloff's *Poetic License*, 309). Howe's comment on Emily Dickinson pertains to her own work as well: "she explored the implications of breaking the law just short of breaking off communication with a reader"; and while Howe certainly goes much farther than Moore (or Dickinson) in this direction, and some may argue that she has overstepped the communicative boundary, this is not her intention.[28]

The explicitly political themes of M. Nourbese Philip (1947–) place her in a different relation to Moore from where Howe stands. Philip's poetry is more openly didactic than Moore's and yet, because of its complex surface texture and multivocality, remains in the realm of oppositional rather than of openly revolutionary poetry.[29] For example, in "The Question of Language is the Answer to Power," Philip plays the two sides of her pages of text against each other, using left-hand pages to present a series of grammar book style "LESSONS FOR THE VOICE" that function as meta-commentary on the rest of the poem. The first "lesson" concerns vowels *"by nature either long or short . . . These vowels are all shaped predominantly by the lips, though the position and freedom of the blade of the tongue affects their quality."* This lesson on physiological constraint presents Philip's dominant theme in this poem, and in much of her writing, namely, how "position and freedom" (historically, legally, and psychologically defined) affect the possibility, clarity, and aesthetic qualities of one's expression. These aspects of positioning are linked in the lesson's phonic examples, each of which refers to the enslavement of Africans—for example, *"OH as in the slaves came by 'boat' (dipthongal)"* (*She Tries*, 70). One sees here that knowledge (say, of how one pronounces certain vowels) is indeed different from the use of that knowledge (the phrases illustrating each sound), although they appear to be inseparable: the "lesson" of English is and does not have to be a lesson about history, racism, and colonization—although articulations of language, history, and identity will always be intertwined. Philip's focus on the details of grammar here resembles the pointed indirection of Moore's descriptions of landscape in "Virginia Britannia," or of the desert rat in "The Jerboa."

The right-hand pages of "The Question of Language is the Answer to Power," in contrast to the left with their "lessons," proceed in two columns that alternately repeat the examples of the poem's first "lesson" and comment broadly on language, so that they read like a dialogue of culturally imposed and inner voices—the cultural lesson visually and psychologically interrupting the speculative thought. The poem ends anticlimactically with Alice in Wonderland talking in a prose of bourgeois fussiness to characters from British children's stories like Winnie the Pooh:

> "The word, the word"
>
> the Red Queen screamed
>
> "Banish the word
> Off with its head—
> The word is dead
> The word is risen
> Long live the word!"

"Oh dear, oh dear," said Alice, "what will Tigger and Pooh and Eeyore and Mrs. Tiggy Winkle think of all this kerfuffle. She does carry on so—that Red Queen." (75)

Like many of Moore's poems, this one leaves the reader with no single point of view, and no possibility of transcendence. Are we to sympathize with the anger (or in Lewis's fable more like hysteria) of the "Red" (hence leftist?) queen as representative of marginal ("other"-worldly) frustration with and dependence on language? Does Alice represent the British empire, the colonizer, at its most pernicious because apparently least threatening—trivializing serious conflict and emotion around issues of language as "kerfuffle" and "carry[ing] on"? Or is it Alice that we finally turn to in "insist[ing]" upon qualities of play, of flex, in language rather than tirades that tyrannize others but accomplish nothing? The first alternative seems most persuasive, especially given the poem's earlier use of commanding language ("I decree [the word] mine . . . till it come to do the bid in . . . this chattel language"; 71, 73); the speaker may be a black and "red," multifaceted, multicolored and multivocal, queen. Still, the choices are not clear-cut, and neither is particularly attractive. It is perhaps more important to note that in this poem, with its title "The Question of Language is the Answer to Power," Philip closes with reference to popular characters conceived by British women and men—those whose power over language reveals itself in the international distribution of their children's literature, but is undercut by Philip's allusion and quotation. Like Moore's "Silence," this may be a poem about speech-acts as acts of power: a story's power over children in developing their conceptions of the world (red queens "carry on"), a grammar's power over the choices possible to speakers of that language, and a poem's power to respond to the history embedded in its language (Philip asks, *Do words collect historical responses?* 74).

Like Moore's, Philip's "I" is abstract; it at times claims a historical, raced, gendered position, or voices desire, need, longing, anger, humor, and opposition, but without calling attention to particularities of selfhood or claiming an authority of experience. Even in Philip's earlier poems—which may refer to aspects of her past (for example, "Cyclamen Girl" traces a young African Caribbean girl's response to first communion, and "And Over Every Land and Sea" deals with an exiled daughter)—the biographical effect is mediated by the abstraction of the language, the difficulty of the syntax, the representativeness of the experience described (thousands of daughters emigrate "north"), and—in the latter poem—repeated quotation of Ovid. Biography, and the more abstract process of characterization, may inform but does not focus these poems. Similarly, Philip's "I" typically uses a vernacular idiom but one including so much repetition, word play, and interrupted syntax that it, like Moore's, remains colloquial while bearing little resemblance to "natural" speech.

Philip quotes frequently from canonical authors, linguists, and a variety of popular sources, although her quotations—like those of Rich, Macdonald, and Howe—maintain their independence as distinct voices rather than becoming pieces in a Moore-like mosaic text. Philip's quotations highlight their source—information she includes, as does Macdonald, within the text of the poem. Yet as is apparent in "The Question of Language is the Answer to Power," such broad-based quotation does not constitute self-authorization through reference to an Eliotian "tradition" or culture, but rather is a Moore-like strategy for juxtaposing cultural authorities with her own experimental and inclusive assertions. In an interview, Philip states that she intends to subvert "all the traditions of poetry" both formally and through thematic inclusion: as she explains,

> Poetry came to us in the Caribbean as another form of colonization and oppression. So . . . in the poem "Discourse on the Logic of Language" I set out to subvert the poem itself. Usually a poem is centred on the page with the margins at both sides clearly demarcated. Also there is the prescription of certain traditions like Eliot's objective correlative: you remove the poem from its morass of history . . . I deliberately set out to put the poem . . . back in its historical context, which is what poetry is not supposed to do.[30]

For Philip, poetry *should* point to and reveal its place in the "morass" of its historical and other context(s); consequently, it does not involve clear demarcation of voices (no "I" fully originates her own language). Poetic (like all linguistic) form is immediately constructed by an individual, but it is not isolated from communal, material, and historical life.

Philip's formulations of the historical, economic, philosophical, and psychological interplay of people's relationships with broader social, cultural, and political issues are both pointed and complex. Consequently, her poetry balances the advantages and disadvantages of not being transparently accessible to a broad audience. For Philip, as for Moore, such balancing involves reconceiving the relation between poet, poem, and audience:

> One possible danger is that I have made the audience for my poetry even smaller than it already is . . . The problem is how to speak these poems when they have become unspeakable? . . . Or is it just that the work is entering a community where I as the poet can no longer speak alone but need other people to help. ("Writing a Memory," 238)

When Janice Williamson, the interviewer, responds to this speculation by suggesting that Philip has "become a chorus," the poet emphatically corrects her: "No, I need a chorus!" Like Moore, Philip does not want to speak *as* or *for* those who concern her but *with* them—quoting them, paraphrasing them.[31]

More than any other poetry I know of, that of Alice Fulton (1952–) bears striking resemblance to Moore's.[32] In particular, for both poets, the realm of science provides startling, factual subject matter and a subject position that steps away from the personal at the same time that it calls attention to the partiality of all observation—the play on "subject" here reflecting the extent to which both poets see the observer's perception as affecting what she (or he) sees. Fulton writes of nuclear particles with the same familiarity as Moore writes of a pangolin, jerboa, or "octopus" of ice.[33] For example, "The Fractal Lanes," "Cusp," "Romance in the Dark," "Scumbling," "Palladium Process," and "Peripheral Vision" all use quantum theory's "complementary" or multiple observations of light as central to their themes: just as light reveals itself paradoxically to be both a particle and a wave under different experimental conditions, human physical existence and moral existence may reveal themselves to be quite different from or "complementary" to what they in some situations appear to be.[34] This leads not to despair or indifference but to heightened sensitivity to questions of trust and faith, and to

225

simultaneous desires to know with precision (hence to be uncertain, because all reality manifests itself multiply) and to act, to live (hence to assert some stability and possibility for meaning).

For example, in "The Pivotal Kingdom," musing on the terrible problems of poverty and homelessness leads Fulton's speaker to abstract questions about the relation of flesh to soul, or death to life, conceived with scientific specifity:

> Does it hold
> eminent domain inside our heads, live in
> vivid ampules under wraps
> of fat, swim through tissue's minnowed shadings,
> the opalescent flecks of cellulite
> like spectral residues
> in flesh? As Socrates said
> life's intrinsic
> to the soul but accidental
> to the body. He said
> if the spirit does exist
> it isn't a good mixer. In my book
> inclusions are not accidents,
>
> though accidents exist.
>
> *(Powers of Congress, 34)*

Moving quickly from biology to philosophy, and later to jazz, botanical history, and pollution—all in the service of understanding what it means to live with spirit and "soul"—Fulton puns on Moore's famous epigraph "Omissions are not accidents" to call attention instead to her digressive inclusions. In both poets' "book[s]," however, what is put in is no more accidental than what is left out. Moreover, both writers emphasize (or even exaggerate) the controlled formalities of poetic structure as well as aspects of language and knowledge beyond their control, and both are playful in linking spiritual and moral questions to the most mundane, apparently trivial, and unnoticed processes or phenomena of living.

Like Moore, Fulton experiments with rhyme, stanza patterns, and other formal elements of poetic structure. "Disorder Is A Measure Of Warmth," for example, uses visually symmetrical (nonmetrical) stanza and sound patterns to suggest the snow crystals that provide its primary metaphor. The first stanza of this poem is typical in its dense combination of alliteration, assonance, and slant rhyme:

> In the window, frost forms cradles
> > more fail-safe than the beams
> > of string kids knit
> > > between their fingers.

Fulton's complex play with sound and stanza structure in this poem has a contradictory effect much like the simultaneously "organic" and arbitrary form of Moore's syllabic stanzas. For example, by enjambing the word "melo- // drama" melodramatically across a stanza break Fulton creates a marvelous punning effect while also calling attention to her obviously arbitrary artifice (here no strict metrical pattern prevents the addition of a few syllables to a line). More generally, this poem establishes the uselessness of perfection while painstakingly maintaining a pattern of line indentations and stanza length that highlights its own arbitrariness.[35] In an extended association of watching window panes with watching soap operas, the speaker sees the TV "blond starlet" "forg[ing] a perfection / older than enzyme or ferment / within the human melo- // drama of protoplasm and cell." Such heroines, like snowflakes, are

> ignorant things
> > that succeed in being
> gorgeous without needing to be
> > alive. How deeply we,
>
> the products of chance collisions
> > between wrinkled linens
> full of eccentricity and mission,
> > want to be like them.
> > > (*Powers of Congress*, 3–4)

Fulton's poems, like "our" lives, are "full of eccentricity and mission"—terms remarkably parallel to Moore's "idiosyncrasy" and "meaning."

Other poems in *Powers of Congress* experiment more obviously with traditional forms. "The Expense Of Spirit" (18), "The Fractal Lanes" (23), and the last section of "The Gilt Cymbal Behind Saints" (22) include acrostics that comment ironically and humorously on their themes.[36] "Silencer" (27–28) uses a justified right rather than left margin and an unusual number of end-stopped lines and lines that coincide with a single phrase or full sentence. "Our Calling" (44–45) uses alternate lines, parallel columns, and differing type to present an undramatized dialogue on language, militarism, and individual responsibility. And "Romance in the Dark" (100–101) consists of stanzas in which every line-end word rhymes, and most lines end with a Latinate and technical word, making almost all rhymes "feminine" (in the first stanza: nebula, umbrella, curricula, specula, flagella, flotilla, tarantella). Formal conventions, in both poets' work, are shown to be arbitrary, are perhaps even parodied in Moore's syllabic stanzas and (for example) Fulton's aaaaaaa rhyme scheme; they provide a kind of base note above and around which the poets' syncopations run.

Most of Fulton's poems involve a dramatized "I" and, like Macdonald's, use a story to frame their questions. Surprisingly, given these narrative frames, Fulton makes several of her speakers ungendered.[37] Often, as with Moore and other poets, this is simply a matter of using an "I" without strong, or with contradicting, gender implications. For example, in "Palladium Process," the speaker—presented as "a cloud / chamber"—punningly refers to her or himself as "Skirted, stalled, / in the realm between feeling and expression" and yet claims to react to "ordinary things / the way a 19th-century gentleman might / start at a glimpse of undraped / limb" (*Palladium*, 62–3). "The Expense Of Spirit" inclusively questions why lovers cannot "praise the otherness / Rising or widening next to one's own / Nude dilations" (*Powers of Congress*, 18). Moreover, because Fulton writes poems in a specifically male as well as specifically female dramatized narrative voice, one cannot assume that an unmarked speaker represents the poet, or is female. Like Moore's, Fulton's nongendering is a matter of fluidity of gender boundaries, of using set categories to show their limitations, rather than the attempted neutrality of ignoring cultural and sexual difference or creating an unsexed thing.[38] In this poetry, which is explicitly sexual and often deals with narratives of romance or sexual coupling, Fulton constructs alternatives to the essentializing categories of popular conceptions of gender.

Perhaps most remarkable in structural connections with Moore is Fulton's increasing interest in experimenting with multivocality in her verse. While this element occurs in her early poems through the wide range of diction and vocabularies she characteristically employs, it appears most dramatically to date in "Point of Purchase," a poem spoken by a pool-playing sculptor consumed, like many of Fulton's speakers, with questions of faith and "vision" (*Powers of Congress*, 73–86). This poem begins with two epigraphs: one typeset, from Emily Dickinson—hence presumably Fulton's, or the speaker's—and a second in handwritten script from Salmon Rushdie, placed parallel to the first but on the margin of the page. The handwriting of this epigraph and that of three other "speakers" appears periodically in the margins of this long poem—all four of these structurally peripheral speakers commenting on the style, words, and implications of the sculptor's, and occasionally also each other's, words. The poem, then, contains its own commentary, or makes the process through which one reads and discusses the text with others formally a part of its process: the reader is literally written into this poem. Moreover, because the various handwritings present different readings of the poem—academic, insistently personal, intertextual, and so on—there is no single or ideal "reader."

Perhaps because of her increased experimentation with multivocal poems, Fulton seems to have become increasingly interested in quotation as well. She has long used epigraphs to preface poems, and several poems quote or allude to sources as diverse as Dickinson and other poets, popular music, scientific theorems, and advertising slogans. Fulton's "Give," a long poem about Daphne, includes multiple speakers—Apollo, Cupid, Daphne herself, the tree that (in Fulton's version of the myth) she is forced to enter, and a commentator (*Sensual Math*, 72–116). Moreover, "Give" quotes and annotates both notably popular or nonliterary and literary sources. In this poem, Fulton echoes the rhythm and lyrics of songs recorded by Frank Sinatra and Elvis Presley and quotes from Moore's "Feed Me, Also, River God," Dickinson's "Safe in their Albaster Chambers," Joyce Kilmer's "Trees," one of her own earlier poems, and Mary S. Lovell's *The Sound of Wings: The Life of Amelia Earhart*. In one of the several ways in which Fulton revises notions of authority and proper behavior in this myth, Daphne speaks the lines of (female) poets and authors, while the dominant note in Apollo's and Cupid's lines is imitation, at times mingled with quotation, of popular singers (Sinatra and Elvis, respectively) and comic-book superheroes, with their comic-vulgar combination of archaic, erudite, and pop slang diction. Not a god and subject to their pursuit and transformation, Daphne nonetheless speaks to the contemporary reader with greater—and specifically female—authority than Apollo, Cupid, or Zeus.

In the last section of "Give" ("A New Release"), Fulton puns on wedding rings, tree rings, shackles, and the rings or grooves of a vinyl record to reposition Daphne. Responding to Cupid's latest record "cut," Daphne comments "Somehow, by the last chill tingle of the cymbal / I wanted / to be the singer rather than the wearer of the ring" (*Sensual Math*, 112). Like Moore's distinction between rights and obligations in "Marriage," Fulton's exploration of choice and freedom in this poem involves not just what the individual enjoys but what he or she is capable of fostering; song functions in multiple ways as the "record" of a star's egotism, as self-expression, and as a form of communication with others—that is, as either oppressive or enabling, depending on what is sung and in what context. In this poem, Fulton implies the difficulty of achieving a nondominating, nonviolating expressive affection in contrast to the mythic (and quotidian) pattern of Daphne's life. As presented in the rock-star scenario, one either "cuts" the latest "hit" or is captive audience, "caught," like Daphne, within multiple invasive and encircling literal and socially (paternally) constructed rings. The choices appear to be between violence and victimization. At the same time, Daphne remembers her mother as a successful and powerful singer (based on Big Mama Thornton, a blues singer whose "Hound Dog"

Elvis/Apollo makes into his biggest hit), and several undercurrents of the poem lead away from the simplistic dichotomy outlined above.[39] At the poem's conclusion, Daphne is caught in nature (a tree) but thereby also freed from the wifehood and childbearing that patriarchy has insisted is her sexual destiny or womanly "nature." Fulton does not rewrite the myth to release Daphne from all captivity, but she does give Daphne a voice, and the last word: she plays, as it were, Daphne's song (recorded in the androgynous tree's, rather than vinyl, rings) with her "diamond-tipped / stylus," or pen, leaving behind the "hits" of the superstar-fathers.

As Fulton writes in the lines I use as an epigraph to this chapter, "In my book / inclusions are not accidents": while a different critic might choose other poets to mark the continued aptness of Moore's poetic for exploring reconstructions of poetic voice and form, those I have included in my discussion demonstrate how broad and how significant the resonances are. Using Moore's poetry as a touchstone for reading the work of late twentieth-century feminist poets will, I believe, greatly enrich our understanding of their similar and various challenges to poetic and cultural authorities. At the same time, such comparative reading underscores the extraordinary vitality of Moore's own questions of authority. Moore has created not just a few superb individual poems, not just a singular combination of features and tones in her poetry, but a poetic that continues to be as profoundly challenging, as acute in its speculations, and as brilliant at the end of the twentieth century as it was in the beginning.

Notes

1. Introduction

Epigraphs: Williams's statement appears in "Four Foreigners," *Little Review* 6.5 (1919). Moore is quoted from conversation in Richard Howard's "Marianne Moore and the Monkey Business of Modernism" (AMM, 8).

1. *Outside in the Teaching Machine* (Routledge Press, 1993), 29.

2. Gerda Lerner, *What Women Thought: The Creation of Feminist Consciousness* (Oxford University Press, 1993).

3. In Chapter 7 I briefly discuss the poetics of Mina Loy, Lorine Niedecker, Gwendolyn Brooks, Adrienne Rich, Heather McHugh, Cynthia Macdonald, Susan Howe, M. Nourbese Philip, and Alice Fulton as bearing significant resemblance in a variety of ways to Moore's.

4. Specifically, one might argue, for example, that Moore turns to Hebrew poetry and philosophy, Gwendolyn Brooks to African American poetic styles, and M. Nourbese Philip to an African spiritual heritage in place of dominant (Western) traditions. On Moore, see John Slatin's *The Savage's Romance: The Poetry of Marianne Moore* (SR), 25–30. Jeredith Merrin similarly argues that Moore's interest in Sir Thomas Browne's prose as a model for her verse stemmed in part from her strong association of this writer with her mother and in part from his peripheral canonical standing and his lack of association with "popular Renaissance themes of sexual assault and seduction"; *An Enabling Humility: Marianne Moore, Elizabeth Bishop, and the Uses of Tradition* (Rutgers University Press, 1990), 137.

5. It is of course possible for a single feature to be enabling or authorizing for a poet herself and at the same time for it to affect adversely, and hence to reduce her authority for, her audience. In particular, eccentricity—what Moore calls "idiosyncrasy," a primary concept of her poetic—has this effect. Singularity in the range of diction, or singularity that encom-

passes extended reference to devalued popular modes, is particularly likely to be interpreted as eccentric rather than experimental in form, and hence to be devalued. It may also be the case that critics more readily judge a woman's language as dismissibly eccentric than as deliberately experimental.

6. See Wolff's *In Defense of Anarchism* (Harper & Row, 1970), 3–4; and McGann's *A Critique of Modern Textual Criticism* (University of Chicago Press, 1983), 48.

7. "Public Power and Authority in the Medieval English Countryside," in *Women and Power in the Middle Ages*, ed. Mary Erler and Maryanne Kowaleski (University of Georgia Press, 1988), 19, 29.

8. *Gender and Genius: Towards A Feminist Aesthetics* (Indiana University Press, 1989), 23.

9. *Revolution in Poetic Language*, trans. Margaret Waller (Columbia University Press, 1984), 59–60.

10. In "The Archaic Mother and Mother and Mother: The Postmodern Poetry of Marianne Moore," *Contemporary Literature* 30, 1 (1989): 25. Brownstein argues that Moore, like Williams, is a postmodern rather than a modern poet. Working through a Kristevan discourse of "preverbal dynamic[s]" and relation with "the archaic mother," as well as with notions of right- and left-brain experience, Brownstein's reading of Moore resembles mine in its basic characterization of the verse—albeit not in its explanations of those characteristics.

11. For empirical studies of both how women talk in particular groups and circumstances, and how men, women, and children typically perceive women's speech, see Chapter 6, note 47.

12. At the same time, as I explain later, these poets use language strategies that resemble especially those described by Hélène Cixous. Here I differentiate between the theories themselves and what I see as their grounding in Freudian, Hegelian, Lacanian thought. For example, by following—even in a transformative way—Lacanian cultural positioning of subjectivity and language, Kristeva continues to define language as a symbolic order in relation to the phallus, and thus even her maternally based "semiotic" order of language is conceived in opposition to this symbolic (*Revolution*). Similarly, while Cixous and Luce Irigaray construct their experimental texts with the explicit purpose of disrupting such "laws," the repeated grounding of their theory in female sexuality suggests the binary of phallic/feminine. Such theory provides useful ways for understanding how the oppositional may enter a text through nonverbal structures, and it de-essentializes "woman" as understood in the phallic economy to focus instead on relations of power—in particular, the relation of phallic domi-

nance to language. Yet the foundational terms of such theorizing suggest that all cultural authority, all public writing, perhaps all grammatical speech, participates in and hence supports the phallic order. See Rita Felski's *Beyond Feminist Aesthetics: Feminist Literature and Social Change* (Harvard University Press, 1989) for an excellent analysis of these feminist theories. Teresa de Lauretis's first chapter of *Technologies of Gender: Essays on Theory, Film, and Fiction* also points persuasively to the problems in collapsing differences of race, sexuality, and gender (Indiana University Press, 1987).

13. Jean-François Lyotard, in *The Differend: Phrases in Dispute* (University of Minnesota Press, 1983), 206.

14. "Verbalizing a Political Act," in *Language and Politics*, ed. Michael Shapiro (New York University Press, 1984), 42.

15. *Feminism and Poetry* (Pandora, 1987), 27.

16. See Cixous's *"Coming to Writing": and Other Essays*, ed. Deborah Jenson (Harvard University Press, 1991) and Irigaray's *This Sex Which Is Not One*, trans. Catherine Porter (Cornell University Press, 1985; originally published 1977). Sabine Sielke uses Cixous to describe this aspect of Moore's (and Emily Dickinson's) art as specifically gendered, commenting that these poets "neither adapt a traditional aesthetics nor take their deconstructive textual practice to Mallarmean extremes, but instead mediate transgression with the reconstruction of new kinds of authority. This inbetween position is a fundamental aspect in the construction of female subjectivity" ("Intertextual Networking: Constructing Female Subjectivity in the Poetry of Emily Dickinson, Marianne Moore, and Adrienne Rich," Ph.D. diss., Free University of Berlin [1991], 458). Jeanne Heuving similarly uses Irigaray's concepts of the specular and of a feminine *écriture* to explain Moore's use of some of the forms of a "specular or symbolic poetry" while she rejects other of its aspects to write a poetry of "self-affection": "woman's existence 'elsewhere' allows her . . . an important, if partial, freedom from the proper or the symbolic"; see *Omissions Are Not Accidents: Gender in the Art of Marianne Moore* (Wayne State University Press, 1992), 23.

17. Foucault, *The History of Sexuality*, I, trans. Robert Hurley (Random House, 1978), 95; Chambers, *Room for Maneuver: Reading the Oppositional in Narrative* (University of Chicago Press, 1991), xiii. Page numbers in this paragraph refer to Chambers's study.

18. Chambers's book focuses on the activity of "reading" the oppositional (in) narrative; I shift his focus to one on the activity of the writer, while still acknowledging the reader's (and my own) complicity in the construction of the "oppositional." As much of Chambers's initial work on oppositionality focuses on the poetry of La Fontaine, it is clear that he sees this structure as operating equally forcefully in poetry and in prose.

19. I borrow "masculist" as the parallel form to "feminist" from Gayatri Spivak's *In Other Worlds: Essays in Cultural Politics* (Methuen, 1987); like "feminist," the ideological "masculist" distinguishes itself from its related gender category ("masculine") more than the (more commonly used) "masculinist" does. I thank Jerold C. Frakes for calling my attention to this term.

20. *The Pursuit of Signs: Semiotics, Literature, Deconstruction* (Cornell University Press, 1981), 146–148, 142.

21. *Death in Quotation Marks* (Harvard University Press, 1991), 4.

22. Quoted in *These Modern Women: Autobiographical Essays from the 20s*, ed. Elaine Showalter (Feminist Press, 1978), 67.

23. See Anne K. Mellor's collection *Romanticism and Feminism* (Indiana University Press, 1988) on British romanticism; Joanne Feit Diehl's *Women Poets and the American Sublime* (Indiana University Press, 1990) on romanticism in the United States; and Margaret Homans's *Women Writers and Poetic Identity* (Yale University Press, 1980) and Marlon B. Ross's *The Contours of Masculine Desire: Romanticism and the Rise of Women's Poetry* (Oxford University Press, 1989) on British and American women writers. Much has also been written about Moore's conscious resistance to the romantic tradition—most recently by Heuving (*Omissions Are Not Accidents*, 25–29) and Merrin (*Enabling Humility*, chap. 3). Page numbers in this paragraph refer to Homans's *Women Writers and Poetic Identity*.

24. Mellor more radically claims that the romantic tradition was established on the basis of gender politics; Blake, Wordsworth, Coleridge, Byron, Shelley, and Keats have been canonized for their gendering of the poetic self: "These six male poets have been heralded because they endorsed a concept of the self as a power that gains control over and gives significance to nature, a nature troped in their writings as female. They thus legitimized the continued repression of women and at the same time gave credence to the historically emerging capitalist belief in the primacy of the individual over the group" (*Romanticism and Feminism*, 8).

25. Joanne Diehl argues that American romanticism (as outlined by Emerson and developed by Whitman) leaves even less opportunity than the British for the assertion of a female voice or power. Rather than continuing the British metaphor of marriage between the masculine imagination and feminine nature or experience, American romantics pair themselves with an "abyss" and usurp the feminine sphere as a part of their own perceiving brains. Woman is identifed solely in terms of biology and the family, as maternal procreator (*American Sublime*, chap. 1).

26. For descriptions of female poets prominent in the nineteenth century, see Emily Stipes Watts's *The Poetry of American Women from 1632 to 1945* (University of Texas Press, 1977); Cheryl Walker's *The Nightingale's Burden:*

Women Poets and American Culture before 1900 (Indiana University Press, 1982), and Joanne Dobson's *Dickinson and the Strategies of Reticence: The Woman Writer in Nineteenth-Century America* (Indiana University Press, 1989). Suzanne Clark's important study *Sentimental Modernism: Women Writers and the Revolution of the Word* (Indiana University Press, 1991) and Walker's *Masks Outrageous and Austere: Culture, Psyche, and Persona in Modern Women Poets* (Indiana University Press, 1991) explore the extension of this tradition into the twentieth century.

27. Dobson is particularly good at showing ways in which various nineteenth-century women poets besides Dickinson departed from conventional "feminine" behavior and forms (*Strategies of Reticence,* 29–34, 38–39).

28. Clark, *Sentimental Modernism,* 2.

29. *The Pink Guitar: Writing as Feminist Practice* (Routledge, 1990), 16, 152, 42. Sandra Gilbert and Susan Gubar provide impressive and persuasive literary and historical evidence for the pervasiveness of gender as an organizing structure of modernist thought, and for the conservatism along gender lines (when not outright misogyny) of many male modernist thinkers. This is the primary argument of their multi-volume *No Man's Land: The Place of the Woman Writer in the Twentieth Century* (Yale University Press, 1988, 1989). This argument has also been made forcefully in two essays by Carolyn Burke—"Supposed Persons: Modernist Poetry and the Female Subject" (*Feminist Studies* 11 [Spring 1985]: 131–148), and "Getting Spliced: Modernism and Sexual Difference" (*American Quarterly* 39, 1 [Spring 1987]: 98–121)—and is the basis for the recent anthology *The Gender of Modernism: A Critical Anthology,* ed. Bonnie Kime Scott (Indiana University Press, 1990).

30. In *Made in America: Science, Technology, and American Modernist Poets,* Lisa Steinman notes that poetry was frequently regarded by both poets and critics of the early twentieth century as feminine, or effeminate, in explicit comparison to "objective" and technical fields like science and engineering. William Carlos Williams in particular frequently regrets that poetry is not as "manly" as science, and may refer extensively to science and technology as a way of masculinizing his poems (Yale University Press, 1987; chap. 1, especially p. 16). Moore, in contrast, as I discuss in Chapter 4, seeks to collapse such stereotyped gender boundaries for various creative endeavors. On this topic, Cleo Kearns comments that "the annihilation of personality for which Eliot was ready to take up the knife looked to Moore at times no more than a desperate quest for a false control"; in "Consanguinities: T. S. Eliot and Marianne Moore" (*Sagetrieb* 6, no. 3 [Winter 1987]: 51). See Celeste Goodridge's *Hints and Disguises: Marianne Moore and Her Contemporaries* for an extended analysis of Moore's disagreements with and critique of Eliot, Pound, Williams, and Stevens (University of Iowa Press, 1989).

31. As Margaret Holley (*The Poetry of Marianne Moore*), Slatin (SR), and Heuving (*Omissions Are Not Accidents*) have persuasively demonstrated, some elements of Moore's style change notably during the sixty-odd years of her writing. I find, however, that Moore's most important convictions and stylistic characteristics remain fairly consistent.

32. *Language and the Poet: Verbal Artistry in Frost, Stevens, and Moore* (University of Chicago Press, 1979), chap. 5.

33. This is the primary argument of Schulman's *Marianne Moore: The Poetry of Engagement* (University of Illinois Press, 1986).

34. Many readers, I think, mistake the didactic elements of Moore's tone for authoritarianism, or dogmatic moralizing; they do not hear the contradicting, contrasting, questioning elements that are also key to her style. Consequently, the poet's surface complexity, her challenges to a reader to take nothing for granted, seem to them signs of elitism.

35. "Portrait of a Writing Master: Beyond the Myth of Marianne Moore" (TCL, 192–209).

36. Hugh Kenner (*A Homemade World: The American Modernist Writers* [Random House, 1974]), Slatin (SR), Lynn Keller (*Re-Making It New: Contemporary American Poetry and the Modernist Tradition* [Cambridge University Press, 1987]), and Heuving (*Omissions Are Not Accidents*, 1992), for example, focus almost entirely on Moore's work of the 1920s and 1930s; Bonnie Costello claims that "the late work lacks sincerity and gusto" (IP, 13); Laurence Stapleton (*Marianne Moore: The Poet's Advance* [Princeton University Press, 1978]), Holley (PMM), and Charles Molesworth (*Marianne Moore: A Literary Life* [Atheneum, 1990]) argue that her poems of the 1940s are her greatest achievement. To my mind, until we have a truly *Complete Poems of Marianne Moore*, it will continue to be prohibitively difficult to make such a judgment. Moore's later poems had no opportunity to undergo the severe knife of her dictum that "Omissions are not accidents" (CP, vii). When all her work is published together and chronologically—the best with the mediocre—we will be able to judge more reasonably whether her later work is truly less strong or simply unweeded.

37. Richard Howard documents the unusual unanimity of this praise in "Marianne Moore and the Monkey Business of Modernism," 5.

38. In *Marianne Moore, Subversive Modernist* (University of Texas Press, 1986), Taffy Martin locates the point at which critics begin to stress Moore's mannerisms as "ironically, just at the time when those very critics [also] began arguing for rigorously analytical treatments of literature"—or with the rise of New Criticism (5).

39. In *Imaginations*, ed. Webster Schott (New Directions, 1970), 317–318.

40. "Her Shield," in CCE, 122.

41. It is worth noting here that this is a typical move toward women in male-dominated professions. Such a woman is seen as neutered, not the same as men but different from women, the proof of her difference being her very presence in that profession.

42. Random House, 1951; p. 146.

43. George Nitchie's recent essay, "Condescension and Affection: Some Observations on Marianne Moore" (*Poesis* [1985]: 35–39), focuses on the tendency of male critics to enter a "border country between affection and condescension" in writing of Moore. Nitchie is unusually self-conscious in describing the "trap" of responding too fully to expectations created by Moore's gender, a trap to which other less self-conscious readers have succumbed (36). Noting his own tendency to perceive her through the romanticized lens of the masculine gaze at the feminine object and noting the number of her contemporaries and later writers who respond similarly, Nitchie warns that "the small-bore academic critic . . . had better be very, very careful about how he lets the personal and the general contaminate one another" (36). He also admits his own flirtation in reading Moore: "As a particular kind of woman, she does things to the particular kind of man that my fantasy versions of myself assure me I really am, and I enjoy the things that she does" (37).

44. In *The Madwoman in the Attic: The Woman Writer and the Nineteenth-Century Literary Imagination* (Yale University Press, 1979), 20, 25. Wallace Stevens in fact calls Moore an "angel" and her style "angelic" (*The Letters of Wallace Stevens*, 290). Moore never represents herself or any woman as "angel," and she shows her impatience with such images even years later. In a 1961 interview, when Donald Hall reminds Moore of Williams's characterization of her as "a rafter holding up the superstructure of our uncompleted building," she objects, "I never was a rafter holding up anyone!" (MMR, 257).

45. Penn Warren's "Jingle: In Tribute to a Great Poem by Marianne Moore," in *Festschrift for Marianne Moore's Seventy- Seventh Birthday by Various Hands*, ed. Tambimuttu (Tambimuttu and Mass, 1964), 103. The "saint" metaphor for Moore was well entrenched. In 1944, in response to Morton Zabel's calling Moore a "saint of American poetry," Louise Bogan repeats the phrase, then modifies it with the same mixture of condescending critique and admiration expressed by her male peers: "Although I feel that saints should be outside their mothers' leading strings, and dance every day before the Lord, and have visions and ecstasies, but also a fine, firm, human and tough point of standing . . . well, we can't have everything, and Marianne's decadence has been channelled off into her life and her prose,

leaving the poetry pretty firm and pure and clear"; quoted in Gloria Bowles's *Louise Bogan's Aesthetic of Limitation* (Indiana University Press, 1987), 56.

46. Martin also makes this claim *(Subversive Modernist)*, as does Carolyn Durham in "Linguistic and Sexual Engendering in Marianne Moore's Poetry" (in *Engendering the Word: Feminist Essays in Psychosexual Poetics*, ed. Temma F. Berg, Anna Shannon Elgenbein, Jeanne Larsen, and Elisa Kay Sparks [University of Illinois Press, 1989]). Durham, for example, mentions Juhasz, Gelpi, and Rich on the feminist side, and Costello, Diggory, and Kammer as non-feminist writers who give positive attention to gendered aspects of Moore's writing without altering at all the male, mainstream perception of her as a "'poet's poet' whose primary interest lies in her mastery of form and technique" (225).

47. See Joanna Russ's "What Can a Heroine Do? Or Why Women Can't Write" for an astute and humorous analysis of such criticism (in *Images of Women in Fiction: Feminist Perspectives*, ed. Susan Koppelman Cornillon [Bowling Green University Popular Press, 1972]).

48. "Efforts of Affection: A Memoir of Marianne Moore," ed. Robert Giroux *(Vanity Fair* [June 1983], 44–61); page numbers in the text refer to this essay. Lynn Keller ("Words Worth a Thousand Postcards: The Bishop/Moore Correspondence," in *American Literature* 55, 3 [1983]: 405–429), Bonnie Costello ("Marianne Moore and Elizabeth Bishop: Friendship and Influence," in TCL, 130–149), David Kalstone *(Becoming A Poet: Elizabeth Bishop with Marianne Moore and Robert Lowell,* ed. Robert Hemenway [Farrar, Straus & Giroux, 1989]), Betsy Erkkila *(The Wicked Sisters: Women Poets, Literary History and Discord* [Oxford University Press, 1992]), and Joanne Diehl *(American Sublime* and *Elizabeth Bishop and Marianne Moore: The Psychodynamics of Creativity* (Princeton University Press, 1993]) have written on Moore's and Bishop's relationship. All acknowledge tension between the two writers and some criticism of the older poet by the younger one, but most seem to regard it as fully justified by what they describe as Moore's attempts to regulate Bishop morally and artistically rather than as part of a pattern of criticism developed long before Bishop knew her well. Bishop's memoir was left incomplete and unpublished at her death (Robert Giroux, however, followed her detailed marginal notes in completing it). As Erkkila speculates, Bishop may have left the essay unpublished because of its uneven tone in relation to Moore *(Wicked Sisters,* 148).

49. One must think in this context particularly of Bishop's inclusion of details like Moore's interest in her underwear. One can hardly imagine a fellow poet writing of, say, Pound's or Eliot's private behavior in quite this way.

50. *The Complete Poems, 1927–1979* (The Noonday Press, Farrar, Straus & Giroux, 1983), 82–83.

51. *On Lies, Secrets, and Silence: Selected Prose 1966–1978* (Norton, 1979), 33–49.

52. Erkkila calls important attention to prudish, decorous, and conventional things that Moore apparently says or in fact writes to Bishop. Yet there is a tendency among critics comparing Moore and Bishop (including Erkkila) to assume that Bishop's memory is flawless and any utterance of Moore's simply reveals her "self." This is patently not the case. It cannot be reiterated too strongly that by the time Bishop met Moore the latter was already in her mid-forties and had begun to cultivate the demeanor that increasingly dominated public images of her and that, as I argue in Chapter 6, attempted to counteract while it also exaggerated the tendencies previously ascribed to her. Bishop was as apt to misunderstand the conscious and political choices, or the incidental and playful remarks, of the older poet as Moore was to misread hers.

53. "'Corpses of Poesy': Some Modern Poets and Some Gender Ideologies of Lyric," in *Feminist Measures: Soundings in Poetry and Theory*, ed. Lynn Keller and Cristanne Miller (University of Michigan Press, 1994), 69–95.

54. The relative lack of interest among feminist critics and theorists in poetry at all, and particularly in nonconfessional and experimental poetry, constitutes the primary topic of Lynn Keller's and my introduction to *Feminist Measures*.

55. Such poets, among recent and contemporary writers, might include among others Lorna Dee Cervantes, Lucille Clifton, Judith Ortiz Cofer, Nikki Giovanni, Marilyn Hacker, Cynthia Ozick, Marge Piercy, Sylvia Plath, Anne Sexton, May Swenson, and Mitsuye Yamada. Poets like Audre Lorde and Judy Grahn—like the earlier Emily Dickinson and H.D.—seem to have a foot in both camps, writing a verse that may be read as confessional and experiential or as distanced from a revealed personal self and focusing on stylistic as well as political/sexual disjunction.

2. "Inquisitive Intensity" in Marianne Moore

1. Moore does in fact try out some conventional verse styles in her early poetry, especially in poems mailed home to her family from Bryn Mawr and never published. These are, however, for the most part light verse styles—limericks, songs, and humorously amorous valentines rather than soliloquies or odes. As Margaret Holley remarks in "'Any Dash for Freedom,'" even Moore's early verses are characterized by acuity and lack all "hand-me-down sentimentality" or heavily perfumed qualities—espe-

cially in comparison with the early Williams (and, one might add, Pound) (*William Carlos Williams Review* 14, 1 [Spring 1988]: 76).

2. In "No Moore of the Same: The Feminist Poetics of Marianne Moore," *William Carlos Williams Review* 14, 1 (Spring 1988): 23. DuPlessis uses "four tropes to define Moore's access to authority and vocation": namely, authority based on gender, on accessibility to cultural hegemony, on otherness/marginality, and on sexual/erotic authority (16). While I argue that Moore rejects notions of authority as based "on" gender, marginality, or sexuality, my conclusions about Moore's politics and poetic of "shared authorial authority" resemble DuPlessis's, and I am indebted to her work.

3. In "Gendered Quotation in the Poetry of Marianne Moore and T. S. Eliot" (unpublished manuscript), 4. See Gregory's *"Imaginary Gardens with Real Toads"'*: *Quotation and Modern American Poetry* (Rice University Press, 1995).

4. In *Painterly Abstraction in Modernist American Poetry: The Contemporaneity of Modernism* (Cambridge University Press, 1989), 260.

5. With its play on rebelling from the "parent block," this poem's controlling metaphor constitutes a delightful anticipation of feminist critique of psychoanalytic—especially Bloomian—notions of literary influence as family romance.

6. Bonnie Costello argues that much of Moore's verse involves a by-process of self-portraiture in the sense that Moore "learns about herself through observation of the external world" but without that self-absorption subverting the observation itself; "The Feminine Language of Marianne Moore," in *Marianne Moore*, ed. Harold Bloom (Chelsea House, 1987), 99. In *Marianne Moore and the Visual Arts: Prismatic Color*, Linda Leavell writes of Moore's poems of collage or selection—especially those of the late 1910s and 1920s—as disguised but intentional self-portraits (Oklahoma University Press, 1995; 126–130), and Jeanne Heuving considers Moore's animal poems self-portraits (*Omissions Are Not Accidents: Gender in the Art of Marianne Moore* [Wayne State University Press, 1992], 149).

7. Laurence Scott quotes the first statement from a personal conversation with the poet (private communication with the author, May 1986); the second occurs in the "Notes" for "Marriage"; the third is the title of a late poem, "In Lieu of the Lyre."

8. Quoted, respectively, by Lisa Steinman in *Made in America: Science, Technology, and American Modernist Poets* (Yale University Press, 1987), 19, and by Rosemary Sprague in *Imaginary Gardens: A Study of Five Poets* (Chilton Book Company, 1969), 185. Most of these statements occur quite late in Moore's career, but this is because that is the period when she was most frequently asked to comment on her work. The previously quoted note to "Marriage"

indicates that Moore publicly distances her work from traditional poetry quite early on.

9. In *The Didactic Muse: Scenes of Instruction in Contemporary American Poetry* (Princeton University Press, 1990), 3, 6.

10. Moore's letters to her family between the years 1910 and 1916 provide remarkable evidence of her determination to publish despite years of having her manuscripts rejected.

11. Erkkila's *The Wicked Sisters: Women Poets, Literary History and Discord* (Oxford University Press, 1992). Costello's groundbreaking essay on Moore's "'Feminine' Language" skirts this view: she argues that Moore manipulates "feminine" virtues so as to show their vitality and force, yet by conceiving those virtues and several aspects of Moore's style within the rubric of femininity (even in quotation marks), she nonetheless perpetuates the boundaries of such categorization in a way that, I believe, goes against the grain of Moore's poetic.

12. Sandra Gilbert similarly states that Moore's questioning "of the historically privileged status of 'poetry'" involves "quiet arrogance" ("Marianne Moore as Female Female Impersonator," in AMM, 42); Robert Pinsky, in the same volume, refers to Moore's forceful promotion of her ideas against an aesthetic of hierarchy and domination ("Marianne Moore: Idiom and Idiosyncrasy," 24). Stapleton also describes Moore as self-confident, frank, and direct from the start of her career, even with famous people (*Marianne Moore: A Poet's Advance* (Princeton University Press, 1978], 110).

13. Celeste Goodridge makes a similar argument in *Hints and Disguises: Marianne Moore and Her Contemporaries* (University of Iowa Press, 1989), 13, as does Taffy Martin in *Marianne Moore, Subversive Modernist* (University of Texas Press, 1986), xiii. Margaret Holley insists throughout her book that "Moore from the beginning sets her own poetry at odds with poetry-in-general" (PMM, 16).

14. *Women Poets and the American Sublime* (Indiana University Press, 1990), 60.

15. As Goodridge points out, this conviction of Moore's contradicts one of the most hallowed tenets of modernism and of New Critical thought: that the text is an object sufficient unto itself. Moore, she writes, "often de-stabliizes the notion of what a text is" and "assumes that every reading is potentially capable of creating the text" (*Hints and Disguises*, 22, 127). The primary argument of Martin's book rests on her claim that Moore is a postmodern in the modern age (*Subversive Modernist*, xi–xiv).

16. An important distinction must be made here, however, between Moore's rejection of authorial mastery and her continued use of authorial signature—that is, while denying she is a poet she nonetheless "signs" her

poems as her own, hence also as written by a woman, in publishing them. On this subject, see Nancy Miller, especially the three essays constituting her part II, "The Subjects of Feminist Criticism," in *Subject to Change: Reading Feminist Writing* (Columbia University Press, 1988); Miller and Peggy Kamuf's debate over the importance of signature, "Dialogue" (*Diacritics* 12, 2 [Summer 1982]: 42–53); and Domna Stanton's "Autogynography: Is the Subject Different?" in *The Female Autograph* (University of Chicago Press, 1984).

17. Lynn Keller calls Moore's verse mosaic and several critics refer to collage-like aspects of her poetry, but the topic receives most extensive and recent discussion in Leavell's *Prismatic Color,* chap. 3 (see Keller's "'For inferior who is free?' Liberating the Woman Writer in Marianne Moore's 'Marriage,'" in *Influence and Intertextuality in Literary History,* ed. Jay Clayton and Eric Rothstein [University of Wisconsin Press, 1991], 219–244). Leavell comments, for example, that "the witty subversiveness of collage would have appealed to Moore as a modernist, as a feminist . . . and as an American—for the impulse of collage is anti-hierarchical and democratic" (117). Heuving claims that Moore's innovative use of collage "may have been instrumental in enabling this form to emerge in the literary arena" and that this use is decisively at odds with that practiced by Eliot in *The Waste Land* (*Omissions Are Not Accidents,* 112).

18. I borrow here from reader-response theory and Umberto Eco's postulation that a text in some sense posits its own reader (*The Role of the Reader: Explorations in the Semiotics of Texts* [Indiana University Press, 1979]). Of course, one may construct exactly this sort of self from Moore's poems, and much of feminist criticism (including parts of this book) attempts to perform this very task. Most of Moore's poems do not, however, offer an easy path toward such reading.

19. Along the lines of the more traditional claim, see Andrew J. Kappel's "Introduction: The Achievement of Marianne Moore," in TCL, v–xxx; Keller's *Remaking It New* (Cambridge University Press, 1988); Charles Molesworth's *Marianne Moore: A Literary Life* (Atheneum, 1990); Erkkila's *The Wicked Sisters;* and Darlene Erickson's *Illusion is More Precise than Precision* (University of Alabama Press, 1992). In *Language and the Poet: Verbal Artistry in Frost, Stevens, and Moore,* Marie Borroff identifies the moral value of "self-effacement" as it is enacted in language with stylistic characteristics of feature article journalism: "We pay little if any heed to [the expounding 'I'] as a personality in his own right . . . the author of the feature article is 'there' to draw our attention to the subject, as the copywriter is there to draw our attention to the product . . . Moore plays the part of a high-minded publicity agent or honest advertiser, one who is giving us informa-

tion for what he sincerely believes to be our own good" (University of Chicago Press, 1979), 83, 132.

20. On masking generally in feminist criticism, see, for example, Hélène Cixous's "The Laugh of the Medusa," *Signs* (Summer 1976): 245–264; Alicia Ostriker's *Stealing the Language: The Emergence of Women's Poetry in America* (Beacon Press, 1986); Florence Howe and Ellen Bass's collection *No More Masks! An Anthology of Poems by Women* (Anchor Press, Doubleday, 1973; recently reissued); and Cheryl Walker's *Masks Outrageous and Obscure* (Indiana University Press, 1991). Ostriker and Gilbert argue that Moore is masked in her poetry (*Stealing the Language*, 52–53, and Gilbert's "Female Female Impersonator") and, in an extreme statement of this view, Erkkila refers to Moore's "endless proliferation of animals, objects, and other peoples' words" as a "shield that she constantly hides behind" (*Wicked Sisters*, 104).

21. Burke writes that Moore, like other of her female contemporaries, saw "the poetic subject as not so much a stable entity/identity but as a 'subject-in-process' (Kristeva's phrase), a shifting, unstable position in language from which to speak the complex ethics and aesthetics of their (female) modernism"; for them, "the meanings of the 'self' in relation to the 'supposed person' [of a text] were always complex and never unambiguous"; "Supposed Persons: Modernist Poetry and the Female Subject," *Feminist Studies* 11 (Spring 1985): 136.

22. Gary Lee Stonum, *The Dickinson Sublime* (University of Wisconsin Press, 1990).

23. "In a Word," an interview with Ellen Rooney, in *differences* 1.2 (Summer 1989): 130.

24. I am reading the "must" in the line "the physiognomy of conduct must not reveal the skeleton" as descriptive rather than imperative. I quote here from the version of "People's Surroundings" in the *Complete Poems* because the earliest versions of the poem do not yet include what I read as a crucial line: "these are questions more than answers."

25. Slatin persuasively reads this poem as depicting Moore's relation to Pound, Williams, Eliot, and Stevens—or, more generally, a poet's relation to the past. I do not concur, however, that it also represents a failed attempt to reconcile contemporary surroundings or the present with that tradition; nor do I see Moore as an "acacia-like lady" who disappears "'like an obedient chameleon,' betrayed by her own mimetic instincts into accommodating herself too readily to alien and hostile—and male—surroundings" (SR, 135).

26. Helpful here is C. Carroll Hollis's claim that the antithetical structures and repeated negation of Whitman's poetry construct an undeniably

affirmative poetic, in *Language and Style in Leaves of Grass* (Louisiana State University Press, 1983). Quoting from W. K. Wimsatt, Hollis writes, "'The negative defines the positive. The more peculiar and complex the affirmation the more it may need the emphasis of negation' . . . the negative is used as an emphasis for the positive; it is a stylistic, a rhetorical, device, . . . and in no way suggests or relates to personal doubts, despair, solipsistic rejection" (136, 138). While I believe that personal doubts, anger, and other feelings that encourage antithesis *do* enter distinctly into Moore's and Whitman's poetic, she (like Whitman) uses structures of negation and antithetical distinction emphatically rather than as set quantities.

27. Joanne Diehl puts this both in more conflictual and in gendered terms, again regarding lack of clarity as part of a tactic of disguise: "To break free of the confines of this engendered trap of language requires the sacrifice of ascriptive clarity . . . Such an obfuscation of point of view bestows the freedom that enables Moore to interrogate as well as to describe the debilitating effects of cultural and aesthetic traditions" (*American Sublime*, 48–49). Slatin, in contrast, argues that "Clarity—poetry—is the ideal Moore holds up not only to herself but to her contemporaries as well; like Paradise, though, it is impossible to attain"; in this view, what she and others write is at best a modern approximation of poetry (SR, 6).

28. *In Other Worlds: Essays in Cultural Politics* (Methuen, 1987), x.

29. As this review implies, such definitions of "clarity" were shared by several modernist poets and artists. Williams writes repeatedly of clarity and in *Spring and All* frames his definition by discussing Moore's work; *Imaginations*, ed. Webster Schott (New Directions, 1970), 101–102).

30. One may also read this poem more sympathetically to the hobo figure, as I do in Chapter 4.

31. "Marianne Moore: 'Transcendence, Conditional,'" in *Modern American Poetry*, ed. R. W. Butterfield (Vision Press, 1984), 118, 120. It is important to note—as Edwards does, but as do few other writers taking Moore's religious views as their theme—that Moore does not promote simple belief in religious structures any more than in anything else. Christian beliefs may be seen to underlie much of what she writes, but she does not insist on the connection. Leavell quotes Moore's mother as writing to her brother, "Marianne herself has never professed to have faith,—has almost *said* her soul was dim with darkness and utter lack of faith" (*Prismatic Color*, 43); like Leavell, I find that many critics are too quick to see Moore's church-going and the piousness of her family and some friends as signs of her own strict adherence to religious doctrine. They seem to me instead signs of her profoundly Christian upbringing and a deeply felt sense of spiritual and

moral presence in the world that takes its most automatic and comfortable (but not only) form for Moore in Christianity.

32. Moore's notes to this poem provide the reader with some of her sources of information—including the *Illustrated London News*, A. Hyatt Verrill's *Lost Treasure*, and F. W. Hutton and James Drummond's *Animals of New Zealand*.

33. See, for example, Holley (PMM, 131) and Randall Jarrell's "Her Shield" (CCE, 114–124). DuPlessis suggests that Moore uses animals to stage an authority of otherness, to "creat[e] otherness as a source of critical knowledge" for herself; Moore, however, also "lump[s] all humans together as exploiters and 'rapers' of animals" who are themselves "unquestionable heroes" ("No Moore of the Same," 19). Heuving sees Moore's animal poems of the 1930s as "her most direct attempts at self-portraiture—and the poetry is among her most traditionally symbolic or specular" (*Omissions Are Not Accidents*, 149).

34. Although arguing in direct contrast to my primary point here, Marie Borroff also notes the lack of realism in Moore's descriptions, even calling them "surreal word photographs" pointing toward "essential form or emblematic significance" rather than toward the thing itself (*Language and the Poet*, 113).

35. For a cogent discussion of "complementarity," see Henry J. Folse's *The Philosophy of Niels Bohr: The Framework of Complementarity* (North-Holland Physics Publishing, 1985). Also useful is N. Katherine Hayles's *The Cosmic Web: Scientific Field Models and Literary Strategies in the Twentieth Century* (Cornell University Press, 1984). I am grateful to Karen Barad for letting me read and discussing with me in manuscript form her essay "Meeting the Universe Half-Way: Ambiguities, Discontinuities, Quantum Subjects and Multiple Positionings in Feminism and Physics," which links poststructuralist feminist and quantum theories (in *Making a Difference in the Natural Sciences: Eliminating Gender and Related Biases in the Content and Practice of Science*, ed. Bonnie Spanier (Indiana University Press, 1995]).

36. Kappel sees "the characteristic action of a Moore poem [as] an act of management" and finds "the poetic consciousness committed . . . to the challenging project of managing the world . . . always equal to the task" ("The Achievement of Marianne Moore," viii). I see Moore's attempts to "manage" as signs of her vivid consciousness that only temporary, subjective, and partial successes are possible; the extraordinary diversity of the world will always exceed any individual's attempt to understand or manage it. Interestingly, while Kappel attributes Moore's self-confident control to her Protestantism, Edwards sees her Protestantism as responsible for

Moore's delight in the imperfect, faulty, and partial nature of any human perception or control.

37. *The Pink Guitar: Writing as Feminist Practice* (Routledge, 1990), 144.

38. Moore does not mention quoting from Stalin in her Notes, but refers to it in "Idiosyncrasy and Technique": the phrase "the citadel of learning" is taken from Stalin (CPr, 512).

39. Although Moore only substitutes "author" for "man" twice, other clues in the poem and notes indicate that the "author" is her primary concern. Most important, she quotes twice from Louis Dudek's "The New Laocoon," an essay on modern verse published immediately preceding a positive review of her *Collected Poems*—the arrangement suggesting that *Origin's* editor saw the striking similarity between the principles of her verse and Dudek's call for a poetry of "working ideas," of commitment that transforms "unexampled chaos . . . a multitude of emotions, words, rightful hates, likes and dislikes—if not loves" into "a new body" (*Origin* 18 [1956]: 118, 119–120). Moore also quotes from Dudek in "Subject, Predicate, Object" (CPr, 505).

40. This is also the argument of "In Distrust of Merits" and several other of Moore's poems, as Costello points out: "Humility is not armor against the aggressions of the world on the self so much as against those of the self on the world . . . To impose the self and its accumulated structures on the world is to narrow the world and trap the self, a self-defeating gesture" ("'Feminine' Language," 93).

41. Moore may, however, pun on feminine power by closing the poem with a phallic figure cast in a "feminine" rhyme—the two-syllable "cower"/"tower." In Chapter 4 I discuss Moore's use of "masculine" language.

42. In manuscript versions of the poem, Moore uses an "I" and refers to the momentum and vitality needed for a poetry of public responsibility—for example, "I am alive fr top / to toe w curiousity . . . Hew to the line & let the chips fall where they may . . . strike till the iron is hot . . . Discouragement is a form of temptation & paranoia is not optimism" (RML I.01.20). These notes make the poem, at least in its initial stages, a series of directives to the poet rather than a celebration of a person or role already "blessed."

43. Although Eisenhower did not come from a wealthy family, he both graduated from West Point and married into a powerful family—that is, he was not born into the American upper class, but no part of his heritage or upbringing prevented him from entering fully and comfortably into it in early manhood. Interestingly, Moore is aggressively defensive about quoting Eisenhower, asking in *The Marianne Moore Reader* if there is "Anything

reprehensible" in what she has quoted from him (xvi). She then strengthens her own identification with Eisenhower by quoting further. When asked if he is a "moralist," Eisenhower replies, "'I think perhaps I am. I do not thrust promises and deeds of mercy right and left to write a lyric—if what I write ever is one'"; Moore then appends her own remark: "a qualification received with smiles by a specialist (or proseur turned poseur)—(leopard and croco-dile)" (MMR, xvii). Although it remains ambiguous whether Moore is a "specialist" moralist or poet ("poseur"), and what it means to link the President of the United States with herself as "leopard" with "crocodile," Moore would clearly argue that the "Blessed Man" or poet should not sacrifice truth to aesthetics—give excessive promises to "write a lyric." Her poem suggests an ultimate distinction between the positions of statesman and poet, but Eisenhower remains a personal hero for Moore.

44. As with other women writers, critics tend to identify Moore with her speakers—perhaps in particular with her because the "I" is understated and thus gives little evidence of being a dramatic persona. The fact that Moore's family apparently read her poetry as being in her personal voice if not specifically about her (and them) no doubt contributes to this tendency. Moore's brother Warner, for example, writes in 1919 that Moore uses "our own special 'language'" in her poems, but "so marvelously handled that the 'aliens' could and can understand" it (RML VI.23.17; May 1, 1920).

45. Slatin reads this poem as Moore's expression of desire to rebel against her mother as her brother has: she longs for the freedom of following her own path, but remains merely "looking" at "Liberty" (SR, 35–36). Similarly, Holley discusses the spatial relations in this poem, concluding that Moore remains trapped between her two alternative spaces (PMM, 29–30). I would argue instead that the poem has a Dickinsonian openness, staging a scene of conflict and questioning without specifying the circumstances that bring the speaker to the point of this scene, and thereby allowing the poem's readers each to imagine their own version of this conflict.

46. Freedom is a topic of ongoing concern in Moore's writing—height-ened particularly during and following World War II. As she states at the beginning of "Humility, Concentration, and Gusto," "In times like these we are tempted to disregard anything that has not a direct bearing on freedom" (CPr, 420).

47. For a fuller account of such revision, see both Holley's *The Poetry of Marianne Moore* and her essay "The Model Stanza: The Organic Origin of Moore's Syllabic Verse" (TCL, 181–190). Jeredith Merrin, Bonnie Honigsblum, and Jeffrey D. Peterson also have essays on Moore's revisions in *Marianne Moore: Woman and Poet*, ed. Patricia C. Willis (National Poetry

Foundation, 1990). These essays are titled, respectively, "Re-Seeing the Sea: Marianne Moore's 'A Grave' as a Woman Writer's Re-vision" (155–167); "Marianne Moore's Revisions of 'Poetry,'" (185–222); and "Notes on the Poem(s) 'Poetry': The Ingenuity of Moore's Poetic 'Place'" (223–241).

48. Moreover, there is no single body of texts that comprises Moore's "complete poems." The volume published under that title contains fewer than two-thirds of the poems Moore published and only one version of each poem (with the exception of "Poetry"); several of her poems remain unpublished. Molesworth counts the number of unpublished poems as "at least seventy-four" (*A Literary Life*, 102).

49. In *Language and Politics*, ed. Michael Shapiro (New York University Press, 1984), 26. Page citations in the following paragraphs are to this essay.

50. *The Poem as Utterance* (Methuen, 1986), 10.

51. As Pocock acknowledges, a speech-act, of course, functions within a particular historical and cultural context which constitutes part of its meaning, hence in part determines the kind of act it is, the degree of power it exercises, and so on. The basic assumptions here are Foucauldian, but I find their articulation through speech-act theory more useful in analyzing Moore's poetry than through discourse theory.

52. Chambers, *Room for Maneuver: Reading the Oppositional in Narrative* (University of Chicago Press, 1991), 70; and "Narrative in Opposition: Reflections on a La Fontaine Fable," *French Forum* 8, 3 (September 1983): 220.

53. Lines from "The Mind Is an Enchanting Thing" and "Charity Overcoming Envy" (CP, 134, 135, 217). In *Vision into Verse*, Willis quotes from a letter in which Moore states that "The Mind Is an Enchanting Thing" emphasizes the "courage to change one's mind, willing to seem to have been wrong—unwise and improvident" (Rosenbach Museum and Library, 1987), 60.

3. An "Unintelligible Vernacular": Questions of Voice

1. In part, this amounts to saying that modernism is more complicated than some definitions of it have been; it is rare (if not impossible) to find a pure representative of a complex literary movement or period—and Moore is not one. See Chapter 6, note 5, on the fact that definitions of modernism were long proposed and refined with little attention to Moore's work, which in part explains why it would not fit comfortably within the boundaries of such definitions.

2. For one of the earliest and strongest statements of this position, see *The L=A=N=G=U=A=G=E Book*, ed. Bruce Andrews and Charles Bernstein

(Southern Illinois University Press, 1984); this is also a repeated theme of Hank Lazar, and of several avant-garde poets, manifested, for example, by Susan Howe in "Articulation of Sound Forms in Time"—a title that in itself mocks traditional notions of language as "voice."

3. *Radical Artifice: Writing Poetry in the Age of Media* (University of Chicago Press, 1991), 10–11. Charles Altieri also questions what it means to attempt to construct "emotional authenticity" in a poem, in *Self and Sensibility in Contemporary American Poetry* (Cambridge University Press, 1984), 10–15.

4. *A Homemade World: The American Modernist Writers* (Random House, 1974), 102.

5. *Marianne Moore: The Poetry of Engagement* (University of Illinois Press, 1986), 21, 45–46. Schulman argues that Moore's verse is "natural" and speech-like: it is structured by rhetorical figures of argument, and on word-stress rhythms that resemble the rhythms of speech, or a dialectical process of thought. She also notes, however, that the increasing "naturalism" in the rhythm of Moore's verse is "gained, paradoxically, through organizing devices that are highly complex" (97). In "The Model Stanza," Holley notes the mixture of tones in Moore's verse: "Moore's skillful opposition of the written and spoken aspects of poetry" balances "the textual with the vocal elements of verse in general" (TCL, 188–189).

6. Among other changes, Moore later altered "autocrats" to "poets." The earlier version of this line pointedly marks her rejection of the role of poet as "autocrat" (as well as her rejection of nongenuine and useless poetry)—as does the later deleted phrase "in defiance of their opinion."

7. In "The Model Stanza: The Organic Origin of Moore's Syllabic Verse," Holley concludes that the syllabic measure "cross[es] the rhythms of the natural voice or nonpoetic passage over the traditional textual appearance of the repeated stanza form": "The effect of this dissociation and yet interpenetration of text and voice in Moore's work is to demythologize the traditional notion of poetry, that is, to show that the metrical rhythms we have customarily assumed to be a necessary, definitive essence of poetry are, in fact, a contingent, conventional attribute of it" (182, 190). Linda Leavell attributes the combination of natural subject matter and abstract form to the influence of Cubism and Moore's interest in the aesthetic of functionalism (*Marianne Moore and the Visual Arts: Prismatic Color* [Oklahoma University Press, 1995], chap. 2). Lisa Steinman describes a similar complexity in Moore's definitions of the scientific and technological in terms of process, evolution, and flux rather than as categories of fixed form or factual knowledge, in *Made in America: Science, Technology, and American Modernist Poets* (Yale University Press, 1987), 114, 123–125. Moore's desire to construct the natural may partially explain her failure

to write effective dialogue in her dramatization of Maria Edgeworth's eighteenth-century novel *The Absentee*, published in 1962. In "Marianne Moore and *The Absentee*: The Poet as Playwright," Bruce Henderson finds no particular gift for dramatic dialogue as it must be produced on the stage but nonetheless concludes that studying this play helps one see all Moore's verse "as a conversational, even dialogic (in a Socratic sense) representation of created and creative speech" (in *Marianne Moore: Woman and Poet*, ed. Patricia C. Willis [National Poetry Foundation, 1990], 283). Similarly, T. S. Eliot's reflection that Moore's speech resembles "the curious jargon produced in America by universal university education" might be interpreted as an acknowledgment of her combination of the natural with the constructed (CCE, 49). Schulman, in contrast, interprets Eliot to suggest that Moore's typical speaker is "an elegant conversationalist" (*Poetry of Engagement*, 49).

8. Moore's essay "Henry James as a Characteristic American" is often read as reflecting qualities of her own verse. For example, Costello uses this essay in her "Epilogue" as Moore's "appreciation of her own virtues as an artist" (IP, 247), and Celeste Goodridge argues that Moore's aesthetic was influenced by James ("Towards a Poetics of Disclosure: Marianne Moore and Henry James," in *Sagetrieb* 6, 3 [Winter 1987]: 31–43). Moore herself writes to Ezra Pound in an early letter that James is one of the few "direct influences bearing upon my work" (RML V.50.06; January 9, 1919).

9. In AMM, 19, 14. Pinsky speculates that "Moore's declining to reproduce something like the social art of conversation in her poems, even parodying that art by an autocratic system of apostrophe and quotation, is a way of refusing the realm traditionally or stereotypically assigned to women of intelligence and force: polite conversation"; later, however, he suggests that Moore refuses and parodies "male assertion" as much as "female charm" (21, 23).

10. "Idiom and Idiosyncrasy," 20; Merrin, *An Enabling Humility: Marianne Moore, Elizabeth Bishop, and the Uses of Tradition* (Rutgers University Press, 1990).

11. See Morton White's *Pragmatism and the American Mind* for a history of pragmatism in America, and on the importance of James's thought to the development of this philosophical school (Oxford University Press, 1973). By the end of World War I, he states, pragmatism's liberal philosophy of society and social science dominated the American intellectual scene. Moore had strong personal links with William James's family, which may have increased her interest in pragmatism; for over a year, she had what amounted to a passion (in Bryn Mawr terms a "smash") for William's daughter Peggy James—a constant subject of letters between the Moores

during 1907–1908 (RML, boxes VI.13a, 13b, 14). Molesworth mentions that Moore read Dewey during the late 1910s and 1920s, and writes of her general attraction to pragmatist thought (*Marianne Moore: A Literary Life* [Atheneum, 1990], xx, 161).

12. I am indebted to LeeAnn Lawrence's "Organisms vs. Machines: Gertrude Buck and the Direction of Early Twentieth-Century Rhetorical Theory" for calling Buck to my attention and for her summary of the development of Buck's career in the context of popular theories of rhetoric (*Women and Language* 15, no. 2 [Fall 1992]: 32–34).

13. As I discuss in Chapter 6, these contrasting models resemble the conclusions of empirical studies about language patterns that tend to be used by single-sex groups of men and women, respectively. It is also a widespread assumption that English-speaking men tend to use battle or military language more frequently than women in describing linguistic interaction (an argument "attacks," "wins" or "loses," and so on); to my knowledge, no empirical work is available on this subject. Carol Cohn's brilliant analysis of the gendered basis for military jargon, "Sex and Death in the Rational World of Defense Intellectuals," with its almost exclusively male speakers, points in this direction (*Signs* 12:4 [1987]: 687–718).

14. See Costello's *Imaginary Possessions*, chap. 4, for a discussion of Moore's use of metaphors of combat.

15. "Verbalizing a Political Act: Toward a Politics of Speech," in *Language and Politics*, ed. Michael Shapiro (New York University Press, 1984), 25; *The Mirror and the Lamp: Romantic Theory and the Critical Tradition* (Oxford University Press, 1953). Buck's rhetoric, like much of speech-act theory and some of Moore's poetry, tends to idealize the relationship between speakers as being based on a fully cooperative relationship of equality between individuals. I argue, for example, in "Moore's Maternal Hero" that Moore to a certain extent focuses her analysis of power relationships, ethics, and communication on individuals and an ideology of personal choice rather than on systemic or institutional abuses and response, although—as I argue later in this book—I think Moore is more savvy to the nuances of systemic power differentials than is commonly recognized. Norman Fairclough cogently critiques this aspect of speech-act theory in *Language and Power* (Longman, 1989), 9–10.

16. York's *The Poem as Utterance* (Methuen, 1986), 7, 13; and Stephen C. Levinson's *Pragmatics* (Cambridge University Press, 1983), 102. Levinson provides a lucid summary of Grice's cooperative principle on pp. 101ff.

17. Quoted in Carroll C. Hollis's *Language and Style of Leaves of Grass* (Louisiana State University Press, 1983), 68. Hollis provides an exemplary analysis of how speech-act theory may illuminate a reading of poetry.

18. The history of this poem is reviewed in the *Marianne Moore Newsletter* 3, 2 (1979): 5–8. According to Holley's count, four-fifths of the poems written in Carlisle address a "you" (PMM, 20). Many of these poems remain unpublished.

19. Of those she reprints in the *Complete Poems*, "To Robert Browning in His Act of Vandalism" becomes "Injudicious Gardening" and "To Bernard Shaw: A Prize Bird" becomes "To a Prize Bird"—titles that at least imply more inclusive address, although nothing else within the poems broadens the frame. Other changes include the alternative titles "To A Strategist" for "To Disraeli on Conservatism" and "Reprobate Silver" for "Blake." Moore did not republish most of the poems written to specific men after *Observations*. In *Complete Poems*, her only poems naming specific people in their titles appear in the 1966 volume *Tell Me, Tell Me* ("W. S. Landor," "Arthur Mitchell," "To Victor Hugo of My Crow Pluto," and "Rescue with Yul Brynner")—and only "Arthur Mitchell" is a poem of direct address.

20. Holley also distinguishes Moore's "I" from that of the "more purely lyric poet": "By not enveloping the entire poem in its awareness, but remaining rather one element among others, Moore's 'I' formally recognizes a world beyond its own consciousness, an environment that is genuinely 'other'" (PMM, 123). In "No Moore of the Same," DuPlessis describes such address as "a syntactic method for entering into 'poetry' while denying the high lyric mode, the invocation or prayer to power, the supposed universality of the lyric 'I'" (*William Carlos Williams Review* 14, 1 [Spring 1988]: 12.

21. Of course, appreciation may also be competitive, in that it implies a stance, and hence a capacity for, judgment. These poems, however, have less to do with the act of judgment than with expressions of pleasure. Their tone is comradely; Moore's authority then seems to lie parallel to that of other poets rather than in competition with it.

22. Holley estimates that Moore uses an "I" in more than half of her poems (PMM, 25). Although she appropriately distinguishes between the "I" of early poems and those of poems from the 1940s on, I also see common elements in Moore's nearly lifelong but typically low-keyed and in various ways communally oriented use of a first-person speaker.

23. Schulman calls attention to this construction under different terms: "Moore's negative statements also have an exhortatory manner . . . especially in their reinforcement of rhetorical shifts and demarcation of rhythmic divisions" (*Poetry of Engagement*, 106); in these places, Moore often begins her sentence with the negating term. As I do in Chapter 2, Schulman also calls attention to Moore's affirmative use of negative constructions.

24. Moore also uses frequent implied negatives. In *Language and the Poet:*

Verbal Artistry in Frost, Stevens, and Moore, Borroff mentions "unextirpated," "unsolicitude," "unparticularities," and "chlorophylless" as the poet's coinages, remarking that her "formations with *un-* . . . are especially frequent" (University of Chicago Press, 1979; 89). The speaker of "A Carriage from Sweden" exclaims, remarkably, "What unannoying / romance!" (*CP*, 131). In "The Plumet Basilisk" Moore describes the Malay dragon, "Among unfragrant orchids, on the unnutritious nut- // tree, *myristica* / *fragrans*, the harmless god spreads ribs that / do not raise a hood" (*CP*, 21). Or, to give a single more extended example, "In Lieu of the Lyre" begins with the semantic negative "One *debarred* from enrollment at Harvard" (emphasis mine) and then continues with direct and indirect negatives ("Brooklyn's (or Mexico's) / *ineditos*," "Lowell House Press—/ Vermont Stinehour Press, rather. (No careless statements / . . . least of all inexactness," "unavoidably lame as I am"), concluding with a repetition of its title—which also implies a negative: her "statements" appear "in lieu of the lyre" (that is, they are *not* a poem; *CP*, 206). Although one might argue that this poem is particularly defensive in topic, given its beginning with the reminder that women were not allowed to enroll at Harvard in Moore's college days, the poem is generally read as a statement of grateful praise, and several other of Moore's poems contain a similar number of contradicting or negative constructions.

25. Joanne Feit Diehl (among others) rightly insists upon Moore's affiliation with Whitman, both through "the immediacy of individual observation" that characterizes both poets and "in her determination to free herself from outmoded forms and non-native styles" (*Women Poets and the American Sublime* [Indiana University Press, 1990], 58).

26. In 1935, Moore writes to Dorothea Gray: "I tend to regard the stanza as the unit of composition rather than the line" (MMN II, 2 [Fall 1978]: 11); she echoes this statement repeatedly—for example, telling Hall that she "consider[s] the stanza the unit" in her "versifying" (MMR, 259).

27. Although this is of course not the case in Moore's free verse, as Robert Beloof remarks, even there Moore does not "direct the reader's voice through typographic guides" as do Pound, Eliot, Cummings, and other of her contemporaries; lines are based on syntactic, not inflectional or spoken (breath) units; in "Prosody and Tone: The 'Mathematics' of Marianne Moore" (CCE, 144–149, 145).

28. "Line Break," in Robert Frank and Henry Sayre's *The Line in Postmodern Poetry* (University of Illinois Press, 1988), 98, 102.

29. See Leavell for the sequence of Moore's development of her stanza and rhyme structures in relation to other visual and poetic modernist experimentation with form, and for an excellent analysis of her stanzaic

forms (*Prismatic Color*, chap. 2). Marie Borroff, in a comparison of the "layout" of Williams's and Moore's poems, attends to "enjambment, syntactically necessitated pauses, punctuation or the lack of punctuation, left-margin justification, indentation or lack of indentation, the spacing out of stanzas, the narrowness or width of the poem as laid out on the page, syllable-counts, rhymes . . . [and] other visual and aural prosodic features" ("Questions of Design in William Carlos Williams and Marianne Moore," in the *William Carlos Williams Review* 14, no. 1 [Spring 1988]: 106). Borroff claims that Moore tends to use such features to slow rather than speed a reader's progress through a poem. Rather than creating the momentum common in Williams's poetry, Moore makes one aware of "the constraints of form" and the liberatory potential of such constraint (110).

30. Paradoxically, this tension between line and phrase in some ways calls more attention to a prose rhythm in her poetry than do her free verse poems, with their coincident line and phrase structures. The tension between line endings and phrasal units in Moore's syllabic verse keeps the reader's ear alert to the driving rhythms of the syntax as they forge through the lines.

31. As Holley writes, this experiment with the "free" form began with Moore's revision of a number of syllabic-verse poems into free verse lines. When she returned to writing poetry in the 1930s, she showed no interest in continuing her experimentation with the free verse line (PMM, 47–51).

32. Moore in fact typically marks her end-rhymes visually by indenting rhyming lines the same number of spaces from the left-hand margin—that is, she marks an aural practice with visual structures.

33. In Chapter 6 I analyze structural or metapoetic ways in which quotation functions to suggest interactive as well as constructed form.

34. Borroff uses the terms "distinctively formal," "distinctively colloquial," and "common" (of native or Teutonic origin) to characterize Moore's various styles. For the purposes of this discussion, the last two may be combined as both characterizing speech-like text. Borroff sees Moore's "formal" style as a product of her Romance-Latinate diction, high use of scientific and technical words, complex syntax, and relatively phrasal or noun- and adjective-dominated descriptions.

35. Schulman argues that Moore, after hearing herself read her poems on records for the first time, began revising syllabic stanzas to make them correspond more closely to the phrasing of speech (*Poetry of Engagement*, 99–100). Nonetheless, the later verse still contains a distinct tension between its formal and illocutionary elements, and the latter still tend to dominate.

36. Howard introduces this list by insisting that "Marianne Moore did not have a great mind, but she aspired to have a whole one, and a whole mind is rarer still, and more important than mere greatness"—another example of taking with one hand what is given with the other, in the context of apparently intended great praise ("Marianne Moore and the Monkey Business of Modernism," 6–8). Why, for example, is not a "whole mind" indeed a "great" one, and doesn't the moral as opposed to qualitative judgment place Moore back in the realm of "poetess" and outside the canon of "mere[ly] great" literature?

37. Some biographical evidence for this reading of Moore's notion of sophistication exists in a letter she writes her brother not long after the publication of this poem (August 1, 1920): "I am at the 'it-takes all kinds to make-a-world-stage' when I doubt whether sophistication really advances one's position more than it hinders" (RML VI.23.22).

38. The source of this line confirms this aspect of its meaning. Moore quotes her brother in a conversation notebook saying, "I don't know. I suppose I'm stubborn—I feel sometimes as if the wave can go over me if it likes and I'll be there when it's gone by—" (RML 1250/23).

39. The association of Apollo Belvedere with male perfection was quite popular in the late nineteenth and early twentieth centuries, thanks to racist extensions of Johann Casper Lavater's (eighteenth-century) theories of physiognomy. Lavater describes Apollo as the highest physical type, and argues that "all members of the human race would eventually share the glad fate of 'becoming Apollo'"; quoted in Martha Banta's *Imaging American Women: Idea and Ideals in Cultural History* (Columbia University Press, 1987), 104. By a century later, this theory had been altered to fit eugenicist claims that only Caucasians were capable of attaining the look, and hence the moral superiority, of the Apollo Belvedere. Moore's rejection of this model for truth may then also mark her rejection of racist notions of human perfection. Moore reveals her familiarity with "Lavater's physiognomy" in "Then the Ermine" (1952) and its accompanying footnote; it is also possible that she knew earlier of the racist association of Apollo with the highest human phenotype without knowing its source. Banta's study provides a detailed portrait of racial and sexual stereotyping during this time period.

40. "Plainness" may also constitute an aesthetic pun contrasting the less attractive complexity of smoke and shadow with the beauty of Adamic light; as I argue in Chapter 4, Moore eschews an aesthetic of simple beauty as uninteresting and perhaps even harmful, constructing a poetic that is deliberately *not* beautiful in traditional terms.

41. Slatin also sees Moore's identification of complexity with women,

and with herself, but reads this identification as "intensely, almost savagely self-critical"; he sees the poet admitting that her own "complexity . . . has been committed to darkness" (SR, 96).

42. Clearly, this campaign had a solid basis in the already established heterosexual commercialism of popular culture. For example, in 1926 the main character of Anita Loos's best-selling *Gentlemen Prefer Blondes* proclaims, "Kissing your hand may make you feel very good but a diamond bracelet lasts forever" (Boni and Liveright, 1925; 101). On diamonds, see Edward Jay Epstein's *The Rise and Fall of Diamonds: The Shattering of a Brilliant Illusion* (Simon and Schuster, 1982), 121–128. My thanks to Ruth E. Gilmore for calling my attention to this volume. Anita Loos's "A Diamond Is Forever" did not become a slogan of the De Beers cartel diamond campaign until 1948, after Moore's poem was published, but the various strategies of advertising used between 1938 and 1947 all point in this direction. The strong association of diamonds with women engaged to be married makes me assume the speaker of this poem is female.

43. The exception occurs of course in wealthy families or royal estates, where jewels are part of the family inheritance, and hence another sign of a patriarchal system: the son gives his mother's jewels to his wife.

44. An interesting gloss on this phrase may be found in a 1927 review, where Moore comments that the new series *The Little Books of New Poetry* published by Lincoln MacVeagh "assumes that we can enjoy what has not had a fuss made about it"—or that one should credit a reader with being able to appreciate without loud touting or advertisement (CPr, 183).

45. The poem's quotation from Paul's letter to the Ephesians—the source of the phrase "love undying"—may also suggest a spiritual love, or love of God, as one of those preferred to romance.

46. The fact that Moore apparently quotes Crane in the poem's first line may also be telling here. Patricia C. Willis observes that Moore wrote in the margin of the manuscript she sent Crane, next to the first line: "Said by you to me, Louise, and now by me to you" (*Vision into Verse* [Rosenbach Museum and Library, 1987], 64). Moore associated Crane with love for women not only because of their friendship but because Crane, too, lived with her mother, and because of Crane's earlier relationship with Elizabeth Bishop. That Moore would not have used the word "lesbian" to describe that relationshop (or others) in no way reduces her knowledge of the importance of such relationships to Crane.

47. As Borroff continues, such language "originates in an investigation of present reality unhindered by reverence and subject to continuing revision"; thus it suggests a willingness to rethink propositions quite different from that of a high lyric mode, with its typically high proportion of

archaisms and hence suggested celebration of values of the past (*Language and the Poet*, 88).

48. Several feminist critics have theorized about the subversive and radical elements of humor or play. For example, in *A Very Serious Thing: Women's Humor and American Culture*, Nancy Walker traces a historical tradition of American women's humor, taking a primarily sociological perspective to argue that women's humor is typically subversive and focusing on ways in which it may disguise both rebelliousness and power by making its users seem harmless (University of Minnesota Press, 1988). Regina Barreca has edited an excellent collection of theoretically focused essays on women's comedy and humor from a variety of literary traditions called *Last Laughs: Perspectives on Women and Comedy* (Gordon and Breach, 1988), and popularizes her own theoretical position in *They Used To Call Me Snow White But I Drifted* (Viking Penguin, 1991). In *Honey-Mad Women: Emancipatory Strategies in Women's Writing*, Patricia Yaeger uses Cixous's "The Laugh of the Medusa" and a more psychoanalytically-oriented theory as the primary basis for theorizing that play establishes a place in the texts of women writers where revolutionary transformation may occur—although her chapter on this subject provides an extensive review of the importance of "play" to a number of other philosophers and psychologists as well (Columbia University Press, 1988).

49. Several critics call attention to humor in Moore's art, although without developing a framework for how it functions. For example, Altieri speculates that "if one replaced the composing will with a more flexible imaginative playfulness, it might be possible to show how the will itself can be understood in terms of virtual and transpersonal energies that an abstract art can display" (*Painterly Abstraction in Modernist American Poetry: The Contemporaneity of Modernism* [Cambridge University Press, 1989], 260). Moore, he argues, "reveals no hidden symbolic forces and works out no deep psychological conflicts. She does, though, define modes of activity where it may be possible not to have to live in the sets of oppositions that are generated by those conflicts" (264). Martin uses the "smile" concluding Moore's "Sojourn in the Whale" as an emblem of both Moore's "stubborn feminine temperament" and her imaginative independence, titling the final chapter of her book "'And You Have Smiled'" (*Marianne Moore, Subversive Modernist* [University of Texas Press, 1986], 136).

50. See her essays "Humility, Concentration, and Gusto" (1949; CPr, 420–426) and "Idiosyncrasy and Technique" (1956; CPr, 506–518).

51. *American Sublime*, 50. As several critics mention, Moore also undoubtedly plays in a great number of poems by embedding what amount to private messages or references for and to her family.

4. "Your Thorns Are the Best Part of You"

Epigraphs: The Moore quotation is taken from "A Letter From Kathleen Raine" in *Festschrift for Marianne Moore's Seventy-seventh Birthday by Various Hands,* ed. Tambimuttu (Tambimuttu and Mass, 1964). The DuPlessis quotation is from "'Corpses of Poesy': Some Modern Poets and Some Gender Ideologies of Lyric," in *Feminist Measures: Soundings in Poetry and Theory,* ed. Lynn Keller and Cristanne Miller (University of Michigan Press, 1994), 71.

1. A substantial draft of this chapter was completed by 1990. Since that time, it has been my pleasure to read several essays by Rachel Blau DuPlessis (especially several drafts of her "Corpses of Poesy") that have helped me sharpen the distinctions this chapter proposes and provided the confirmation of finding similar analysis in someone else's work. Much of the overlap in our approaches is based on the coincidence of our both (re)discovering material of Moore's that begs for such analysis; for the rest, as elsewhere in this study, I have tried to acknowledge my debts to DuPlessis specifically—although particularly with small details it at times became difficult to remember whose words came first. Hence I want to begin this chapter with a general statement of my indebtedness to her writing about gender and the lyric poem during the modernist period.

2. Altieri writes similarly that the context of noniconic art helps explain why Moore testifies to the importance of gender without making overt gender identifications: she experiments with "establishing an aura of gender as a property, not of the content of experience, but of its formal structure within the reflexive space of the poem" (*Painterly Abstraction in Modernist American Poetry: The Contemporaneity of Modernism* [Cambridge University Press, 1989], 262).

3. Linda Leavell gives the best description to date of the importance of Mary Norcross to the Moore family and to Marianne's intellectual and social-political development, in *Marianne Moore and the Visual Arts: Prismatic Color* (University of Oklahoma Press, 1995), 14–16. Norcross influenced Moore's decision to attend Bryn Mawr (her own alma mater) and tutored her in preparation for the entrance exams. Norcross generally spent a great deal of time in the Moore house, set up her loom there in what had been Warner's room after he moved out to attend Yale, and participated in family activities; she was often included in the address of family letters. As the letters between them reveal—especially between 1901 and 1909—the relationship between Mary Norcross and Mary Warner Moore had erotic overtones of the type described as relatively common between women in the nineteenth century (see Carroll Smith Rosenberg's *Disorderly Conduct*

[Oxford University Press, 1985]); the two women even contemplated buying land and building a house together.

4. See, for example, letters of January 20 and January 25, 1908 [RML I.14.01], where both are basilisks; January 5, 1909 [RML I.15a.01] and several letters of 1911 [RML VI.17 box], where both are Weaz; and several letters in 1914 [RML VI.20 box] where both are Bruno.

5. A complete listing of the family nomenclature as it shifts over the years would fill several pages. For decades, though, Marianne remains primarily "Rat" in self reference and to her mother, although Warner's names for her change frequently.

6. Bryher also participates in referring to Moore with animal names and as male; in a conversation notebook, Moore reports her as saying: "The dactyl is a boy and must be fed before we broach the business of the evening" (RML 1250/25). Later Bryher writes that Moore is a "Marco Polo detained at home" (quoted by Harriet Monroe in "A Symposium on Marianne Moore," *Poetry* 19, 3 [1921]: 209).

7. According to Charles Molesworth, the female Moores conceived their life as one of Christian "service" in conjunction with the more formal work of the male pastor; in *Marianne Moore: A Literary Life* (Atheneum, 1990), 129, 137–138, and throughout. This seems to me accurate of Mary Warner Moore, but not of Marianne. Jeredith Merrin claims more moderately that Moore's poetry is companion work to Warner's Christian ministry, in *An Enabling Humility: Marianne Moore, Elizabeth Bishop, and the Uses of Tradition* (Rutgers University Press, 1990), 23.

8. Moore may also be referring to herself in the masculine in an early, never published poem, "Am I a Brother to Dragons and a Companion to Owls?"

9. This is not to say Moore has no gender anxiety—only that not too much should be made of her family's playfulness in isolation from other factors that affect gender dynamics. For example, I find Darlene Erickson's assertion that "Moore always experienced an amazing stability" exaggerated; but because women's anxiety in attempting to write poetry tends to be more emphatically developed than any corresponding sense of their confidence and empowerment, I focus primarily on the latter here (see *Illusion is More Precise than Precision* [University of Alabama Press, 1992], 221). Carolyn Burke makes a similar argument about Moore's and other modernist women's fluid construction of self ("Getting Spliced: Modernism and Sexual Difference," in *American Quarterly* 39, 1 [Spring 1987]: 98–121). In the particular context of gender fluidity one should also note that Moore later uses a male pseudonym—"Peter Morris"—in a 1927 review of Sachev-

erell Sitwell's *All Summer in a Day*, and she refers to herself (or the "generic" reviewer) as male ("the gentle reader, in his eagerness") in her 1918 "Comment" on Eliot's *Prufrock and Other Observations* (CPr, 143, 35). The isolated occurrences of this usage and the common use of pseudonyms among *Dial* editors, however, make it less telling than it might otherwise be (MMN I.1 [1977]: 14–15).

10. The information in the following paragraphs is taken from "The New Woman as Androgyne: Social Disorder and Gender Crisis, 1870–1936," the last chapter of Smith-Rosenberg's *Disorderly Conduct*.

11. In *The Spinster and Her Enemies: Feminism and Sexuality, 1880–1930*, Sheila Jeffreys analyzes the motives for not marrying among the large number of British "spinsters" during this same period, claiming that until the end of World War I, many women made a consciously political choice not to marry (Routledge and Kegan Paul, 1985; 86–89). For example, Christabel Pankhurst argued that no "spiritually developed woman" should mate with "men who in thought and conduct with regard to sex matters are their inferiors" (89); spinsterhood marked a political position. It is not clear that this was the case for Moore and her peers.

12. William Drake, for example, writes that "one need only compare Babette Deutsch's Class Day poem, with its affirmation of 'Something . . . in us to answer the thrill / Of things untried' with Eliot's youthful exhaustion and malaise—'Do I dare?'—to realize that what appears as beckoning possibility to the oppressed seeking freedom is frightening to the reactionary clinging to his security"; in *The First Wave: Woman Poets in America 1915–1945. The Loves, Friendships and Politics That Sparked a Revolution in Women's Creativity* (Macmillan, 1987), 162. Gilbert and Gubar reiterate this difference in *No Man's Land: The Place of the Woman Writer in the Twentieth Century* (Yale University Press, 1988, 1989).

13. Cott argues that by 1910 the "Woman movement"—with its emphasis on homogeneity of women's experiences and lives—was breaking into "Feminism" and what has become the *women's* movement, with its emphasis on the diversity of women's experiences; "feminists offered no sure definition of who woman was; rather, they sought to end the classification *woman*" (*The Grounding of Modern Feminism* [Yale University Press, 1987], 8). This early feminism seemed to maintain "divergent emphases" without major conflict—being "like" men while remaining "loyal politically and ideologically to their own sex" (49).

14. Writing of a later time in these younger women's lives, Gloria Bowles comments that "it is surely too simple to say that feminism died utterly after the vote was won; rather, feminism was expressed in different ways, depending on the color, the class, the economic situation and the

location of the women involved. In New York, the white, middle-class, upwardly mobile woman saw that it was in her interests to identify publicly more with men than with women"; in *Louise Bogan's Aesthetic of Limitation* (Indiana University Press, 1987), 39. Elaine Showalter makes a similar point in her introduction to *These Modern Women: Autobiographical Essays from the 20s* (New York: Feminist Press, 1978).

15. These figures are for the years 1889–1908. It may be in large part the effect of M. Carey Thomas, a brilliant and radical feminist, that this college has a slightly higher average than others of women who chose careers over marriage. Moore admired Thomas extravagantly, as did her classmates. Helen Horowitz's *Alma Mater: Design and Experience in the Women's Colleges from Their Nineteenth-Century Beginnings to the 1930s* also provides valuable information about women's colleges of this period (Beacon Press, 1984).

16. *Intimate Matters: A History of Sexuality in America* (Harper & Row, 1988), 175–176.

17. Sandra Gilbert finds that Moore's poetry, while feminist, "stands entirely outside sexuality," and that Moore herself never found "what Adrienne Rich has called 'compulsory heterosexuality' . . . either 'compulsory' or compelling" ("Marianne Moore as Female Female Impersonator," in AMM, 35). Such a reading, like mine, works from pragmatic and cultural understandings of sexuality, including a Foucauldian conviction that one must understand historical changes in such discourse (what seems essential to the late twentieth century did not necessarily seem so ninety years earlier). Moreover, even if the women surveyed all lied about their sexual interest, their responses indicate the extent to which sexuality was still conceived in reproductive and heterosexual contexts.

Cyrena Pondrom, who writes persuasively of the importance to Moore of "female community," makes a veiled suggestion that H.D. may have considered Moore to be lesbian (H.D. calls a character based on Moore "one of the tribe" to which two lesbian poets belong), but although Moore seems indeed to figure on Adrienne Rich's "lesbian continuum" in that she identifies herself more strongly with women than with men, I find no evidence for speculating that she desired or sought a sexual relationship with other women ("Marianne Moore and H.D.: Female Community and Poetic Achievement," in *Marianne Moore: Woman and Poet*, ed. Patricia C. Willis [National Poetry Foundation, 1990], 379); see Rich's "Compulsory Heterosexuality and Lesbian Existence," in *Blood, Bread, and Poetry: Selected Prose 1979–1985* (Norton, 1986).

18. In addition to her correspondence, Moore's 1909–1914 Scrapbook contains repeated evidence of her interest in and acute analysis of gender

issues—including a 1912 letter from the Civil Service Commission saying Moore could not take the civil service exam because she was applying for a position specified as "male." Leavell discusses Moore's interest in the Arts and Crafts movement as an indirect expression of feminist principles as well as of aesthetic and moral appreciation of simplicity, solid workmanship, and nonhierarchical respect for "craft" (*Prismatic Color,* 16).

19. Mary Norcross was active in suffrage activities, and may also have influenced Marianne in this area. Mary Warner Moore occasionally participated as well, and one sees evidence of gender consciousness in her correspondence. For example, she writes her son that the *The Dial*'s closure may have been inevitable after women started working there: Alyse Gregory and Marianne insisted on "responsibility; an everlasting deciding of vexing questions; strap-quick-jerk everywhere"; they were the "serken" [serpent] in *The Dial*'s "Man Paradise" of ease (undated [February 1929?]; RML VI.30.01).

20. William Drake describes this talk in *The First Wave,* 194–196.

21. *The Man-Made World, or, Our Androcentric Culture* (Charlton, 1914), 79, 84.

22. Unlike Moore, however, Gilman and, erratically, Woolf, did see gender-bias in using "generic" or prescriptive masculines to represent the human community.

23. Although most types of careers claimed objectivity in work evaluation and hiring, only the professions were ideologically founded on this assumption, and only the professions insisted on their sex neutrality. Nonetheless, from the perspective of late twentieth-century feminism, Cott argues that, although it was not perceived as such, there was a conflict between the gender-neutrality touted by professionalism and that conceived by early feminists. This made it imperative for women to choose primary loyalty to one or the other, and choosing a profession essentially dictated that a woman accept its standards, not just those of sex neutrality but of rational, impersonal—that is, historically male-defined—standards of judgment. It would be extremely interesting to study Moore's private and public correspondence and reviews during the years she edited *The Dial* to see the extent to which she may have perceived such a conflict, and responded to it.

24. *Women Poets and the American Sublime* (Indiana University Press, 1990), 60, 82.

25. See Heuving's *Omissions Are Not Accidents: Gender in the Art of Marianne Moore* (Wayne State University Press, 1992) and Erickson's *Illusion.* As mentioned in Chapter 1, Betsy Erkkila, too, invokes standard conventions of femininity to describe Moore in *The Wicked Sisters: Women Poets, Literary*

History and Discord (Oxford University Press, 1992). Sandra Gilbert, like Diehl, sees both gain and loss in Moore's deliberate play within and against traditional gender categories ("Female Female Impersonator"); Taffy Martin sees Moore as playing against stereotypes of feminine passivity and indecision to assert her own power and control (*Marianne Moore, Subversive Modernist* [University of Texas Press, 1986]); Sabine Sielke discusses the limitations of Moore's repeated uses of maternal examples or tropes for the feminine ("Intertextual Networking: Constructing Female Subjectivity in the Poetry of Emily Dickinson, Marianne Moore, and Adrienne Rich," Ph.D. diss., Free University of Berlin, 1991). DuPlessis's "No Moore of the Same: The Feminist Poetics of Marianne Moore" (*William Carlos Williams Review* 14, 1 [Spring 1988]: 6–32) and "Corpses of Poesy" argue that Moore's poetic breaks down conventional categories of gender.

26. In *Marianne Moore*, ed. Harold Bloom (Chelsea House, 1987), 91, 93.

27. Interestingly, in *Imaginary Possessions*, Costello does talk at length of Moore's reference to battle metaphors; she focuses, however, on the concept of "armor" in discussing gender in Moore's work.

28. In *The Line in Postmodern Poetry*, ed. Robert Frank and Henry Sayre (University of Illinois Press, 1988), 104, 106.

29. Of course, my contextual frame is also that of late twentieth-century feminism. To see Moore only in these terms, however, does not do justice to her achievement in constructing a poetry that consciously inscribes an earlier feminist approach to gender difference.

30. Joan Retallack comments in an early version of ":RE:THINK-ING:LITERARY: FEMINISM:" that "it's only 'now' that for the first time this project can actively unfold—the formation of a new literature which comes from the power rather than the fear and defensiveness of women: the feminine in female hands. We are no longer clearly disenfranchised, no longer clearly victims . . . Woman's power is in a complex realist pragmatism that is connective rather than exclusive" (in *Feminist Measures*, 344–377). Moore, I believe, felt such enfranchisement in the 1910s and 1920s.

31. Leavell brilliantly suggests that Moore's "Comments" and "reviews" for *The Dial*—as well as her entire editorial production—may be seen as prose poems, or as creating alternative kinds of collages (*Prismatic Color*, 134). Given this suggestion, one might also examine her prose record for indications of her continuing analysis of gender relationships and constructions, even though they could not as directly be linked to Moore's reconception of the lyric poem per se.

32. Moore mentions gender issues and sex in several early reviews— most often in chastising authors, including Eliot, Pound, and other of her well-known contemporaries, for their sexism, but at times commenting

more generally. Celeste Goodridge's *Hints and Disguises: Marianne Moore and Her Contemporaries* remains the most important study of Moore's prose writing (University of Iowa Press, 1989), but notices of sexism in her reviews are also discussed by Martin in *Subversive Modernist* (chap. 2) and Sielke in "Intertextual Networking" (chap. 1.2.2). To give two brief examples of Moore's positive mention of such matters, in a 1926 review of Gertrude Stein's *The Making of Americans*, Moore writes that "the power of sex which is palpable throughout this novel, is handsomely implied" in a particular passage which she then quotes (CPr, 130). In 1931, she attributes "impassioned observation of emotion" and "an important mind" to Alyse Gregory in a novel about "three phases of sex antagonism: that between man and woman; that between man and man; and that between a woman and a woman" (CPr, 278). In other words, and despite frequent critical assertions that Moore is prudish, she recognizes the "power" of sex without embarrassment.

To my knowledge, no one has examined the feminist implications of Moore's editorial activity, which would be invisible in a perusal of her published writing: I wonder, for example, if as editor Moore may have been more inclined to accept work by (especially unknown) women, and less inclined to accept sexist work by anyone, than were her male editorial peers. Leavell, for example, speculates that Moore's objections to material she considered improper may be feminist; for example, an entry in one of Moore's notebooks indicates that she believed nudes degraded a person's (usually a woman's) individuality—although she published art containing nudes in the issues she edited (*Prismatic Color*, 49, especially n. 86).

33. Moore copies out a similar comment in her reading notebook for 1916–1921, namely, "There is almost as much difference between men & women as between men and men" (from *Life*, December 15, 1920; RML VII.01.02, p. 161).

34. This may also constitute a late instance of the long-running, joking competition between "gators" and "turtles" which the two siblings play out in mock-epics, dramas, cartoons, and newspapers enclosed with their letters.

35. In this chapter, I present in full the poems that Moore did not republish in her *Complete Poems*, but quote only passages of most poems reprinted there. Where my argument is chronological, as it is for much of this chapter, I use the earliest book publication of even briefly quoted poems. For poems never collected in a book, I use the first published version.

36. Erickson reads another early, uncollected poem similarly—"Diligence Is to Magic as Progress Is to Flight" (1915). Here Moore's female

subject, riding upon an elephant rather than a magic carpet, opposes herself to "scarecrows / of aesthetic procedure" whom Erickson identifies with defenders of the poetic status quo (*Illusion*, 120–123).

37. Heuving links this poem with two others ("My Lantern" and "Elfride, Making Epigrams") written respectively around 1910 and 1914—both also referring to Hardy's novel and having to do with gender power relationships (*Omissions Are Not Accidents*, 47–48). DuPlessis makes the same link more briefly ("No Moore of the Same," 20–21).

38. Stanley Lordeaux speculates that "certitude" and "attack" may allude to the aesthete's pose and to "a particular kind of popular poetry called the physical force school, the literary voice for nineteenth-century British jingoism" respectively; certainly the latter would support my more general association of "attack" with a poetic of warmongering, or with war itself (MMN II.2 [Fall 1978]: 13).

39. Moore makes a similar statement in the draft of a letter to Alyse Gregory: "Physical disrepair . . . can't disenchant us from that which is enchanting any more than Ziegfeld follies beauty can obsess us with admiration for beauty which has for us never had force" (December 4, 1929; RML V.23.05).

40. DuPlessis and Heuving suggest that this poem may be more immediately written in response to the misogynistic masculine superiority of Pound's "Portrait d'une Femme" and Eliot's "Portrait of a Lady" ("Corpses of Poesy"; *Omissions Are Not Accidents*, 31–32). For an extended discussion of the *blason* form, see Sielke's "Intertextual Networking," chap. 1.2.2.

41. Another fascinating study (begun by Sielke in *Intertextual Networking* but still to be pursued in detail) is the link between Moore's and her family's frequent invocation of the metaphors of "armor" and weaponry, the poet's physical presentation—in photographs, her style of dress—and her articles on or several epistolary references to female fashion and dress.

42. Lawrence J. McCaffrey describes even middle-class Irish Americans as typically supporting the move for Irish independence in 1916, partly out of a misunderstanding of the roots of the prejudice against them in the United States; many seemed to think that the end of colonial status for Ireland would gain Irish Americans greater respect and easier assimilation (*Textures of Irish America* [Syracuse University Press, 1992], 35–40). As a Protestant rather than Catholic Irish American, and because of her solidly middle-class circumstances, Moore seems not to have suffered the discrimination directed against many Irish at the turn of the century.

43. The phrases not belonging to "Roses Only" are taken, respectively, from "So far as the future is concerned . . ." (1915), "Critics and Connoisseurs" (1916), and "Poetry" (1919), the latter poem containing the phrases

"imaginary gardens with real toads in them" and "the raw material of poetry in / all its rawness and / that which is, on the other hand, / genuine" (1921; P, 22).

44. For extended readings of this poem, see Keller and Miller's "'The Tooth of Disputation': Marianne Moore's 'Marriage'" (in *Sagetrieb* 6.3 [Winter 1987]: 99–116); Diehl in *American Sublime*; Keller's "'For inferior who is free?' Liberating the Woman Writer in Marianne Moore's 'Marriage'" (in *Influence and Intertextuality in Literary History*, ed. Jay Clayton and Eric Rothstein [University of Wisconsin Press, 1991], 219–244); Erickson's *Illusion*; Heuving's *Ommissions Are Not Accidents*; and Sielke's *Intertextual Networking*.

45. In her working notebook for this poem, Moore notes: "this division into masculine and feminine compartments of achievement will not do" (RML 1251/7).

46. Eileen Moran quotes an early Moore limerick on a similar theme, in reference to Elizabeth Barrett: "There was a young lady named Liz / Who made writing poems her biz / But when she met Bob / She gave up the job / It took all her time to read his" ("Portrait of the Artist: Marianne Moore's Letter to Hildegarde Watson," in *Poesis: A Celebration of H.D. and Marianne Moore* [Bryn Mawr College, 1985], 127; RML 1250/1).

47. Moore reports in correspondence that she does not share the sentiment of this passage: "*I* did not say 'I am such a cow . . .' That was a neighbor" (November 1, 1963, to Mary Schneeberger; from the Macpherson Collection, Ella Strong Denison Library, The Claremont Colleges).

48. Here I differ strongly with Heuving's argument that after 1930 Moore turns to a poetic mode of overstatement, both disregarding the social context of her work and ceasing to interrogate the contradictions of social constructions and phenomena (*Illusion*, especially chap. 6).

49. This is generally attributed to the collapse of the women's movement after women got the vote and no longer had a clear goal around which to unify; the extreme conservatism fostered by the depression of the late twenties and thirties also had a devastating effect on the women's movement (Cott, *The Grounding of Modern Feminism*, chap. 2).

50. For general information about American women poets of this period, see William Drake's *The First Wave: Woman Poets in America 1915–1945*. Gillian Hanscombe and Virginia L. Smyers's *Writing for Their Lives: The Modernist Women 1910–1940* is also useful but deals more with prose writers than poets, and equally with British and American writers. The poets discussed in Drake's study are Lola Ridge, Kay Boyle, Edna St. Vincent Millay, Sara Teasdale, Louise Bogan, Angelina Weld Grimke, Elinor Wylie, Marjorie Seiffert, Gladys Cromwell, Babette Deutsch, Adelaide Crapsey, Harriet Monroe, Eunice Tietjens, Grace Hazard Conkling, Amy Lowell, H.D.,

Genevieve Taggard, Georgia Douglas Johnson, Helene Johnson, Gwendolyn Bennett, Clarissa Scott-Delaney, Margaret Conklin, and May Sarton.

51. Predictably, this period marked an even more dramatic decline in publishing for black than for white women, although for a similar mixture of personal, economic, and political/ideological reasons. According to Maureen Honey, who addresses this topic in her introduction to *Shadowed Dreams: Women's Poetry of the Harlem Renaissance*, the loss of the "female support system" that black women writing poetry had constructed during the twenties, and the loss of or shifted focus of their male peers and mentors, caused much of this silencing (Rutgers University Press, 1989; 24–31).

52. There are obvious exceptions to this generalization—including Moore's friendships with H.D., Edith Sitwell, and the younger Elizabeth Bishop. But with the first two in England and the latter mostly in Florida or Brazil, these long-distance friendships hardly replaced the frequent contact with other women professionally active as poets in New York that Moore had enjoyed for over a decade. That Moore did not particularly admire what some of these women wrote does not subtract from what the fact of their presence must have added to her sense of her own. As has been far more extensively documented, Moore had supportive friendships with male poets and editors (local and long-distance) throughout both these periods.

53. The phrase "mothering the eggs" is not part of the 1941 version of this poem; in *What Are Years*, Moore writes "he has sat on the eggs" (6). The link with mothering is clear, though, from her preceding "maternal concentration."

54. Moore may be remembering a statement M. Carey Thomas made when Moore was at Bryn Mawr about an earlier Harvard president's opposition to women's education, as well as Harvard's own exclusionary admission policy. Moore writes home quoting Thomas as saying "'of course we cannot give Pres. Elliot [*sic*] a platform [as a commencement speaker] upon which to express his reactionary views upon the subject of woman's education—'" (April 7, 1908; RML VI.14.09).

55. Reading this poem as a woman's statement—as I do above—one may see its argument as replicating, in brief, that of the first part of Virginia Woolf's *A Room of One's Own*, where she is prevented from following a train of thought by being shooed off the grass and barred entrance to the library at an elite male educational institution because of her sex. While the speaker of both Woolf's and Moore's works are honored guests, Moore's speaker has been invited to speak rather than to eat, and so may be both more "grateful" and more ironic.

269

5. "The Labors of Hercules"

1. The turn of the century was characterized by a Progressivist belief in the powers of education and the inevitability of social change with its transformation of American society; moreover, Progressivism dovetailed with much of turn-of-the-century feminism, especially in its stress on rational argument, social reform, and the powers of education. While she later became cynical about any such inevitability, Moore never lost her faith in education or social reform. On the Progressive era, see the introduction to Richard Pells's *Radical Visions and American Dreams* (Wesleyan University Press, 1989). Lisa Steinman sees social reform as the "primary goal" of Moore's redefinitions of values (*Made in America: Science, Technology, and American Modernist Poets* [Yale University Press, 1987], 131).

2. As I discuss later in this chapter, Moore does romanticize racial or national communities in some poems, but she to some extent undercuts the dangers of such characterization within those poems as well. For a detailed examination of Moore's racial politics as they play themselves out in her life and in her prose and poetry, see my "Marianne Moore's Black Maternal Hero: A Study in Categorization," *American Literary History* 1, no. 4 (Winter 1989): 786–815. Where that essay focuses particularly on the racist and xenophobic context in which Moore lived and wrote—especially early in the century—and on the degree to which she implicitly or explicitly condones and combats racism, this chapter focuses on the didactic pluralism constructed in her poetry. That essay also contains an extended reading of "Virginia Britannia," discussed briefly here. To my knowledge, the only other published work on Moore and race is David Kadlec's essay "Marianne Moore, Immigration, and Eugenics," *Modernism/Modernity* 1, 2 (1994): 21–49.

3. For example, and apart from the record of her concern documented in her poems, in 1932 Moore drafted a brochure statement for the racially integrated Bryn Mawr Summer School for Women Workers in Industry (RML V.08.09). In 1940 or earlier, she contributed to the Scottsboro Defense Committee (RML I.03.23); toward the end of her life she wrote publicity statements for the St. James (Harlem) School of the Arts (RML V.24.24); and her long record of speaking out publicly and privately against anti-Semitism and for Jews is attested to by Jacob Glatstein in "Marianne Moore," *Yiddish* 6.1 (Spring 1985): 67–73. Although she did not seek the job for any politically motivated reasons, Moore also taught at the Indian School in Carlisle for a few years after graduating from Bryn Mawr, which may have affected her later support for marginalized groups. For anti-racist commentary in her reviews, see, for example, CPr, 206, 303–304, 540–541, and innumerable reviews of books or movies dealing with foreign cultures

or the work of non-Euro-American writers and artists. It may also be a mark of Moore's active commitment to racial equality that in 1953 Langston Hughes referred to her as "the most famous Negro woman poet in America"—although this remark is obviously also ironic given its context as response to Robert Lowell's praise of Moore as "the best woman poet in English" (quoted in the Foreword by Maxine Kumin in AMM, viii). The brief but warm correspondence between Moore and Hughes shortly before his death suggests that they had known each other for some time (RML V.29.38). Moore's private letters to her mother and brother reveal her occasional willingness to participate in racist discourse, but the context of extreme language play and the infrequency of such discourse indicate that it is not representative of her attitudes about race.

4. Rachel Blau DuPlessis claims, in contrast, that Moore does invoke an "authority of otherness/marginality" in "consider[ing] marginalities parallel to the female" ("No Moore of the Same: The Feminist Poetics of Marianne Moore," in *William Carlos Williams Review* 14, 1 [Spring 1988]: 11–12). I agree, however, that Moore's own marginal positioning no doubt makes her sensitive to the interplay of derogatory and empowering categorizations.

5. The first and third quotations are taken from *The Post-Colonial Critic: Interviews, Strategies, Dialogues,* ed. Sarah Harasym (Routledge Press, 1990), 56; the others occur, respectively, in Spivak's "Can the Subaltern Speak?" in *Marxism and the Interpretation of Language,* ed. Cary Nelson and Lawrence Grossberg (University of Illinois Press, 1988), 285, and "In a Word." Interview with Ellen Rooney, *differences* I.2 (Summer 1989), 56. Kadlec makes a similar, although more narrowly focused, point about Moore's writing: "Moore's aesthetic of inclusive selection, and her distinguishing technical features—her elaborate stanzas, complex nominal compounds, abrupt lineation, and the strong tendency in her poems toward punningly metonymic modes of reference—these formal and rhetorical qualities can be usefully seen as a biologist-poet's response to the nativist controversy over immigration selection"; Moore holds to "fluxional" rather than essentialist notions of identity ("Marianne Moore, Immigration, and Eugenics," 24, 28).

6. "In a Word," 146. This is, I realize, not Spivak's intent in the passage cited earlier. Moore's concurrence with Spivak goes only so far as her not presuming to speak "for" an unempowered group, recognizing that she will inevitably appropriate what she tries to represent thus.

7. As Linda Leavell suggests in private correspondence, Pound was probably joking (May 25, 1994). Moore, however, responded with a serious—if also somewhat exaggerated—portrait. Not to have done so would

have made her complicitous in his joke, or in the racist attitude that assumes such jokes may be exchanged.

8. This is a short section of a very long poem. For its complete publication, and the earlier letter inquiring about Moore's race, see *The Gender of Modernism: A Critical Anthology*, ed. Bonnie Kime Scott (Indiana University Press, 1990), 359–365.

9. Philip Gleason writes at length on the politics of racial and ethnic pluralism, and the relationship of early twentieth-century "cultural pluralism" to the end of the century's "multi-culturalism" in *Speaking of Diversity: Language and Ethnicity in Twentieth-Century America* (Johns Hopkins University Press, 1992). See also Werner Sollors's "A Critique of Pure Pluralism" in *Reconstructing American Literary History*, ed. Sacvan Bercovitch (Harvard University Press, 1986; 250–279), and *Beyond Ethnicity: Consent and Descent in American Culture* (Oxford University Press, 1986). On the eugenics craze in the United States at the turn of the century, see Daniel J. Kevles's *In the Name of Eugenics: Genetics and the Uses of Human Heredity* (University of California Press, 1985). As Kevles explains, because eugenics promoted women's greater control over marital and sexual choices, birth control, and higher education for women, and because of its interest in a wide variety of health and social issues, it attracted even such social radicals as Emma Goldman. Kadlec documents Moore's familiarity with primary issues in this field, as well as her rejection of its essentialist logic ("Marianne Moore, Immigration, and Eugenics").

10. Alain Locke is quoted in Werner Sollors's "A Critique of Pure Pluralism", 273. See Hurston's stories and some of her essays as collected in *Spunk* (Turtle Island Foundation, 1985) and *I love myself when I am laughing . . . and then again when I am looking mean and impressive*, ed. Alice Walker (The Feminist Press, 1979); Larsen's novel was published by Knopf in 1929.

11. "Editor's Introduction: Writing 'Race' and the Difference It Makes," in *"Race," Writing, and Difference* (University of Chicago Press, 1985), 5. In more recent publications, the problem of invoking "race" as a fixed, defining category is a repeated subject of Cornel West's *Race Matters* (Beacon Press, 1993). In "Doing Things with Words: 'Racism' as Speech Act and Undoing of Justice," Claudia Brodsky Lacour brilliantly demonstrates how the mention of "race" may prevent discussion of the actual effects of racism (in *Race-ing Justice, En-gendering Power: Essays on Anita Hill, Clarence Thomas, and the Construction of Social Reality*, ed. Toni Morrison [Pantheon Books, 1992], 127–158). Such analysis is also part of the ongoing project of bell hooks, most recently in her *Black Looks: Race and Representation* (South End Press, 1992), who has for years challenged blacks and "non-black allies and friends" to "imagine, describe, and invent" ways to break down colo-

nized/colonizing definitions of black/non-black cultural identity, or "to look away from the conventional ways of seeing blackness and ourselves" (2, 4).

12. This conjunction is most recently and persuasively articulated in Linda Leavell's 1990 essay "Marianne Moore and Georgia O'Keeffe: 'The Feelings of a Mother—a Woman or a Cat,'" in *Marianne Moore: Woman and Poet*, ed. Patricia C. Willis (National Poetry Foundation, 1990), 297–319.

13. In a letter to Louise Crane, Moore explains this linkage by referring to these musicians punningly as "champions of harmonious speed" (August 2, 1952; RML V.13.04).

14. Willis notes that Moore purchased a 1936 biography of Selassie, who was known as the "Conquering Lion of Judah" and kept several lions at his palace, and marked several passages while reading it (*Vision into Verse* [Rosenbach Museum and Library, 1987], 62). Because this biography was written before Selassie's return to Ethiopia after the Italian occupation in 1941, let alone decades before his deposition by a military coup in 1974, Moore thought of Selassie in glowing terms as a ruler devoted to modernizing and democratizing his country rather than as a repressive and status-conscious monarch. And, as later reading no doubt informed her, in 1941 Selassie indeed instituted a written constitution giving power to elected officials, and reasserting his earlier priorities of education and universal employment. Moore also made note of the historical error that connected Presbyter John with Ethiopia. Several details of "His Shield," about Presbyter John, seem to refer to Selassie as well. Darlene Erickson also discusses this connection (*Illusion is More Precise than Precision* [University of Alabama Press, 1992], 173).

15. See Arthur R. Ashe, Jr.'s *A Hard Road to Glory: A History of the African-American Athlete* (Warner Books, 1988), 11–13. My thanks to Susan Porter for calling this fact to my attention.

16. Linda Leavell called the racial reference of this poem to my attention.

17. Again, Moore seems either not to notice or not to care about what end-of-the-century scholars regard as the racism of Rodgers and Hammerstein's *The King and I*, merely mentioning Brynner's regal role as a point of contrast to his acts of service.

18. *Reading Race: White American Poets and the Racial Discourse in the Twentieth-Century* (University of Georgia Press, 1988). This is also the topic of Toni Morrison's *Playing in the Dark: Whiteness and the Literary Imagination* (Harvard University Press, 1992) and her introduction to *Race-ing Justice*. For example, in the introduction to the latter volume, she writes of the effects of speaking only English—or an imposed, colonizing language—for black people; in speaking the "master's language," "[o]ne is obliged to

273

cooperate in the misuse of figurative language, in the reinforcement of cliché, the erasure of difference, the jargon of justice, the evasion of logic, the denial of history, the crowning of patriarchy, the inscription of hegemony; to be complicit in the vandalizing, sentimentalizing, and trivialization of the torture black people have suffered" (xxviii–xxix). Obviously, Morrison's conclusions are equally valid for descendents of the colonizers, insofar as "there is no other language to speak" (xxix).

19. On this topic, see John Higham's *Strangers in the Land: Patterns of American Nativism 1860–1925* (Atheneum, 1963); T. Jackson Lears's *No Place of Grace: Antimodernism and the Transformation of American Culture 1880–1912* (Random House, 1981); Ronald T. Takaki's *Iron Cages: Race and Culture in Nineteenth-Century America* (University of Washington Press, 1979); and Sucheng Chan's *Asian Americans: An Interpretive History* (Twayne, 1991). Kevles's study of eugenics is also extremely useful for understanding the various forms racism assumed during these decades, and its tenacity.

20. According to Nielsen, "seldom in our literary history has blackness so occupied the imaginations of white artists as during the rise of modernism" (*Reading Race*, 49). Similarly, according to Barbara Johnson, "'Representing the Negro race for whites' was . . . in many ways the program of the Harlem Renaissance"; Johnson quotes from Langston Hughes ("Thresholds of Difference: Structures of Address in Zora Neale Hurston," in Gates's *"Race," Writing, and Difference*, 319).

21. To give a brief review, in *Reading Race* Nielsen writes of Stein's romanticism of race in *Melanctha* (21–28); of Eliot's unwillingness to admit the richness of any but unadulterated Anglo-European culture, and his representation of the nonwhite as "a Conradian area of spiritual darkness associated . . . with death" (58–60); of Stevens's ethnocentrism and exoticization of the black subject (60–64); of Williams's liberal politics but invoking of blacks for local color (72–84; Nielsen does not note that much of Williams's objectification of blacks is of black women, and is parallel to his treatment of white women in his verse); of H.D.'s similarly liberal politics but perpetuation of racist stereotypes through appropriative identification with blacks as "other" (85–89); and of Pound's being "one of the very few publishing white poets of his time who had bothered to acquire any scholarly knowledge at all about Africa and Africans" although he was also prone to "blistering racial insult" in his private and published writing (65–72). On H.D. see also Susan Stanford Friedman's "Modernism and the 'Scattered Remnant': Race and Politics in the Development of H.D.'s Modernist Vision"; in *H.D.: Woman and Poet*, ed. Michael King (National Poetry Foundation, 1986), 91–116. Nielsen does not mention Moore.

22. Costello argues the opposite: "For [Moore], representation steers

dangerously toward prejudice (black is evil) and needs constant revision" (IP, 41). Although I agree that "light" is emblematic of enlightenment for Moore, I do not find that she associates spiritual light with whiteness; rather, such light is much more apt to be of "prismatic color" and is not typically opposed to darkness in a binary scheme. Leavell, too, associates Moore with "prismatic color" rather than whiteness, and makes this argument key to her extended reading of "In The Days of Prismatic Color"; moreover, as the title of her book indicates, this poem is key to her reading of Moore generally (*Marianne Moore and the Visual Arts: Prismatic Color* [University of Oklahoma Press, 1995]).

23. According to the *Concordance* based on her *Complete Poems*, Moore uses "white" (50) more often than any noun or than any adjectives except "more" (57) and "some" (56); "black" (32) appears more often than all but 6 nouns and a few more adjectives. The next most frequently used color-adjective is "green" (27), then "blue" (17).

24. It may be that Moore also calls attention to color in her translation of the Greek "Melancthon" to English: "black earth" (a process initiated by Melancthon himself, who translated his German name—Schwarzerd—into Greek, a practice common among theologians and philosophers at the time). Also seeing self-portraiture in this poem, Slatin calls the elephant "a persona, a mask which conceals the features while amplifying the voice of the actor," or the poet (SR, 78).

25. In this locution, one may again see indirect racist discourse; it was to be another forty-five years before the slogan "Black is beautiful" would become popular. One may also, however, read this locution as acerbically refuting contemporary stereotypes, with a defiant and insistent "but."

26. Slatin also talks of this elephant's skin as a text or kind of speech (SR, 82). Typically, this poem is read as the failed attempt of a proud but hopeful speaker to achieve a "renaissance" of illumination or received light. See, for example, readings by Bernard F. Engel (*Marianne Moore* [Twayne, 1989; rev. ed.], 20–24), Costello (IP, 57–62), and Slatin (SR, 77–88, 93–97). Taffy Martin, in contrast, sees the elephant as successfully receptive to communication/knowledge (*Marianne Moore, Subversive Modernist* [University of Texas Press, 1986], 19–21). It seems to me that Moore sidesteps the question of how desirable a "renaissance" would be. Although some part of her would "stand up and shout," its coming would also imply her loss of the "blemishes" and "patina of circumstance" that now define her. Leavell's argument that Moore is typically critical of the Renaissance era with its emphasis on mimetic representation would support such a mixed view (*Prismatic Color*, 153).

27. Like the Song of Songs—which can be read (among other interpre-

tations) as a set of lyrics between lovers who anticipate, wish for, and then postpone their rendezvous rather than hastening it—Moore's poem flirts with the unities of its apparent opposites, its body and spirit appearing analogous to a lover and beloved, or speaker and poem. I am indebted to Marcia Falk's *The Song of Songs: Love Poems from the Bible* for my reading of that poem (Harcourt, Brace, Jovanovich, 1977).

28. In *diacritics* 17:2 (Summer 1987): 65–81. Page references in the following paragraphs are to this text.

29. I simplify Spillers's argument here for the sake of contrast. She, of course, recognizes that both body and flesh exist within the realm of discourse, but she constructs her "grammar" to recover for African-American women (and men) a name for a lived experience that cannot so easily be etherealized through language play. She attempts to recoup, as it were, a dimension of experience that is primary—like the building blocks of grammar—a basis for later deconstruction rather than always manipulable text ("body") itself.

30. In response to Randall Jarrell's remark that "like the *Literary Digest*, Moore sent postcards to only the nicer animals," Sandra Gilbert writes of this poem: "Seeking to imagine alternatives to the voracity and ferocity of history, the jerboa's celebrant strives to depict the alternative history that might be constructed by what Jarrell contemptuously calls 'the nicer animals'" ("Marianne Moore as Female Female Impersonator," AMM, 41). Moore, she claims, "was liberated" by her knowledge of both the history of European imperialism and of botanical and animal nature "to imagine civilizing alternatives to 'civilization'"—characterized as it is by "possession and enslavement, arrogance and ignorance" (41, 40).

31. "American SF and the Other," in *The Language of the Night: Essays on Fantasy and Science Fiction*, ed. Susan Wook (Putnam, 1979), 99.

32. I do not find this a particularly successful poem, perhaps in part because its epigrammatic and rhyming style seems so at odds with the poem's subject. Moore may, however, have intended an ironic discrepancy between her short-lined, rhymed stanzas and such complex subject matter, so that the form would call attention to the genre's limitations: as she says, "(Don't speak in rhyme / of maddened men in starving-time)"—or of their victims.

33. A 1938 entry in a conversation notebook makes this point more vigorously: "In ancient times, people (barbarous) razed cities and murdered the innocent. One is faint before it and these people are with us now. One does not feel detached by one's horror—even if they are not of our country. They are *we*. They are of our kind" (quoted in Susan Schweik's *A Gulf So*

Deeply Cut: American Women Poets and the Second World War [University of Wisconsin Press, 1991], 35–36).

34. As Leavell describes "New York": "On the one hand is America's idealized, noble 'savage' suggested by teepees (New York Indians never lived in teepees), war canoes, and Indian geographical names; on the other is the savagery of commerce plundering the state's bountiful resources . . . This is then the paradoxical 'savage's romance': to romanticize the 'savage' is itself savage" (*Prismatic Color,* 124).

35. This is the standard reading of the poem; see, for example, Grace Schulman's *Marianne Moore: The Poetry of Engagement* (University of Illinois Press, 1986), 61, and Slatin (SR, 198–201).

36. In a draft of this poem, Moore more clearly states, "What is liberty? To succeed in being captive to the right thing" (RML I.04.21).

37. See Oscar Handlin's *Boston Immigrants, 1790–1865: A Study in Acculturation* on early anti-Irish sentiment (Harvard University Press, 1979), and Laurence McCaffrey's *Textures of Irish America* (Syracuse University Press, 1992) for their transformation in the early twentieth century from despised to respectable ethnic group. The Irish (and Jews) occupied a middle ground in the late nineteenth century—themselves ignoring and discriminating against non-whites, while also victim to increasing Anglo-Protestant nativism (both were, for example, targeted groups of the Ku Klux Klan). In the United States, anti-Catholic sentiment typically expressed itself in racist rhetoric, and its primary focus was the Irish. By the end of World War I, however, the transition was under way, and there were an increasing number of journalistic, fictional, and film portrayals of patriotic, respectable, middle-class Irish (McCaffrey, *Textures of Irish America,* 35–36, 40–41).

38. An early Moore *Newsletter* suggests that she took the tone of this poem from Maria Edgeworth's novels (one of which, *The Absentee,* she later rewrote as a play) and was, like Edgeworth, attempting to place the Irish "'in a more favourable light than they had been placed hitherto, and . . . to produce sympathy for their virtues, and indulgence for their foibles'" (quoting Sir Walter Scott; MMN IV.2 [Fall 1980]: 9). Yet Moore's comment in a draft of the poem, "I'm less & less in love with / Ireland," restated in the margin as "Irld never took my fancy less than now," makes this intention questionable—or points to an unarticulated ambivalence in the poem, perhaps explaining the resonance of the concluding "I'm dissatisfied, I'm Irish" (RML I.04.21). Moore's dissatisfaction with Ireland could well be caused by its neutral stance in the war against fascism—its placing of national issues (rebellion against Britain) above international ones. It is also

perhaps noteworthy that Moore wrote her two poems about Ireland during periods of "world war"—1917 and 1941.

39. Moore might, for example, have questioned whether dependence on enchantment and "obduracy" result from colonialism, or whether stubbornness and "genius for disunion" are "Irish" characteristics as seen by hegemonic power (the named "British" of the earlier poem), which would be viewed differently by the Irish themselves, or even how talent for fly-tying, knitting, and other domestic crafts preserve important values.

40. Margaret Holley points out that this international, if not by contemporary terms multicultural, representativeness of the bridge was precisely Moore's point: she refers to Richard S. Storrs's remarks at the Opening Ceremonies of the bridge in 1883 as reported by Alan Trachtenberg in the book to which Moore calls her readers' attention in her first "note" on the poem. Storrs stated, "Built by a German, it stands next to the figure of Liberty, the work of a Frenchman; it 'represents that fellowship of the Nations which is more and more prominently a fact of our times'" (quoted in PMM, 174).

41. "A Carriage from Sweden" was already accepted for publication before King Gustav V "'open[ed] the doors of his country to the Jews of nearby Denmark'" (quoted in a letter to JWM, March 1, 1944; RML VI.37.04). Upon learning this fact, Moore immediately revised her poem and sent the *Nation*'s editor her changes, believing it "greatly improved" by this addition. As Laurence Stapleton points out, the appearance of Washington and Gustavus Adolphus in the poem anticipates Moore's knowledge of Sweden's asylum for Jews: the former "had attended the first Jewish synagogue in Newport, Rhode Island, and Gustavus Adolphus . . . stood for religious toleration in the Thirty Years' War" (*Marianne Moore: The Poet's Advance* [Princeton University Press, 1978], 128–129). Learning of King Gustav's offer confirmed Moore's sympathy for Swedish politics—identified here with all things Swedish—rather than providing the basis for it.

42. Schweik notes the extent to which Moore succeeded in speaking generally in this poem: "In Distrust of Merits" was frequently held up by her contemporaries during the 1940s as "the single exemplary war poem"— a fact remarkable given both the amount of war poetry published and that it was written by a civilian and a woman (*A Gulf So Deeply Cut*, 31, and chap. 1 throughout).

43. See "In Distrust of Merits" and most of the other poems of *Nevertheless* (1944) for Moore's refusal to equate might with right: the title poem proclaims, "Victory won't come // to me unless I go / to it" and "The weak overcomes its / menace, the strong over- / comes itself"; "The Wood-Weasel" is "his own protection from the moth, // noble little warrior"; in "Ele-

phants," Moore observes "the defenseless human thing sleep[ing] as sound as if // incised with hard wrinkles . . . made safe by magic hairs!" in contrast to the elephant, which "expounds the brotherhood / of creatures to man the encroacher" (CP, 125–126, 127, 128, 129–130).

44. It is perhaps worth noting that this is one of the few places where Moore includes "white" as a possibly hated race, thereby implying that her "we" does not exclusively represent a privileged position from which only "others" are susceptible to categorization by race.

6. Quotation, Community, and Correspondences

1. Margaret Holley distinguishes Moore's poems of the late 1940s from those of the mid-1950s on, particularly in their length and experimentation with increased end-rhyme (PMM, 47–48). For my more general purposes, I consider both these periods "late." Moore critics share no agreement about when Moore's late period begins.

2. Slatin argues that from the 1930s on, Moore attempts to forge an ideal American community (SR, 11). Maybe all conception of community is to some extent ideal; in Moore's late poems, I do not think the ideal is essentially American.

3. See, for example, Sandra Gilbert's essay "Marianne Moore as Female Female Impersonator" (AMM, 27–46). Although Gilbert does not distinguish between the young and the older Moore, her examples of Moore's self-portrayal and of others' responses to this portrait are all drawn from the later period of her life. Gilbert notes that, although Moore's gender had always figured in descriptions of her art, during the 1950s and 1960s there was a marked increase in critical emphasis on her poetry's stereotypically "feminine" qualities, and a concomitant decline in her literary reputation (31). Charles Molesworth also describes well the negative effect of Moore's public persona on the reception of her art (*Marianne Moore: A Literary Life* [Atheneum, 1990], 397, and chap. 5 passim).

4. In *William Carlos Williams Review* 14, 1 (Spring 1988): 86–103. In the following paragraphs, references to Slatin are to this essay.

5. It is tricky to talk about Moore's reputation during the last twenty years of her life because she was both famous, a figure in the poetic world clearly to be dealt with, and yet always somehow dismissable—perhaps not the first to be dropped from an over-full anthology or course syllabus but rarely a point of focus. Similarly, several books on modernist poetry mention Moore only in passing, and some omit mention of her altogether—in the first category, for example, Stanley Sultan's *Eliot, Joyce and Co.* (Oxford University Press, 1987) and Julian Symons's *Makers of the New:*

The Revolution in Literature, 1912–1939, which dismisses Moore as considered "a modernist only by those whose ideas about poetry were set in the nineteenth century" (Random House, 1987; 176). In the latter category, see Thomas Parkinson's *Poets, Poems, Movements* (UMI Research Press, 1987), Andrew Ross's *The Failure of Modernism: Symptoms of American Poetry* (Columbia University Press, 1986), Ricardo Quinones's *Mapping Literary Modernism: Time and Development* (Princeton University Press, 1985), and Aldon L. Nielsen's *Reading Race: White American Poets and the Racial Discourse in the Twentieth-Century* (University of Georgia Press, 1988).

6. It is notable that during the one early period of her life in which she filled a central spot in this establishment, she wrote no poetry at all—namely her years as editor of *The Dial.* Then her centrality was defined by her role as editor, not directly as poet.

7. "Portrait of the Artist: Marianne Moore's Letters to Hildegarde Watson," in *Poesis: A Celebration of H.D. and Marianne Moore* (Bryn Mawr College, 1985; 130, 129).

8. "Efforts of Affection: A Memoir of Marianne Moore," in *Vanity Fair,* June 1983, 44–60, 59.

9. Important exceptions to keep in mind include, for example, Moore's relationship with Bishop—where she clearly plays the guiding and encouraging role—and with H.D., where this dynamic does not enter in at all.

10. Quoted in Laurence Stapleton's *Marianne Moore: The Poet's Advance* (Princeton University Press, 1978). Holley (PMM) also uses Moore's letters to Watson as evidence of her dissatisfaction and self-denigration at this time. While Stapleton notes that the late 1940s and 1950s were "a time of grief and inward struggle" for the poet, she quotes a draft of a (never finished) poem as indicative of Moore's mood: "We fail and fail and fail (there is a touch of portraiture in this) and after all, prevail" (189). That Moore, in the midst of such acclaim, could perceive of herself as "fail[ing]" at all may manifest the doubt of an ambitious poet—one by definition never satisfied with poems already produced—and at the same time an at least subliminal recognition that something is askew in the balance of that acclaim: she has become famous without being widely regarded as "great." Moore may also have recognized sexism in editors' continuing refusals of poems written by one of the most celebrated poets of the age.

11. As Slatin (SR) and Joanne Feit Diehl (*Women Poets and the American Sublime* [Indiana University Press, 1990], among others, have noted, Moore may link both this concept of originality and her use of quotation back to Emerson. As Emerson writes, "There is no pure originality. All minds quote" or "Next to the originator of a good sentence is the first quoter of it. Many will read the book before one thinks of quoting a passage. As soon as he

has done this, that line will be quoted east and west"—hence the quoter is an advertiser of what has already been said, a notion that would please Moore ("Quotation and Originality," in *The Works of Ralph Waldo Emerson*, 8 vols., ed. Edward W. Emerson [1903; Boston, 1909], 182).

12. Bonnie Costello refers briefly to this poem's "prompt precision," commenting that "the poem's white-water surface may finally drown interpretation" (IP, 163, 177). Jeanne Heuving calls the poem perhaps Moore's "most disruptive of prevailing meanings," having "little paraphrasable meaning outside of its disclosure of qualities which are palpable and phenomenal rather than symbolic" (*Omissions Are Not Accidents: Gender in the Art of Marianne Moore* [Wayne State University Press, 1992], 114).

13. Moore may have made this revision to underline her reference to "precisionism" in the visual arts. See Costello (IP, chap. 7), Linda Leavell (*Marianne Moore and the Visual Arts: Prismatic Color* [University of Oklahoma Press, 1995], chap. 5), and Darlene Erickson (*Illusion is More Precise than Precision* [University of Alabama Press, 1992], 61–63) for a discussion of "precisionism" in relation to Moore's art.

14. Henry Gifford similarly describes Moore's verse as interactive in comparison with Dickinson's: Moore's "affinities are with conversation" of the kind described by "heightened consciousness"; they are "nothing if not shared"; Dickinson "utters a few astonishing words from behind the door" ("Two Philologists" in CCE, 173).

15. Heuving calls "Bowls" "Moore's first published collage poem" (*Omissions Are Not Accidents*, 114). See Chapter 2, expecially note 17, on Moore's use of collage.

16. In *Observations*, Moore notes: "'appear the first day': advertisement in French magazine." A reading diary quotes this source in its original French, and reveals that Moore changed the magazine's publication date from the last to the "first day of the month" (MMN II.2 [Fall 1978]: 18). This *Newsletter*'s brief entry on "Bowls" also notes that "Matilda" is "queen of William the Conqueror whose French influence marked a significant shift in the development of modern English" (19). This poem may be another of the multiple instances where Moore includes but does not call attention to the influence of particular women or activities and attributes stereotyped as feminine: here she traces her genealogy as etymologist back to a queen.

17. The most important interpretive work on Moore's quoting practices appears in Slatin's *The Savage's Romance* (throughout, and especially 86–93 and 138–155); Holley's *The Poetry of Marianne Moore* (37–43 and throughout); Taffy Martin's *Marianne Moore, Subversive Modernist* (University of Texas Press, 1986; 105–112); Erickson's *Illusion Is More Precise than Precision* (chap. 3); and in essays by Lynn Keller ("'For inferior who is free?' Liberating the

Woman Writer in Marianne Moore's 'Marriage,'" in *Influence and Intertextuality in Literary History*, ed. Jay Clayton and Eric Rothstein [University of Wisconsin Press, 1991; 219–244]) and Elizabeth Gregory (in an unpublished essay version of "'Imaginary Gardens with Real Toads'": *Quotation and Modern American Poetry* [Rice University Press, 1995]). Virtually all of Patricia C. Willis's critical work deals with this issue, although often from a primarily descriptive rather than interpretive vantage.

18. On the differences between Pound's, Eliot's, Williams's, and Moore's uses of quotation, allusion, and annotation, see Martin (*Subversive Modernist*, 125–131), Holley (PMM, 16 and passim.), Slatin (SR, and "'Something Inescapably Typical'"), Rachel Blau DuPlessis ("No Moore of the Same: The Feminist Poetics of Marianne Moore," in the Moore issue of the *William Carlos Williams Review*, 6–32), and Lynn Keller ("'For inferior who is free?'"). Leonard Diepeveen's *Changing Voices: The Modern Quoting Poem* (University of Michigan Press, 1993) also discusses Moore's poetry at length, although because he insists that quotation entails precise repetition of a source and because he does not acknowledge the mosaic rather than merely juxtaposed qualities of Moore's quotation, I find his work less useful regarding Moore than the other poets he discusses.

19. See Chapter 1, note 4, for Slatin's and Merrin's suggestions of non-Western and non-poetic traditions Moore may have turned to for models enabling her poetic oppositionality.

20. See Keller's "'For inferior who is free?'" (220). I do not mean to imply here that it is irrelevant where Moore finds her quoted material. On the contrary, studies like Slatin's (SR), Willis's "The Road to Paradise: First Notes on Marianne Moore's 'An Octopus'" (TCL, 242–266), and Keller's indicate the interpretive riches to be gained by tracing Moore's acknowledged and unacknowledged literary and popular allusions.

21. The single best source for information about ways in which Moore has altered her citations remains the *Marianne Moore Newsletter*, edited by Patricia C. Willis and staff at the Rosenbach Museum and Library from 1977 to 1983.

22. Slatin demonstrates that Moore is in fact much more likely to give credit to a local newspaper, travel brochure, or obscure work than to any work by major predecessor poets. Moore's literary borrowing is the primary topic of *The Savage's Romance*.

23. See Holley (PMM, 69–72), and again the *Newsletter* and Willis's work on quotation.

24. *Hints and Disguises: Marianne Moore and Her Contemporaries* (University of Iowa Press, 1989), 129. These views stand in direct contrast to Slatin's, who argues that Moore's "quotation has become the form of the 'historical

sense'" or what bears the past into the present. Slatin sees Moore's verse as moving toward "the ends of 'truth' and vision," as dependent on remembering and marking both history and origins (SR, 141).

25. Holley writes of Moore's quotation and Notes as extending the author's province or authority beyond her text, although she also reads this apparatus as acknowledging something like "a selective sharing of a sense of each poem's genealogy, its communal authorship in the public world of words" (PMM, 69–70, 191).

26. Moore recorded what would become the beginning lines from a conversation at a 1919 party: "This fineness of early civilization art. I have never seen such primeval color. It is color of the sort that existed when Adam was there alone and there was no smoke and nothing to modify it but the mist that went up"; the end stems from a remark of her brother Warner's, recorded in the same conversation notebook as "I don't know. I suppose I'm stubborn—I feel sometimes as if the wave can go over me if it likes and I'll be there when it's gone by—" (RML 1250/23).

27. Similarly, Leavell notes that Mary Warner Moore frequently uses the language of "waves" and "spectrums" (*Prismatic Color*, 12), another common idiom of the poet's; Warner's career as Navy chaplain also associates him with the sea.

28. See March 6 and November 3, 1914—RML VI.20.04 and 12; December 26, 1915—RML VI.21.13; for the use of "basilisks," see the 1908 correspondence (VI.14 box). Such references are also frequent in Warner's later letters (see, for example, August 25, 1957; RML VI.40.26). One should remember in this context as well that the family represents both Bryn Mawr and Yale students as armored animals—gators and turtles, respectively (discussed in Chapter 4).

29. Moore even occasionally refers to what "a friend" or "acquaintance" has said in the text of a poem without attributing the comment to a particular person in her notes—for example, in "The Monkeys," "Snakes, Mongooses, Snake-Charmers and the Like," "Rigorists," and "Values in Use." Patricia Willis commented in 1990 that she had already found 131 borrowed lines in Moore's poem "The Octopus" (only 231 lines long)—and was still finding more, although Moore acknowledges only 50 or 60 lines as "quoted or interpolated" (AMM, 120).

30. This acknowledgment appears in the Postscript to Moore's *Selected Poems* (Faber & Faber, 1935), 122.

31. "Verbalizing a Political Act: Toward a Politics of Speech," in *Language and Politics*, ed. Michael Shapiro (New York University Press, 1984), 28.

32. "Rigorists" also consists largely of quotation—this time from an unnamed "friend"—but as Moore provides no category of identity for this

friend, the poem's power relationships play a less prominent, and less clear, role. Molesworth speculates that Bryher may be this unnamed friend (*A Literary Life*, 324). Willis notes in contrast that the poet knew this story from her childhood (*Vision into Verse* [Rosenbach Museum and Library, 1987], 56). Moore refers to hearing Sheldon Jackson speak at the Carlisle Indian School in 1905.

33. Slatin's is still, I think, the best extended reading of this poem (SR, 150–155). He also links the father's particular suggestions of what "superior" guests should visit with a "moribund" patriarchal tradition ("Longfellow's grave" and "the glass flowers at Harvard"—an all-male university when Moore wrote this poem; SR, 154).

34. *Painterly Abstraction in Modernist American Poetry: The Contemporaneity of Modernism* (Cambridge University Press, 1989), 269, 270.

35. *The Poem as Utterance* (Methuen, 1986), 25; the concept of "presupposition" assumes that a "sentence contains within its formulation an account of the world about which it is making a claim, and which is a condition for the appropriacy of the utterance" (22–23).

36. A marvelous archival example of the "imperfection" of Moore's quotation in this poem as opening the way for egalitarian or challenging response lies in the fact that Moore does not either quote precisely from Homans or acknowledge fully her quoted sources. Willis documents that Moore found the line "The deepest feeling ought to show itself in restraint" in a notebook of her mother's, opening the poem to interpretation dealing with daughters and mothers, disguised as fathers ("The Road to Paradise," 259). Heuving interprets this poem by contrasting the words Moore initially records Homans as having spoken with her heavily revised "quotation" in the poem, and through reference to earlier drafts of the poem (*Omissions Are Not Accidents*, 119). For Moore's original quotation of Homans, see reading notebook VII.01.02 [NB 1250/02]).

37. One might, in this context, also consider Moore's epigraph to her *Complete Poems*: "Omissions are not accidents." As several empirical studies of gender and language reveal, not speaking or omitting response or information may be as much an act of power toward another as the act of speech itself. See especially Susan Gal's "Between Speech and Silence: The Problematics of Research on Language and Gender" on the ways in which silence may indicate either lack of power or empowerment, depending on the context of the interaction (in *The Women and Language Debate: A Sourcebook*, ed. Camille Roman, Suzanne Juhasz, and Cristanne Miller [Rutgers University Press, 1994], 407–431).

38. As Willis ("The Road to Paradise," 260–263) and Diehl (*American Sublime*, 79) both discuss, Moore alludes to Milton's *Paradise Lost* in her

exploration of an American "paradise" in this poem, and may indeed construct her poem partially as an oppositional response to his—much as she does in "Marriage." For other allusions in "An Octopus," see Willis's essay.

39. Joanne Diehl argues further, on the basis of a long passage omitted from Moore's final published version of "An Octopus," that Moore identifies this style, and the mountain itself, as female—making it even more clearly emblematic of her poetic (*American Sublime*, chap. 5).

40. *Gossip* (University of Chicago Press, 1985), 17.

41. Yet regardless of how interactional its emphasis is, gossip also functions as an act of power toward someone. In an essay entitled "Female Consciousness and Collective Action: The Case of Barcelona, 1910–1918," Temma Kaplan writes that "gossip exchanged during shared work, for example, provides an opportunity for women to think out loud . . . Through gossip, women both express and find reinforcement for their thoughts, which then influence what they do" (*Signs* 7.3 [1982]: 548). As she suggests, gossip may also function as an act of power toward the speaker; she is affected by her own process of putting her thoughts into words—that is, the speech-act occurs simultaneously between the two speakers, who help each other, and between the speaker and her own words. Pocock also describes the effect of a speech-act on the speaker in "Verbalizing a Political Act" (26–29).

42. Costello writes of "Bowls" and others of Moore's poems that "the reader of good sense" will remember "the words, not the subjects" (IP, 234), and in her essay "The 'Feminine' Language of Marianne Moore" she calls Moore "'gossipy' and chatty, passing on bits of hearsay and borrowed phrases" (in *Marianne Moore*, ed. Harold Bloom [Chelsea House, 1987], 90). Hartman, too, writes that Moore "represents herself as a gossip on the baroque scale" (quoted in Costello, IP, 177).

43. In an essay entitled "Quoting Poetry," William Flesch argues that there is always a metapoetic element in quotation: "the [quoted] word sloughs off the transparent content it has in context and takes on some of the opacity or refractoriness of form" (*Critical Inquiry* 18 [Autumn 1991]: 45). As I do, he also sees the act of quotation as one of clashing authorities. Because Flesch gives only instances of quotation in metered poetry and conceives of authority in binary terms—"the question will always be which is to be master"—his analysis is not finally very useful for Moore's poetry, which is not metered in the sense Flesch uses and does not seek mastery in a hierarchy of types of language within the literary tradition. As Kenneth Burke writes, Moore's "independence" is of an "unchallenging" or noncompetitive mode ("Likings of an Observationist," CCE, 126).

44. Costello makes a similar observation in nearly opposite terms, arguing that Moore's poems "draw our attention away from reference and toward the fact of composition" (IP, 9).

45. *A Concert of Tenses: Essays on Poetry* (University of Michigan Press, 1986), 181, 173.

46. Marilyn Brownstein argues that there is also a psychoanalytic one in "The Archaic Mother and Mother and Mother: The Postmodern Poetry of Marianne Moore" (*Contemporary Literature* 30, 1 [Spring 1989] :13–32). Using Kristeva's theorizing of the maternal, Brownstein argues that Moore's verse is essentially "preverbal" from that "infantile 'place'" which "contains the mother/daughter amalgam and a world view based on all points of view, or at least as many as one can get with porous boundaries and the concomitant fusions and partings which persist throughout the lives of mothers and daughters" (26). She sees Moore's poetry as radically "unsafe" because of her faith in "the maternal" and feminine/feminist *jouissance* (29–31). As is clear from my reading of "Silence," I do not believe that Moore outright rejects the paternal or hierarchically embraces "the maternal"—either culturally or psychologically—yet am sympathetic with the general direction of such a reading.

47. Most of these studies have been conducted on primarily white, middle-class speakers in the United States, although fictional texts by black women (like Paule Marshall's *Reena* and Toni Cade Bambara's *Gorilla, My Love*) suggest that similar patterns of conversational exchange may exist for African Caribbean and African American women. On the problematics of any set characterizations of either men's or women's language as such, see three excellent recent essays approaching the issue from cross-cultural anthropological, historical psycho-linguistic, and socio-linguistic perspectives, respectively: Susan Gal's "Between Speech and Silence," Nancy M. Henley and Cheris Kramarae's "Gender, Power, and Miscommunication," and Penelope Eckert and Sally McConnell-Ginet's "Think Practically and Look Locally: Language and Gender as Community-Based Practice," all reprinted in *The Women and Language Debate*. Recent collections on this subject include *Women in their Speech Communities: New Perspectives on Language and Sex*, ed. Jennifer Coates and Deborah Cameron (Longman, 1988); Cate Poynton, *Language and Gender: Making the Difference* (Oxford University Press, 1989); and Marsha Houston and Cheris Kramarae's *Women Speaking from Silence*, a special issue of *Discourse & Society* 2, 4 (1991).

48. For an excellent explanation of this phenomenon in very clear terms, see Francine Frank and Frank Anshen, *Language and the Sexes* (State University of New York Press, 1983), or the Henley and Kramarae essay mentioned in note 47.

49. Diehl juxtaposes characteristics of silence and excess in describing the political effectiveness of Moore's verse: "It is Moore's prescriptiveness, aphoristic neatness, and willfully idiosyncratic rhyme that delimit the rigorous interrogations embodying the rebellious aspect of the poems. And yet the rhetorical digressions, overspecificity of descriptions, and proliferating negative constructions themselves function to divert the reader from the poems' true radicalism" (*American Sublime*, 50).

50. See Leavell for an excellent description of Moore's participation in the Stieglitz and other art circles in New York (*Prismatic Color*, chap. 1).

51. *The First Wave: Woman Poets in America 1915–1945. The Loves, Friendships and Politics that Sparked a Revolution in Women's Creativity* (Macmillan, 1987), 69. According to Drake, some poets of this generation even used women's clubs as the most extensive means of organizing support for women in the arts (69)—and although Moore was never as active in this respect as Harriet Monroe, Eunice Tietjens, or Amy Lowell, she did give several lectures at women's colleges and to women's community groups as well as publishing in the women's magazines mentioned earlier. Like the other poets Drake describes, Moore placed great importance on her relationship with her mother as a source of confidence and strength, and tended to model her friendships on family relationships rather than on resistance to family (9). Drake finds that the majority of women poets coming to prominence between the wars did not have children, and found their most satisfying and enduring relationships in friendship, or more intimate bondings, with other women.

52. See note 48 in Chapter 1 for publications on Bishop and Moore's friendship.

53. Molesworth states that at the time Moore met Bishop she was already offering assistance to Mary Jones, Catherine Flagg, and Esther Tennent. He mentions no younger male poets whom she was advising at the time (*A Literary Life*, 261). Poets she encouraged or assisted later include Judith Farr and Mary Barnard.

54. Such collaborative activity, of course, also occurred among male poets—Pound's editing of *The Waste Land* and his extraordinary energy in helping writers he admired find publishers being the most obvious examples. Goodridge mentions that Moore sent Williams a draft of a Pound review (*Hints and Disguises*, 62), and Molesworth notes that Moore volunteered to pay for publishing work written by Pound in *Poetry* (*A Literary Life*, 410). It remains a question for further study whether the female community of this time was in fact more community-minded in its offers of assistance and support than the male or whether their communal-mindedness has simply been better explored because of current feminist interest in this topic.

55. Jones also sent money regularly to Moore, as did Bryher, and, less regularly and more in the form of gift-giving, Crane. With characteristic warmth and exaggeration, Warner Moore acknowledged Jones's help on October 30, 1947: "And let me say that but for the actual money, Katherine, you have so continuously given us, we would now be seriously in debt," as well as adding his deep gratitude that Jones and her companion Marcia Chamberlain invited Moore to stay with them for a few months following her mother's death (RML V.31.05). After Mary Warner Moore's death, Marianne and Katherine verbalized their mutual dependence playfully by addressing each other and signing themselves "Baby Moore" and "Baby Jones" (see 1947 correspondence), and Marcia referred to herself as "Mama Chamberlain" (Molesworth, *A Literary Life*, 335). Crane later became the executor of Moore's estate.

56. As mentioned earlier, Moore wrote long and frequent letters to her family whenever she was separated from them. In addition, in her later years, Moore complained of receiving as many as forty or fifty letters a day (letter from Alyse Gregory, December 12, 1955; RML V.23.05). Similarly, in a miscellaneous piece at the end of the *Collected Prose*, Moore describes herself as having, one evening, spent "an hour and a half just opening my letters. In the morning I look at them. Sometimes in the past I didn't eat until about noon, I was so determined to get my mail answered" (CPr, 665).

57. "Marianne Moore and H.D.: Female Community and Poetic Achievement," in *Marianne Moore: Woman and Poet*, ed. Patricia C. Willis (National Poetry Foundation, 1990), 371–402. Pondrom admits that Moore appeared to be much more eager for the publication of her poetry when the project was first broached in 1916 than by the time it appeared; she was apparently disheartened by the long delay. This corresponds with evidence in the poet's notebooks and family correspondence. On February 7, 1915, Moore announces to her brother that she has decided to compete in a series sponsored by the *Atlantic Monthly* to "issue a series of one-man volumes (60 or 80 poems each)," and on the 21st of the month, reports that she has submitted her manuscript (RML VI.21.03). On October 13 of the same year, she reports a conversation with her mother: "I said to Mole, 'now with what poems I have published and my general welbeing [*sic*], I could publish a book any time.' Mole said 'I wouldn't publish.' I said, 'Never?' Mole said, 'After you've changed your style.' 'Huh!' I said; 'you would omit all these things I prize so much?' 'Yes,' said Mole 'they're ephemeral'" (RML VI.21.11). It may be some indication of the importance of this conversation to the poet that she records it in a conversation notebook a week or more before reporting it to Warner (RML 1250/23;

not in regular sequence). By 1919, Moore is telling people that she no longer cares to publish.

Molesworth frequently mentions the importance of gift-giving to Moore, stating that "the circulation of gifts, tokens, and well-chosen words, all seen as both personal testament and cultural ritual, had always been a key part of her personal ethic, and in her later years . . . [i]f anything, her attention to it increased" (*A Literary Life*, 359).

58. In Pondrom's "Female Community and Poetic Achievement," 401. One might even speculate that the common Anglo-American cultural practice in which the kind of letter writing meant purely to maintain relationships (writing to relatives, to children away from home, to friends rarely seen) falls to women may result from women's greater practice in an exchange in which what matters is the contact, the acknowledgment of continued intimacy, more than the specifics of information exchanged. As Moore suggests in "Bowls," as well as in her correspondence, the act of writing back itself may matter most in some structures of relationship.

59. An unexplored element of this translation is suggested by Ross Chambers's description of La Fontaine as a master of oppositional narrative (*Room for Maneuver: Reading the Oppositional in Narrative* [University of Chicago Press, 1991], chaps. 2 and 3). Chambers presents La Fontaine as preeminently concerned with matters of authorial posture, power relationships between audience and poet (as well as between characters within the fables), and with narrative tactics of undermining the apparently absolute power of the monarchy (or the noble and royal classes). Such oppositionality, played out in witty and subtle, often emblematic, forms would undoubtedly have appealed to Moore and may have abetted her interest in theorizing the structure of community through the apparatus of quotation.

60. While it is only in her later years that Moore writes what could be called "love poems," albeit not love poems of a traditional sort, love has been a fairly consistent topic in her poetry. According to Gary Lane's *A Concordance to the Poems of Marianne Moore*, Moore uses "love" 35 times and across the whole range of her verse—10 times in the *Selected Poems*, 14 times in her poems published from the 1940s on, and 9 times in the three fables included in that volume of her poetry (Haskell House, 1972). Especially when combined with her 7 uses of other forms of "love" (loved, lover, loves, love's), this is among Moore's most frequently used nouns, exceeded only by her uses of "man" (48) and "nothing" (39).

61. I am indebted here to Lynn Keller's analysis of Marilyn Hacker's revisionary love poems, "Measured Feet 'in Gender-Bender Shoes': The

Politics of Poetic Form in Marilyn Hacker's *Love, Death, and the Changing of the Seasons*," in *Feminist Measures: Soundings in Poetry and Theory*, ed. Lynn Keller and Cristanne Miller (University of Michigan Press, 1994), 260–286.

62. Interestingly, Moore revised the poem to disrupt her rhyme scheme in this way. In *The Collected Poems* (1951), the first stanza ends with the lines "though at no real impasse, / would gladly break the glass"—a rhyme exactly parallel (in chiasmus) to the *sight / delight* of the poem's last lines. Changing "glass" to "mirror" creates an intensely jarring effect at the end of the first stanza, which in turn emphasizes the fullness of the rhyme at the conclusion of the poem. There is, of course, no evidence that Moore has gender in mind here, but she certainly is conscious of the sequence and crescendoing effect of her rhymes.

63. Other examples of Moore's writing poems as an act of immediate exchange include "Old Amusement Park," which was written in response to a photograph enclosed in a letter from Brendon Gill, suggesting she write a poem about it: she wrote the poem "as part of an exchange of appreciation," thanking him in her return letter as the "Producer of unaccidental Masterpieces" (MMN, I.1, 5–6); "St. Nicholas" was written in response to a postcard from Barbara Church; Moore then mailed a draft of the poem with a letter thanking Church (MMN I.1, 10). Moore also uses gifts as subjects of poems—most famously, the paper nautilus given to her by Crane but also, for example, the postcard of a Flemish tapestry from Laurence Scott that inspired "Charity Overcoming Envy." Moore's dedication of "Avec Ardeur" to Pound, while not a product of direct exchange, reflects her sense of their lifetime of exchanges: her use of a phrase from a poem by Madame Boufflers—a poem Pound had translated from French to English—as her poem's title, demonstrates and underlines her sense of literary interdependence as well as her gratitude.

7. Questioning Authority in the Late Twentieth Century

1. Although Moore's poetic may be useful to the understanding of a large number of contemporary female poets, only a relatively small percentage of them construct a poetic markedly resembling hers; I focus on such poets here. Similarly, one might illuminate the poetic I have developed in reading Moore by examining its manifestation in contemporary male as well as female poets. Because I see a restructuring of gendered elements of the poet's role and poetic form as key to this poetic, however, and because such feminist work continues to be predominantly that of women, I restrict my discussion to female poets.

2. See my discussion of this effect in Chapter 3, note 47.

3. This version of "Dock Rats" appears in *Observations* (54). In *Poems*, Moore writes: "shipping is the / most congenial thing in the world" (20)—an even less sublime category than that of interest.

4. Moore's admiration for her more famous peer H.D. is well documented in her several reviews of her friend's work and in their long correspondence. Yet while both are concerned with history and the events dominating national and international politics, and while both certainly experiment with traditional forms in ways that rewrite gendered aspects of these forms, H.D.'s leaning toward the personal and the conventionally lovely in verse, and her constant return to relationships between men and women as the emotional vortex of her work, mark her poetry as fundamentally different from Moore's.

5. Burke in *American Quarterly* 39, 1 (Spring 1987): 98–121; DuPlessis in *Feminist Measures: Soundings in Poetry and Theory*, ed. Lynn Keller and Cristanne Miller (University of Michigan Press, 1994), 69–95.

6. In *The Last Lunar Baedeker*, ed. Roger L. Conover (The Jargon Society, 1982), 9.

7. *Baedecker*, 91. Burke quotes an earlier version of this poem in her essay, calling attention to what Loy called her "mental spatiality" as it manifests itself in the unusual use of white space to separate words within lines; for example, the first and last lines of this section, as Loy published them in *Others*, 1917, contain unusual spacing: "Spawn   of   Fantasies. . . . Coloured   glass" ("Getting Spliced") (108–111, 119). Conover regularizes Loy's spacing and capitalization in *The Last Lunar Baedeker*.

8. *"Between Your House and Mine": The Letters of Lorine Niedecker to Cid Corman 1960 to 1970*, ed. Lisa Pater Faranda (Duke University Press, 1986), 75. I thank Rachel Blau DuPlessis for calling Niedecker's repeated reference to Moore to my attention, in this collection of letters and in *Niedecker and the Correspondence with Zukofsky, 1931–1970*, ed. Jenny Penberthy (Cambridge University Press, 1993).

9. Reprinted in *The Norton Anthology of American Literature*, 3rd ed., vol. 2 (W. W. Norton, 1989), 2384.

10. In "Community and Voice: Gwendolyn Brooks' 'In the Mecca,'" Gayl Jones characterizes Brooks's poetry by its simultaneous "move[ment] both away from, and . . . toward speech; hers is an aggregate language that runs the gamut of 'elevated' and 'street' without devitalizing either" (in *A Life Distilled: Gwendolyn Brooks, Her Poetry and Fiction*, ed. Maria K. Mootry and Gary Smith [University of Illinois Press, 1987], 195). Jones argues that Brooks's language sets itself apart from community while also directing us to it. Perhaps because of the multivocality of Brooks's work, she—like Moore—became famous and widely touted without becoming the focus of

serious critical study. On this topic see both Mootry's "'Down the Whirl-wind of Good Rage': An Introduction to Gwendolyn Brooks" (1–20) and Houston Baker's "The Achievement of Gwendolyn Brooks" (21–29) in this same collection of essays.

11. The poems mentioned in this paragraph are from *Blacks* (The David Company, 1987), 64, 71, 69, and 73. Betsy Erkkila accurately identifies the mixing of tones, issues, and voices of Brooks's poetry written during the 1940s, 1950s, and 1960s as problematic for Brooks after her conversion, as it were, to a black nationalist and more nearly separatist aesthetic and political ideal in the late 1960s (*The Wicked Sisters: Women Poets, Literary History and Discord* [Oxford University Press, 1992], 201–202). Brooks, and several of her critics, seem to have regarded the earlier work ambivalently, as though it were not sufficiently focused on issues of race and social oppression. I would argue that Brooks's early poetry indeed fully engages these issues, but it does so in the context of other aspects of discrimination and personal difficulty (for example, intraracial prejudice, sexism, poverty, and ambivalent nationalism) that receive less attention in her later work.

12. In her early verse, Brooks turned away from the Harlem Renaissance's celebration of unique racial values. As she put it, she wished "to prove to others (by implication, not by shouting) and to such among themselves as have yet to discover it, that [African Americans] are merely human beings, not exotics"; she resented "pure propaganda, and [would] *try* (!) not to perpetuate it myself" (in George E. Kent's *A Life of Gwendolyn Brooks* [University Press of Kentucky, 1990], 64). Although her later verse focuses more narrowly on urban black communities, Brooks still does not write as though her own experience grounds her authority.

13. My sense of the parallels between these two authors is confirmed by the essays on Brooks collected in Mootry and Smith's *A Life Distilled*, which claim for Brooks much of what I claim for Moore. For example, Mootry writes that critics have "neglected, undervalued, or misunderstood the role of gender" in Brooks's art and her fundamental commitments to both an experimental aesthetic and social justice (10). Hortense Spillers writes of Brooks's "refus[al] to make easy judgements," and of her "shrewd opposition of understatement and exaggeration"; she concludes that Brooks "restores the tradition of citizen poet" (224, 233, 235; in "Gwendolyn the Terrible: Propositions on Eleven Poems"). Essays by Erlene Stetson and Gary Smith stress the influence of Elizabethan and Jacobean poets on Brooks's art—particularly Donne, Milton, and Jonson. It may also be significant that Brooks, like Moore, came to poetic maturity during years characterized by extreme American optimism—the older poet immediately preceding (and during) World War I and the younger one in the early

1940s, at the beginning of U.S. involvement in World War II. Both periods were also characterized by particular optimism in relation to women's roles and capacities.

14. Quotation from Brett C. Millier's *Elizabeth Bishop: Life and the Memory of It* (University of California Press, 1993), 67. Recent critics especially interested in biographical readings of Bishop's poems include Millier (not surprisingly, for a biographer); Lorrie Goldensohn in *Elizabeth Bishop: The Biography of a Poetry* (Columbia University Press, 1991); David Kalstone in *Becoming a Poet: Elizabeth Bishop with Marianne Moore and Robert Lowell* (Farrar, Straus, and Giroux, 1989); the collection of essays edited by Marilyn May Lombardi, *Elizabeth Bishop: The Geography of Gender* (University Press of Virginia, 1993); and to a lesser extent Victoria Harrison in *Elizabeth Bishop's Poetics of Intimacy* (Cambridge University Press, 1993). The extent to which this reading has become standard, however, can be seen in Lynn Keller's *Re-Making It New: Contemporary American Poetry and the Modernist Tradition* (Cambridge University Press, 1987), where she characterizes the distinction between Moore and Bishop as a shift in focus from the visual "eye" to the emotional landscape of the "I" (98).

15. In "When We Dead Awaken"; see chap. 1, n. 32.

16. *Your Native Land, Your Life* (W. W. Norton, 1986), 33. The other two volumes were also published by Norton, in 1989 and 1991, respectively.

17. As Joanne Diehl and Sabine Sielke suggest by including both Moore and Rich in *Women Poets and the American Sublime* and "Intertextual Networking: Constructing Female Subjectivity in the Poetry of Emily Dickinson, Marianne Moore, and Adrienne Rich" (Ph.D. diss., Free University of Berlin, 1991), and as Cynthia Hogue suggests in linking these poets (along with Dickinson and H.D.) as part of a tradition of "scheming women," a more extensive study of the convergences between these two major poets might be illuminating to both their works.

18. Brooks, as Erkkila points out and as is obvious from George Kent's excellent biography, was apparently never troubled by a crisis of identity in negotiating her multiple positioning as black, female, mother, community activist, and poet (*Wicked Sisters*, 192; *A Life of Gwendolyn Brooks*, throughout).

19. *Stealing the Language: The Emergence of Women's Poetry in America* (Beacon Press, 1986). Ostriker comments, for example, that the poetry being written by women from the 1960s on "constitute[s] a literary movement comparable to romanticism or modernism," and mentions Muriel Rukeyser, Anne Sexton, Adrienne Rich, Sylvia Plath, Margaret Atwood, Mona Van Duyn, Gwendolyn Brooks, Diane Wakoski, Maxine Kumin, and Carolyn Kizer—as well as, later, Lucille Clifton, Audre Lorde, Nikki Giovanni, June

Jordan, and Judy Grahn—as influential in establishing this tradition (7). While Ostriker does not write exclusively about poetry that takes women's lives as its theme or that speaks in a personal voice, such poetry dominates her discussion.

20. *Shades* (Wesleyan University Press, 1988). This series is in section II. All further references to McHugh's poetry are to this volume.

21. These poems appear, respectively, in *(W)holes* (Knopf, 1980), *Transplants* (Braziller, 1976), and *Living Wills: New and Selected Poems* (Knopf, 1990); all the poems I cite later appear first or are reprinted in *Living Wills*.

22. Interview with Daniel Bourne, "Artful Dodge Interviews Cynthia Macdonald," *Artful Dodge* 18–19 (1990): 85.

23. In her interview with Bourne, Macdonald mentions her research for poems and the importance of a sense of community to her writing. More telling, with Moore-like tact, she does not respond to Bourne's several questions about his "having to suspend my command of what is going on" in reading her poems or the degree to which she plays games of mastery with her readers, making them "follow" her, or herself going "after a coup in terms of trust" ("Artful Dodge Interviews Cynthia Macdonald," 81, 82). Instead, Macdonald stresses the need for a poet to "earn the right to be difficult" and yet write poems that people can understand, and that mean something (82).

24. *Singularities* (Wesleyan University Press, 1990). Howe describes her debt to mathematician Rene Thom and mathematical theory in her interview with Edward Foster ("An Interview with Susan Howe" in *Talisman* 4 [Spring 1990]: 30–31). To give a sense of her range, on the same pages she also mentions (among others) Schoenberg writing about his music, the colonial minister Hope Atherton, Emily Dickinson, and Increase and Cotton Mather. The quotation within her poetry, however, tends to be much more focused—centering, often, on a single text or writer.

25. See Marjorie Perloff's "'Collision or Collusion with History': Susan Howe's *Articulation of Sound Forms in Time*" for an analysis of the effect of this sequence of sounds, in *Poetic License: Essays on Modernist and Postmodernist Lyric* (Northwestern University Press, 1990), 304–305.

26. While providing no simple answers to present or past historical/cultural dilemmas, Howe nonetheless expresses hope that "the truth will out"—a hope manifested in her poetry through her continued return to, and research in, historical documents and literature ("An Interview with Susan Howe," 17).

27. *The Pink Guitar: Writing as Feminist Practice* (Routledge, 1990), 133.

28. *My Emily Dickinson* (North Atlantic Books, 1985), 11.

29. Philip's poems containing the features I discuss here appear primar-

ily in the second half of *She Tries Her Tongue* (Ragweed Press, 1989). My "M. Nourbese Philip and the Poetics/Politics of Silence" discusses her more recent experimental writing (in *Semantics of Silences in Linguistics and Literature*, ed. Gudrun Grabher and Ulrike Jessner; collection under review).

30. "Writing a Memory of Losing that Place"—an interview with Janice Williamson in *Sounding Differences: Conversations with Seventeen Canadian Women Writers* (University of Toronto Press, 1993), 227–228.

31. What is equally important, "community" or "chorus" for Philip, as for Moore, does not imply only people who might conventionally be defined as "like" her: not just African Caribbeans, women, poets, and so on. She addresses herself to all who can hear. In her interview with Williamson, Philip comments on the racism of the (commonly held) assumption that writers of color write only for their similarly raced communities while similar work by white writers is assumed to address all readers.

32. Fulton denies that Moore has influenced her writing, and claims Emily Dickinson as her only important female influence. As I show later, however, Moore has at least begun to enter Fulton's verse. I quote below from Fulton's *Powers of Congress* (David R. Godine, 1990), *Palladium* (University of Illinois Press, 1986), and "Give" (*Sensual Math* [W. W. Norton, 1995]). Fulton generously made the manuscript of this poem available to me.

33. Although Fulton has no formal training in physics, she notes in correspondence (November 2, 1993) that undergraduate work in photography may have whetted her interest in precise observation and technical processes (similarly encouraged by Moore's college work in biology; unlike Moore's, Fulton's education focused almost entirely on the fine arts—creative writing, photography, quilt-making, music, and theater). Also echoing Moore's recognition of the importance of the environment at Bryn Mawr to her later assertiveness, Fulton comments in the same letter: "I don't know how I could have become a writer without the ideas held forth by feminism. I was lucky to be young in those years, when women were being encouraged to create."

34. These poems appear, respectively, in *Powers of Congress*, 23, 96, 100, and in *Palladium*, 61, 62, 66. On this subject see my essay "'The Erogenous Cusp' or Intersections of Science and Gender in Alice Fulton's Poetry," in *Feminist Measures*, ed. Keller and Miller, 317–343. There I argue that Fulton uses quantum mechanics as theoretically analogous to some aspects of feminism, or at least as supportive of elements of feminist theory, in its insistence on "complementarity." The kind of essentializing responsible for historical gender constructions (or classic notions of scientific knowledge) is undercut by quantum theory's fundamental claim that the structure of

the experiment, hence the perspective of the observer, will always affect its outcome, or the properties visible to the observer.

35. In "To Organize a Waterfall," Fulton comments that "perfection has a dead center, while the work of a living poet is too mutable to free-frame. That something is provisional doesn't lessen it . . . Things that change hold my interest" (*Parnassus* 16, 2 [1991]: 304).

36. The acrostics, respectively, read: "TRY A LITTLE TENDERNESS," "BOWLING DEVELOPS THE RIGHT ARM," and "THIS THINGS BIG-GER THAN BOTH OF US" (*Powers of Congress*, 18, 23, 22). Other poems referred to in this paragraph are also from *Powers of Congress*.

37. In private correspondence, Fulton has confirmed her intention not to assign gender: when "writing 'Between the Apple and the Stars' [1983], I came to these lines in the penultimate stanza: '. . . The scientist passes / a hand like a wand / over the wondrous button. . . .' And I remember . . . thinking will it be 'her hand' or 'his hand' and deciding on the article instead. This was in 1979 or 1980. It was a decision made consciously, to keep the gender blurred" (letter dated "August 30–September 9, 1992").

38. This is even the topic of one of Fulton's poems, "Cherry Bombs," in which the speaker remembers her childhood distrust of strongly gender-marked behavior: "I hated the world's complicitous *give / in, give in*. / Though the shot // silk slips, Lilt perms, and Ambush / scent seemed lusciously adult / a suspicion lingered they were lures // to an unfixable forever / I deeply didn't want . . . It wasn't that I wanted to be not / female. I wanted to be female / as I was" (*Powers of Congress*, 37, 39).

39. As another aspect of dichotomy undercut, Fulton implies that Daphne is black (the daughter of a blues singer)—in apparent contrast to her origin in Greek myth, although perhaps she is using this contrast, and Daphne's heritage, with Moore-like pointed understatement to suggest that African American culture is as powerfully originary as Greek myth.

Index